MILTON, MANNERISM AND BAROQUE

S. Maria della Salute, Venice

MILTON, MANNERISM and BAROQUE

Roy Daniells

UNIVERSITY OF TORONTO PRESS

The illustrations appear with the kind assistance
and permission of Alinari, Florence, with the
exception of the panorama of the Grand Canal
for which thanks are due to Editions Sun, Paris

FOR LAURENDA, WITHOUT WHOM...

Preface

THIS BOOK would not have been written but for the generosity of the Canada Council, from whom in 1959 I received a Special Senior Award, and of the Board of Governors of the University of British Columbia who granted me leave of absence for a year.

The work has been published with the help of a grant from the Humanities Research Council, using funds provided by the Canada Council. I am indebted to the University of Toronto Press for a grant from its Publications Fund and to the editor, Miss Frances Halpenny, for assistance and advice. Many errors of fact or form were caught in the manuscript by Mrs. Eleanor Cook. That the index is intelligible I owe to Inglis Bell.

My debts to Arthur Woodhouse are so many and of such long standing they can neither be itemized nor summed up. My thanks are due to Malcolm Ross for criticism and encouragement.

Common sense has been allowed to prevail over strict consistency where ease of reading seemed to demand it. The customary form "St. Peter's" has been used, though names of less familiar Roman churches have not been anglicized. Quotations whose source is obvious have not been formally identified. Footnotes have been kept to a minimum; they are supplemented by a brief, highly selective bibliography.

Permission to incorporate material from my article "Humour in Paradise Lost" in the *Dalhousie Review* (Autumn 1953) is gratefully acknowledged.

R. D.

Vancouver
Easter Sunday, 1963

Contents

Illustrations

MILTON, MANNERISM AND BAROQUE

ɪ. INTRODUCTION

NOT LONG AGO, any attempt to relate literary criticism to the concept of Baroque was received with polite derision. Today even the wide public to which paperbacks are directed takes the relation for granted. Critical discussion now brings together without a sense of strain the schematic evaluation of European art and the categories of literary form. Comprehensive histories of style employ the concept of Baroque with increasing precision. It has produced categories of Early, High, and Late Baroque and the useful independent concept of Mannerism. In the pages that follow, I have attempted a clarification of the Mannerist traits in Milton's earlier work and the Baroque elements in his great poetic trilogy.

These pages are only incidentally concerned with Milton's sources and I am aware that to some readers this will appear as a disabling limitation. It would seem, however, that something quite as important as sources is the manner and spirit in which the derived materials are employed. Even so triumphant a piece of identification of sources as Lowes's *Road to Xanadu* has receded into a perspective which invites other and complementary approaches to Coleridge.

If an apology is still needed for criticism which takes for granted analogies among the arts it can be argued that the arts of a given period form a total pattern, the same impulses expressing themselves in a variety of forms. Sometimes there can be no room for doubt. What Blake or Morris or Rossetti is saying in words he is also saying in line and colour. Sometimes the visual arts of a whole area or period can be shown to echo in imagery or iconography the philosophers and poets. Sometimes the attempt to relate the arts produces only generalized and unconvincing statements, but this may be for lack of a vocabulary flexible enough to take care of the relationships explored. The academic habit of keeping disciplines for pedagogical reasons in their own compartments has discouraged the formation of a flexible set of terms.

One thing is clear: the effort to relate the arts to one another continues to be made. The desire for wholeness of conception persists. Spengler, Hauser, and their like never lack readers. Tradition tells us that the Muses dance together to the same melody; their steps are felt to be part of a combined movement.

In the academic world misgivings about the validity of a search for analogies between the arts die very slowly. Their departure should be hastened by certain successful efforts, which have brought real illumination. Such is Panofsky's analysis of parallels between Scholasticism and Gothic architecture. He establishes the intention of each, states the principles governing structures, produces convincing chronological parallels, and substantiates his argument by a wealth of reference to actual buildings.

Panofsky argues that Scholasticism derived its expository method from "the postulate of clarification for clarification's sake" and was accordingly obsesssed by such devices as systematic division and subdivision, methodical demonstration, consistent terminology, parallel structure (even to rhyming words). In High Gothic architecture the same desire for *manifestatio* showed in what might be called the principle of transparency. As Scholastic philosophy separated faith from rational knowledge yet desired to express the objectives of faith in rational terms, so the architects of High Gothic made shapes of their interiors shine through the fabric of the building. "The cross-section of the nave can be read off from the façade."

In its scope the High Gothic cathedral, like the Scholastic *Summa*, embodied the totality of Christian experience. In its arrangement it corresponded to the subdivision of Scholastic argument into homologous parts and parts of parts, from nave, transept, and choir to the very arrangement of mouldings. In some instances the organization of the whole system may be inferred from the cross-section of a single pier. But *manifestatio* is only half the story. The rest is contained in the desire for *concordantia*. Contradictions in authoritative sources had to be resolved by logic and apparent opposites reconciled. This Scholastic habit had its parallel in the High Gothic resolution of architectural problems. After much conflict between the circular shape of the rose window and the inherent shapes of Gothic, the rose was contained within a pointed arch which was itself a window. Other and more complex illustrations of the same principle conclude Panofsky's essay. His observations apply to the period, not much more than a century, following the undertaking of St. Denis by Abbot Suger in 1135.[1]

It is not likely that any scheme so adroit and complete can be produced for the relationship between literature and architecture in the seventeenth century until many attempts have perfected an analytical procedure. But Panofsky's essay provides, by its clarity, economy, and fruitfulness, a heartening demonstration of what can be done.

In the discussion of Milton and Baroque which follows, I have tried to stick to a small set of fundamental principles, to stay with a limited number of the best works of Bernini and his contemporaries, to embark on no flights of fancy. On the literary side, the text of Milton's major poetic works is kept constantly in view, a method which their strongly and self-consciously formal character facilitates. In the chapters on Milton and Mannerism it has not been possible to proceed within such safeguards. Literary Mannerism has not yet received enough critical attention to permit any but tentative conclusions.

Whatever his final measure of agreement may be, it is hoped that the reader will find himself rereading Milton's actual work, which, as Hazlitt said, is the answer to many preconceived objections.

1. Another useful analysis of Gothic as "petrified scholasticism" may be found in Worringer, *Form Problems of the Gothic*, 115–36.

2. MANNERISM

IT HAS TAKEN over thirty years for the term Mannerism to become current in criticism of the arts. There was initially little interest in Dvorak's use of it to describe El Greco[1] or in Pevsner's perception that what had been thought of as early Baroque might better be termed Mannerist. But a great change has taken place. Readers of Sir Kenneth Clark's special article on El Greco in the *Sunday Times* (September 27, 1959) are expected to take casual references to Mannerism quite in their stride. The application of the term to works of literature has been a slower development but is encountering less resistance, on both sides of the Atlantic, since the appearance of popular books such as Pevsner's *European Architecture* and Sypher's *Four Stages of Renaissance Style,* both of which in paperback editions have achieved wide distribution.

There is general agreement that Mannerism flourished, and was perhaps the leading style, between 1520 or 1530 and 1590 or 1600. There is also a fairly satisfactory consensus of opinion that certain works of Michelangelo are *loci classici* of Mannerism, that Pontormo, Rosso Fiorentino, and Parmigianino are at the centre of the movement, and that both Tintoretto and El Greco are outstanding practitioners of the style. Bronzino, Beccafumi, Cellini, and Bruegel are also reckoned in.

It is possible to separate the products of Mannerism into groupings associated with form, or content, or geographical location, or all of these. Michelangelo is regarded as the progenitor of tragical and mystical forms. An aristocratic Florentine form is associated with

1. A. Hauser, *The Social History of Art,* I, 357.

Vasari and the court of the Medici. The influence of Rome after the Council of Trent is manifest in an official religious form. The emotional and ecstatic painting associated with Barocci forms a final division.

The student who feels that Mannerism is a concept useful in the criticism of English or French literature has thus a number of steeds he may mount and there is considerable risk that they may be prepared to start off in different directions. An agile rider may leap from one to another. In two books by Imbrie Buffum this method is used with great address and to good advantage. In Wylie Sypher's book already mentioned the effect is of a cross-country gallop. Exhilarated and shaken, the reader thinks he will retrace part of the marvellous journey on foot.

In the pages that follow I try to arrive at a definition of Mannerism consonant with the judgement of reputable art critics and at the same time applicable to English literature. The specific works of art appealed to, whether poetic or plastic, are very few in number and are of the very first rank. The sacrifices entailed by this conservative approach are considerable. The temptation to pass directly from the experience, say, of Parmigianino's "Madonna del Collo Lungo" in the Pitti Palace to a consideration of John Donne is almost irresistible. But it has been resisted.

The starting point for a study of Mannerism is the recognition that the Mannerist artist invariably employs traditional themes and materials and frequently gives the impression that he is about to employ them in a traditional way. Giulio Romano, creator of the Palazzo del Tè at Mantua, may be regarded as "an artist who all the time takes every care to preserve the dehors of classical correctness, a care which has deceived observers of several centuries."[2] A simultaneous eagerness to employ traditional forms and determination to rupture their prescribed rules is not often recognized in the criticism of English writing. Coleridge and Wordsworth, we feel, signalled their change of direction clearly and set up the expectation that their predecessors will have done the same.

Pevsner observes that a "tendency to enforce movement through space within rigid boundaries is the chief spatial quality of Mannerism." Even when a breakthrough seems to be achieved it is not the

2. N. Pevsner, "The Architecture of Mannerism," *The Mint*, 116–38.

expansion into the heavens easily achieved in Baroque painting. "The layer of opened-up space is shallow and clearly confined in depth."[3] Mannerism creates "an uneasy neutrality rife with potential disturbance everywhere." It "either breaks symmetry deliberately or overemphasizes it until it becomes monotony."[4]

It is in the handling of figures in space that Mannerism painters are most clearly opposed to their predecessors. The scene presents itself as an accretion of separate parts with different internal organizations. The size of the figures may contrast sharply with their thematic importance; the leading theme, in consequence, may be veered away from. "The final effect is of real figures moving in an unreal, arbitrarily constructed space."[5]

Mannerism "sets against Renaissance human form excessively elongated figures, sometimes over-graceful sometimes ascetic."[6] The bodies not infrequently turn and twist to give the *figura sepentinata*. "Thus there arises a new beauty, no longer resting on real forms measurable by the model or on forms idealized on this basis, but rather on an inner artistic reworking on the basis of harmonic or rhythmical requirements."[7]

Those who seek to define Mannerism have not only been willing to point out technical criteria by which buildings or paintings may be judged; they have also suggested social causes which induced subjective states in the artist which could themselves become criteria. Among these external causes were the new authoritarianism of the popes and the complex of means, persuasive and regressive, which were employed to establish ecclesiastical absolutism in Italy. The Inquisition and the Society of Jesus were simply two of the outstanding forms taken by this movement. If we need a reminder that Counter-Reformation policies had their effect upon the arts we may turn to the *Instructiones Fabricae et Supellectilis Ecclesiasticae* of St. Charles Borromeo. How far such external operations of policy and propaganda can be made responsible for, let us say, the emotional instability, apprehensiveness, and melancholy of Pontormo is an open question. Certainly in him the artistic goal was "measurable only by insatiable

3. N. Pevsner, *An Outline of European Architecture*, 164, 166.
4. Pevsner, "The Architecture of Mannerism."
5. Hauser, *The Social History of Art*, I, 358.
6. Pevsner, "The Architecture of Mannerism."
7. Friedländer, *Mannerism and Anti-Mannerism in Italian Painting*, 8.

subjective criteria,"[8] and certainly in the whole group of Mannerists, from Michelangelo to El Greco, there are evidences of intense inner compulsions. "The whole bent of anti-classic art is basically subjective, since it would construct and individually reconstruct from the inside out, from the subject outward, freely, according to the rhythmic feeling present in the artist, while classic art, socially oriented, seeks to crystallize the object for eternity by working out from the regular, from what is valid for everyone."[9]

It remains to add that most Mannerist work, from its very nature as part of religious ceremonial, was of a public kind. The artists may have been self-centred and vastly concerned with their own techniques and personal feelings. But because they worked for patrons, if for no other reason, they expressed an aristocratic, intensely cultured, and international sentiment. It is possible to claim that the Mannerism of the courts is "the particular form in which the artistic achievements of the Italian Renaissance are spread abroad."[10]

The relation of Mannerism to the classicism of the High Renaissance is difficult of elucidation, in part for a reason already mentioned, the artist's desire to preserve the conventions of classicism whatever new use he may be putting them to, and in part because no literature remains to explain what the originators of Mannerism were trying to do.[11] A similar absence of formal statements of intention confronts the student of the English Metaphysicals, who is constrained to look into such odd works as the *Mythomystes* of Henry Reynolds to find any critical basis for the practice of Donne and his followers.[12]

According to Hauser, Mannerism amounts to a simultaneous imitation and distortion of classical models, to a replacement of the harmony and normality of classical art by more subjective and more suggestive features. At one time there is the vision of a new spiritual content in life, at another an exaggerated intellectualism; sometimes a fastidious epicureanism produces forms of extreme subtlety and elegance. But always the structure depends on classicism with a completely self-conscious style.[13]

8. I. L. Zupnik, "The 'Aesthetics' of the Early Mannerists," *Art Bulletin*, XXXV (Dec, 1953), 302–6.
9. Friedländer, *Mannerism and Anti-Mannerism*, 10.
10. Hauser, *The Social History of Art*, I, 361.
11. Zupnik, "The 'Aesthetics' of the Early Mannerists."
12. See also Sir Anthony Blunt, *Artistic Theory in Italy, 1450–1600*, 135–6.
13. Hauser, *The Social History of Art*, I, 356.

A final problem, one which has not received enough attention, is the derogatory sense which the term Mannerism has acquired. The pejorative senses which have attached themselves to this word and the word Baroque are in part explained by critics having used as a starting point the late, bad practitioners in each of the styles. (A similar situation in the criticism of English poetry put the term Metaphysical into bad repute.) As the terms are carried back in time to the originators of the style, there is less or no cause for a continued pejorative use. But this is no means the whole truth about the denigrating use of the term Mannerism. Vasari's condemnation of Pontormo in his life of that painter points to deeper causes of dislike. Pontormo, says Vasari, has copied Dürer, losing the sweetness and grace of his own earlier manner; he has abandoned a good style which pleased everyone. The torsos (in a picture Vasari particularly dislikes) are mostly large and the legs and arms small, not to speak of the heads, which lack the singular grace and elegance Pontormo used to give. We see, continues Vasari, that when men wish to force Nature they ruin their natural endowments.

In theory it should be easy for a critic to accept the situation in which an artist suffering from external pressure and inward distress so modifies the conventional forms with which he composes his work that they disappoint the expectation of traditionalists and awaken a new set of responses to the ultimate general enrichment of the art in question. In practice, however, most critics seem to imply that the Mannerist artist is somehow weak, perverse, and blameworthy. For example, we need go no further than to Jonson's remark that Donne for breaking of accent deserved hanging, and to a recent edition of the *Britannica*, which informs us that Donne's influence upon English literature was "almost wholly malign" and that "the first impression of an unbiassed reader who dips into the poems of Donne is unfavourable." In the tradition of words like Gothic, Baroque, Metaphysical, and Romantic, the term Mannerist must serve an apprenticeship in which it receives derision and abuse. The key to its emancipation is presented to us by Hauser, who insists on the dissociation of the descriptive and qualitative elements. The explicitness of his plea and its common sense make it worth quotation:

Mannerism came so late into the foreground of research on the history of art, that the depreciatory verdict implied in its very name is often still taken to be adequate, and the unprejudiced conception of this style as a purely historical category has been made very difficult. In the case of other names given to historical styles, such as Gothic and Renaissance, baroque and classicism, the original—positive or negative—valuation has already become completely obliterated, but in the case of mannerism, on the other hand, the negative attitude is still so strongly active that one has to fight against a certain inner resistance, before one can summon up the courage to call the great artists and writers of this period "manneristic." Not until the concept of the manneristic is completely separated from that of the mannered, do we get a category that can be used in the historical investigation of these phenomena. The purely descriptive concept of the species and the qualitative concept, which have to be distinguished from each other here, coincide over certain stretches, but intrinsically they have almost nothing in common.[14]

Mannerism canvasses the elements of a fixed traditional pattern, unexpectedly combines them to achieve effects of dissonance, dislocation, and surprise, and illuminates the reader's mind, enabling him to reconsider the whole traditional pattern of their relationship. Mannerist works, even when they appear by classical standards to be unfinished, perverse, or inscrutable, do succeed in reflecting a real side of our psychological life.

If the concept of Mannerism did not exist we should by now be compelled to invent it. The old concept of the Renaissance as a long florescence exhibiting an extended succession of blooms and only slowly fading has now disappeared. In its place we have the concept of the High Renaissance as a "narrow ridge" of a couple of decades only. In "the short span of barely twenty years,... there actually remains only a relatively small number of works in which normativeness and balance of high classic style can be demonstrated."[15] Such a theory of Italian painting will surprise least of all the student of English poetry of the sixteenth and seventeenth centuries. From the *Shepheardes Calender* to the last of the true miscellanies there extend two decades in which the High Renaissance enjoys its brief and splendid maturity.

If the concept of Mannerism is accepted, it is possible to see Donne and the Metaphysicals in a new and achromatic light. No longer does

14. *Ibid.*, 353.
15. Friedländer, *Mannerism and Anti-Mannerism*, 4. Cf. Hauser: "The High Renaissance was of short duration; it covered no more than twenty years" (*The Social History of Art*, I, 352).

their style seem like an aberration, even a splendid one, but rather as the logical development from Spenserian or Sidneyan smoothness and the necessary bridge from this island of stability to the Baroque terra firma on which the larger works of Milton are erected.

It may be objected that Wölfflin long ago supplied the concept of an art which perpetuated and yet rebelled against High Renaissance modes and that he applied to it the name Baroque. This is true and no one familiar with Wölfflin's contribution, its massiveness and richness, would be willing to disparage it. It is undeniable however, that Wölfflin's conception of the Baroque style was over-extended and has benefited by a withdrawal to the later part of the period he investigated, leaving much that he once subsumed under the Baroque to achieve self-government under this other concept of Mannerism. The most striking single instance of this operation is probably the recognition of the Gesù in Rome as a Mannerist, and definitely not a Baroque, structure.

It is interesting to find Wellek in 1946 discriminating between two main literary manifestations of Baroque,[16] "that of the mystics and tortured souls such as Donne and Angelus Silesius and another baroque which must be conceived as a continuation of rhetorical humanism and Petrarchism, a courtly 'public' art which finds its expression in the opera, the Jesuit drama and the heroic plays of Dryden." In the days when Wölfflin's original grand concept prevailed unmodified some such conclusion was almost inevitable. Subdivisions with clearly different characteristics made themselves felt in any survey of the Baroque in Wölfflin's sense of the term.[17]

Reference has already been made to the recognized place of Michelangelo among the Mannerists. So vast a genius as his cannot be contained within this term any more than Shakespeare can be labelled a Mannerist because *Hamlet* and other plays show the familiar Mannerist pattern. What is certain and incontrovertible is that the "Last Judgement" in the Sistine Chapel (referred to by one critic as "that overwhelming paradigm of Mannerism"), together with two Floren-

16. R. Wellek, "The Concept of Baroque in Literary Scholarship," *Journal of Aesthetics and Art Criticism*, V (2), 77–109.
17. See M. W. Croll, "The Baroque Style in Prose," *Studies in English Philology*; P. Meissner, *Die geistesgeschichtlichen Grundlagen des englischen Literaturbarocks*; R. Daniells, "Baroque Form in English Literature," *University of Toronto Quarterly*, XIV (4), 393–408.

tine works, the Laurentian Library and the Medici Chapel, can be accepted as prototypes of Mannerist art.

The circumstances in which Michelangelo laboured to create a memorial for the Medici in the chapel constructed beneath the Church of San Lorenzo are well known. The sack of Rome in 1527 and the ensuing expulsion of the Medici from Florence, the siege of Florence itself, the extinction of its republican liberties, the departure of Michelangelo from the city in 1534, never to return: these events help to account for the incomplete complex of sculpture and architecture which the student of the Medici Chapel now encounters. But when allowance has been made for this, the fact remains that the statues of Giuliano and Lorenzo, together with their two pairs of attendant figures and the architectural setting afforded by the chapel itself, which Michelangelo devised as a sepulchral memorial, are an overwhelming embodiment of his intentions and a matchless demonstration of his technique. We must only observe the precaution of not attributing to Mannerism such blanks and lapses in the design as were the result of political upheavals.

Michelangelo's avoidance of colour adds emphasis to the appeal of the forms, both architectural and sculptural. There is a strong intellectual component in this appeal, a surprise, a shock at the palpable change in the handling of conventions, an extremely stimulating sense of a fresh and powerful hand at work, a sense of being startled into fresh sensibility, obliged to reconsider familiar facts, asked in a highly personal idiom to reconsider some important issues, a sense of being drawn out into alertness, of finding nothing which rests satisfactorily or soothes the mind, of meeting that breaking of accent which deserves not hanging but the closest attention and response. The logic of construction responds to what in another field we should call wit.

The chapel is high for its size yet there is no Baroque undulation or expansiveness. The four supporting figures seem ready to slide from their marble couches. The line of their heads is neither above nor below the cornice but is cut by its horizontal. Yet we are neither disturbed nor amused. Here innovation is handled with sobriety, intensity, and complete mastery. The heads of the two male figures are left rough, one of them is scarcely disengaged from the block. The female figures are both androgynous and they share with the male figures a pervading ambiguousness. Twilight is presented as a male figure, night as female; similarly dawn as female and day as male. Like the figures of Lorenzo and Giuliano above them, each seems wrapped in a dream appropriate to his own person and powers. They have no regard, like the figures of a Baroque tableau, for each other, nor any for the spectator. The Medici figures themselves are not portraits, nor do their attitudes, that of pensiveness for Lorenzo and that of expectancy, as of the moment before action, for Giuliano, correspond to their known characters and proclivities. They are wholly idealized, the denizens of their creator's personal world. It is a world from which a sombre and passionate intelligence looks out and takes this occasion of the death of princes to argue with the heart. It makes free with the rules of harmony to sound its own chord, sustained here with an unbelievable resonance.

The architecture of the chapel exhibits niches with angular surrounds displaying a variety of planes and, similarly, sharply bounded panels recessed into certain pilasters. There are similarities between it and the ante-room of the Laurentian Library, to which we must next turn our attention. The effect of the chapel is to put the spectator on the alert, to rouse the expectation that some message of extreme and sombre urgency is about to be transmitted. If one is asked to say in plain prose what this message is, one can only stumble about, protesting at the inadequacy of words to convey the power of plastic forms. One could hazard that here a creative spirit of incomparable power, neglecting all popular appeal and facile repetition of traditional effects, is telling us something about death. The Medici themselves mean less to Michelangelo here than Edward King to Milton, but they demonstrate that even princes fall under death's dominion, that no powers of action or of intellect can save them. The Child hiding his face in the breast of the Virgin supplies an answer to death's depredations, but not here and now, in this atmosphere of tense realization of death's power. There is a paradoxical reversal and denial in this chapel. The Virgin and Child, flanked by the saints Cosmo and Damien in reverential attitudes, together with the altar in the recess opposite them, would seem designed to affirm orthodox doctrines of hope and of release from death's sway. But unsubdued by such representations, death, as it were, suffuses the central volume of the edifice before the two dead princes and their mysterious flanking allegories. The import of these latter teases us out of thought. Dawn is represented by a female waking, her face filled with weariness; Evening by a male figure with a virile body and wearied head. Day is wrathfully aroused and the unfinished eye sockets glare. Night, with symbolic adjuncts of owl and moon and tragic mask and sleep-inducing fruits, is sorrowfully sleepless, in uneasy and unstable posture. And if we turn from allegory to actuality, the wretched life of Lorenzo and the frustration of Giuliano's hopes by his early death as a consumptive make only more acute our racking sense of death's immediacy. Such consolations and escapes as the statue of the Virgin and Child or the altar offer open up only to close again.

It is less necessary to consider this chapel further than to turn to that other work of Michelangelo's associated with the Church of San Lorenzo. This is the so-called Laurentian Library.

The views advanced by contemporary art historians concerning this structure may seem to some readers to spring from too close and ingenious an examination of its elements just as the criticism of metaphysical poetry has suffered from over-reading of the texts. It should therefore be emphasized that Wittkower's critique,[18] a classic of its kind, is based upon a wealth of documentation and close observation and agrees in its conclusions with the less detailed analysis put forward by Pevsner.[19] It is important to notice that Riegl,[20] as early as 1908, was pointing the student of this architecture in the direction of similar conclusions. It is also of interest to see that Vasari had words of discriminating praise when the Library possessed the simple novelty of newness. "Artists therefore," he writes in his *Life*,

owe Michelangelo a great debt for having broken the chains which made them all work in one way. He showed it even better in the library of St. Lorenzo, in the handsome disposition of the windows and ceiling and the marvellous vestibule. Nothing so graceful and vigorous in every part was ever seen, comprising the bases, tabernacles, corners, convenient staircase with its curious divisions, so different from the common treatment as to excite general wonder.[21]

The vicissitudes to which Michelangelo's original concept for the

18. R. Wittkower, "Michelangelo's Biblioteca Laurenziana," *Art Bulletin*, XVI (2), 123–218.
19. Pevsner, "The Architecture of Mannerism."
20. A. Riegl, *Die Entstehung der Barockkunst in Rom*.
21. Vasari, *Lives of the Painters*, IV, 133–4.

Library and its ante-room (the Ricetto) were subjected were both lengthy and tortuous. Wittkower is nevertheless able to show the reader of his analysis of this "most important and influential Italian secular building of the sixteenth century" that Michelangelo's intentions came through unimpaired (page 205): "Our investigations have shown that the change of plan, necessitated by purely external reasons, which led to the present arrangement of the Ricetto and the stair is of decisive importance. The external necessity for change is, however, merely the occasion for an intensification of ideas already contemplated by Michelangelo in the first stage of the plan." To take the extreme example of the staircase: Michelangelo submitted a drawing in the spring of 1524 and it was early in 1559 that he sent from Rome a terracotta model to Ammanati, who was by this time in charge of the work. Yet Wittkower demonstrates that "Anyone who has followed the manifold development of Michelangelo's ideas for the stair will be able to see elements of their every stage in the completed building" (page 179). As for the Library itself, the conclusion reached is that the scroll which Cosimo I affixed above the entrance to record his completion of the work remains "the sole element in the room to disturb the absolute dominion of Michelangelo's ideas of form" (page 200).

The Library and particularly the Ricetto, if they can now be accepted as embodying the intentions of a great and revolutionary architectural genius, deserve the closest attention. Wittkower demonstrates that we are presented, particularly in the Ricetto, with insoluble conflicts. The storey at the entrance level (the floor of which is some three metres below the floor of the library proper) contains the staircase, which stands clear of its walls and occupies the available space so as to make of the walls of this storey the "shell of a sculptural kernel." Above this level, however, are two more storeys, clear of the stair, which simply serve as boundaries to the volume of the room. But if we consider each of the four walls of the Ricetto from floor to ceiling it is clear that the treatment is by the use of classical orders completely unified. The two functions of containing the stair and enclosing the room are never accommodated to one another.

The controlling theme of the whole building is, indeed, an unresolved alternation between extremes. The wall stands before the orders so that they are prevented from exercising their proper function of bearing burdens and articulating wall surfaces. The steps fall in a "cascade" from the library door; such is the effect of the central section. The two side flights, however, give the effect of climbing upward and where the three meet the directional uncertainty is unresolved. There is a species of cleavage effected upon the doorways; door frame and gable, for example, are prevented from uniting. In the framing of the tabernacles normal relations of stress have been reversed. The capitals depend from the entablatures which they ought to support. Triglyphs hang "like dewdrops" below their pilasters. Niches are made to look each like a smaller rectangular box encased within a larger one but if we follow the perimeters round we find this is not so.

As already indicated, there is an extended conflict between interpretations of the room: as a series of separable storeys and as a totality with vertical emphasis and articulation. The piers themselves may be regarded as a range of articulating members that could be stripped from the wall "like a net" but considered from above they are seen to form a homogeneous continuum with the topmost stretch of wall.

There is no suggestion in this analysis that the ante-room or the Library as a whole should be regarded as possessing Baroque movement. On the contrary, the impression the spectator receives is that of eloquent tension between opposites. "The whole Laurenziana is fundamentally," says Wittkower (pages 215–16), "a static structure.... The particular character of the Ricetto comes, however, from the fact that in so small a room such strong relief should be used and the wall so deeply broken up. This gives the effect of an overwhelming oppression, and from it the unstable conflict derives its powerful domination."

If we are willing to accept an analysis of this kind, certain conclusions follow inevitably. It is possible, we must admit, for a genius of the very first rank to create a major work of striking effect and pervasive influence, upon principles which would seem totally perverse. It is possible, in other words, to employ the familiar components of some conventional form of construction, to use them all in ways which it is almost impossible to avoid labelling as "wrong" or "unacceptable," and yet to produce effects of strange and enduring beauty.

To enter the Laurentian Library is to confront an architectural

statement of extreme, perhaps unique, intensity. Within these subdued gray and white walls, reminiscent of the Medici Chapel, something extraordinary is going on. Michelangelo, "being dead yet
speaketh." The first effect is simply one of strangeness. Then gradually
and with increasing clarity the eloquence of the architectural utterance
makes itself heard. For eloquence it is, in the familiar language of
classical structures, as conventional, after two thousand years of use
and modulation, as the grammar of the classical languages with which
it is inevitably associated. The message of these two apartments, the
Ricetto and the Library proper, is neither of repose nor release. We
are drawn up by the great height of the former only to be sucked as
it were into the long avenue of the reading room with its thirty-foot
ceiling. There are no Baroque tricks of illumination or illusions of
illimitable space, only the mind exploring its own limited possibilities
of levitation and penetration, only the creative imagination recombin-
ing the given elements of structure to suggest the nature of its own
struggles, its paralyses of will, its displacements of energy and stress.

Beside this architecture the monuments of Baroque with rare excep-
tions seem rhetorical and assertive. It has been said that lyric poetry
should not be heard but overheard. And when we enter either the
Medici Chapel or the Laurentian Library, through doors which seem
to open by accident and refuse to proclaim themselves as portals, we
slip in as it were to regions where the dialogue of Michelangelo's mind
with itself is proceeding. It is saying that the familiar forms can be
deployed to different ends, that the mind baffled by time and fate
may nevertheless with inconceivable ingenuity and virtuosity express
that bafflement to the everlasting enrichment of its own endurance
and comprehension. Absenting himself voluntarily from the facility
and felicity of Renaissance style, Michelangelo will draw his breath
in pain to tell a complex and infinitely rewarding story.

If, then, the possibility can be conceded that a genius of the first
rank may employ the modes and devices of reorganization which we
are calling a Mannerist use of classical elements, if in so doing he may
construct masterpieces which centuries later amaze and delight the
beholder, if this style is seen to be not the sole one of which he is
capable—for Michelangelo's work *in toto* goes far beyond Mannerist
confines—then perhaps we may in this context turn to Milton.

3. *COMUS* AND *LYCIDAS*

THE THOUGHT that Milton might be a Mannerist will be instantly repellent to many of his readers, but this natural aversion to a shocking idea may perhaps be tempered by the thought that Michelangelo—who is not inferior to Milton compare them how one will—now bears the same stigma. It is, after all, not unreasonable to expect from Milton one or two Mannerist pieces. He was a strict contemporary of the Metaphysicals and exposed to the same cultural influences and climate of opinion. That his later style is by no stretch of imagination to be called Mannerist need cause no confusion for it is now recognized that metaphysical and Baroque styles may appear successively in the same writer and need cause no more disturbance to the critic than the discovery that Bernini's early sculpture of Aeneas leaving Troy is Mannerist in its whole conception and design.

Comus

Comus will provide a convenient beginning, though not the first instance of Mannerism in Milton, and we can perhaps best approach this familiar territory by rehearsing some dicta of A. S. P. Woodhouse's with which few will now disagree.[1] Milton is highly imitative, steeped in Virgil and Horace and Ovid and able to make a most effective use of Homer and Hesiod, Pindar and the Greek tragedians and pastoral writers. His palpable model is almost always one of the recognized genres but the traditional form is only his starting point: what he makes of it is wholly his own. He is pre-eminently a creator

1. From a speech given by A. S. P. Woodhouse to the Milton Society in September 1957.

of structures; he "builds the lofty rhyme"; everything depends for meaning and effectiveness on its place in the structural pattern. Structure and not imagery is the starting point for elucidation. How firm a base this is for a consideration of *Comus* appears from the fact that critics from the eighteenth century onward have conducted attack or defence on this terrain.

Traditionally recognized as a work of much importance, *Comus* has nevertheless evoked a persistent dissatisfaction in the critics. It is neither a good masque nor a good play. The villain is a more attractive figure than the heroine so that his name stands as title by general agreement. Even what Milton intends by "chastity" or "virginity," although absolutely central to an understanding of the piece, has puzzled the commentators. From Johnson on, admiration has been tempered with uneasiness, which from time to time has burst out in complaint, even exasperation.

An example of this reaction to *Comus*, remote enough from both Johnson on one side and from modern criticism on the other to stand on its own feet, is to be found in the critique written by Richard Cumberland the dramatist for the performance of *Comus* in 1808. With regard to the audience for whom *Comus* was written, Cumberland concedes that Milton was "well assured that whilst he regaled them with fine poetry, they would receive him with candour and good breeding. He risqued nothing, therefore, so long as he wrote well, for even allegory and metaphysics (ingredients above all most hostile to the constitution of the drama) were to be rendered palatable to the Lord President and his company, when administered through the vehicle of his dulcifying poetry." This rich and flowing style is not, however, a dramatic style. Had Milton written professedly as a dramatist, that is, for public representation, he must have taken one of two courses, either to develop a new dramatic technique of his own or to outwrite the Elizabethans and Jacobeans in their own way. "He did not openly and avowedly commit himself to either of these undertakings."

Cumberland proceeds from this tempered praise into outright attacks upon Milton's performance. "The morose philosophizing humour of the poet shows itself through the finely wrought veil which he has cast over it." The Attendant Spirit "gives a very bad account of the people under his care" and his opening harangue concerning the

Medici Chapel, Florence, tomb of Lorenzo

Medici Chapel, Florence, tomb of Giuliano

gods would have the gods of the gallery either asleep or in open rebellion. Comus as shepherd "still preserves his dithyrambic roll, and the Lady listens to a clown, who addresses her in the language of Apollo, and never suspects that she has been talking to a counterfeit." As for the Brothers, while their poetry is flowing profusely their search stands still and notwithstanding the ostensibly superior argument of the elder, the younger has the better common sense of the two. "The severest critic will find gold enough in it to repay his search; but even the most candid will confess, that there is an abundant proportion of tinsel."

The version used in the 1808 performance was the abridgement used at the Theatre Royal in Covent Garden in 1774. It endeavours by excisions and additions to overcome some of Milton's deficiencies as a dramatist. The speeches of the Attendant Spirit, particularly his lengthy initial monologue, are shared with a second spirit called Philadel (or in another place Lycidas). The Brothers are tempted by a female of Comus' train in a fashion parallel to the Lady's temptation. Other fresh characters are Euphrosyne, Bacchanals, and Bacchantes. The alterations, designed to turn *Comus* into a more lively and better-knit piece, with more spectacle and less moralizing, show clearly enough that Milton was regarded as a great poet who has composed a poor play.

We might suppose that *Comus* is a poor play because it is a good masque. Such assumptions, however, have been demolished by Enid Welsford. *Comus*, she argues, although it has such essential masque features as the poetic induction, the two anti-masques, the main masque, and the epilogue, suffers from radical deficiencies which forever deny it the status of a successful example of the genre. There are, to begin with, no masquers; the Lady and her Brothers are already pre-empted by the slight dramatic action. It is possible, more-over, to read *Comus* and hardly realize that there are dances. The hinge of the action is not revelation or a metamorphosis but an act of free will: the piece is indeed a dramatized debate. Even so, there is a fundamental incongruity epitomized by the fact that the masque, presided over by Hymen, sorts ill with the sage and serious doctrine of virginity. The golden world of beauty ruled over by Hymen, having at its heart the rituals of Springtime found in the entertain-ments of the Renaissance, "is emphatically not the right symbol for

Milton's harsh creed in which goodness is identified with power rather than with love, and evil is identified with sensuality rather than with cruelty or selfishness...."[2] This objection ramifies into specific difficulties; for example, Milton repeatedly tells us that Comus is evil, yet there is in the presentation very little to suggest this.

If *Comus* is a bad play and a bad masque, it is perhaps a good poem with an acceptable moral conclusion. Such an assumption is exposed, however, to a powerful assault from still another critical quarter. Strong objection is taken to Milton's conduct of his ideology. An especially cogent expression of such objection is put forward by Malcolm Ross, who sees in the association of Chastity, not Charity, with Faith and Hope (lines 213–15) "the reduction of the highest supernatural grace to a secondary practical virtue." Even this would not prevent the play from achieving dramatic success if it were not that when Milton attempts finally to release his heroine and to symbolize concretely, as he must, the high doctrine of virginity, "he does so with a kind of bastard ritual which combines pagan and Christian elements." The Christian and pagan elements in Milton's resolution do not pull together. The Christian images are denatured by Milton's failure to evoke Christian charity and divine love. The pagan elements cannot be elevated as the form requires, but remain merely magical, decorative, or accessory. The epilogue shifts the focus and has no relation to the character or behaviour of the Lady, and the ethical life it envisages is still conceptually tenuous.

In *Comus*, on one level, Milton expresses the exhilaration of the dedicated moral self. On the other level, he is entangled in the treatment of a restrictive moral technique. On one level, the riches of classical and natural allusion are employed with unambiguous daring. On the other level, obsolescent Christian images collide with classical allusion. Milton fails to unify the two levels in any comprehensive and comprehensible purpose. Thus the note of exhilaration and the note of restraint remain distinct.[3]

From such discoveries in the realm of Milton's shortcomings there would seem to be only three directions in which the critic could proceed: toward the conclusion that the piece is a structural ruin on which the wild flowers of some fine poetic nevertheless flourish; or to the notion that this masque is a simple thing written to entertain

2. Enid Welsford, *The Court Masque*, 321.
3. M. M. Ross, *Poetry and Dogma*, 201.

the Bridgewater family (in the words of Robert Adams, "*Comus* as a masque presenting a clear story, a simple allegory, and a graceful compliment embroidered with a fluid imagery seems to me worth ten fretworks of strained conceit and forced interpretation"[4]); or finally to the belief that diligent search will reveal a true and underlying consistency in both Milton's ideology and his tectonics.

The first and second alternatives are on examination so improbable that we should accept either of them only if all proof of alternatives fails. The structure of all Milton's minor works is superb. It is hard, indeed, to think of any poem, except "The Passion" and some undergraduate efforts, that does not upon repeated reading and the closest kind of examination disclose a fabric both firm and delicate enough to satisfy the most exacting. And, similarly, the longer one is acquainted with Milton the deeper grows the conviction that nothing he composed was simple. It is hard, indeed, to believe that the poet of *L'Allegro–Il Penseroso* and of *Lycidas* should between these two have spent his energies on a simple piece of graceful entertainment. The unlikelihood of these two possibilities may be put thus summarily as a reason for exploring alternatives. The third possibility, already mentioned, has been elaborated convincingly by A. S. P. Woodhouse.[5]

The intellectual frame of reference which Woodhouse provides for *Comus* is that of the order of Nature and the order of Grace. Nature provides doctrines of temperance and of continence. Grace provides the doctrine of Virginity in the sense of complete dedication. Between these and partaking of both nature and grace is the doctrine of Chastity, grounded in nature, elaborated in Platonic thought, taken over then by Christianity and carried to a new plane.

If we follow this plan, we find Comus, by appeals to nature, seeking to undermine continence. In rebuttal the Lady also appeals to nature and goes on to show how nature supports the further virtue of

4. R. M. Adams, *Ikon: John Milton and the Modern Critics*, 34. And cf. J. C. Maxwell, "The Pseudo-Problem of *Comus*," *Cambridge Journal*, I, 376–80; e.g., "At various stages virtue reveals itself in different contexts as chastity, as virginity, as temperance, as continence. The patterning of these is important, and Professor Woodhouse has taught us much about it, but there has never been any real danger of destroying the unity of the whole."

5. Woodhouse, "The Argument of Milton's *Comus*," *University of Toronto Quarterly*, XI (I), 46–71, and "*Comus* Once More," *ibid.*, XIX (3), 218–23. See also W. G. Madsen, "The Idea of Nature in Milton's Poetry" in *Three Studies in the Renaissance: Sidney, Johnson, Milton*, 181–283.

Temperance. She then moves on to argue the cause of chastity, a virtue to which both nature and grace contribute and the natural foundation of which has been already elaborated to the audience by the Elder Brother. At the apex of this series of concepts there now shines forth the sage and serious doctrine of virginity, "the ideal culmination of an ethical scheme whose foundations are laid in the order of nature, and which ascends through the whole range of human experience." Sabrina, symbol of divine grace, brings the water of life to effect the Lady's ultimate liberation. The epilogue summarizes the succession.

First, the beauty of nature, with all its gracious associations, which Comus perverts; secondly, in the image of Venus and Adonis, the powers and processes of nature, which Comus (like Acrasia) would prostitute and thwart; thirdly, in the image of Cupid and Psyche, ascent to the highest virtue and wisdom accessible on the natural level, or rather ascent to an area common to nature and grace: thus far the summary has proceeded. But there is one more step to take:

> Mortals that would follow me,
> Love Virtue: she alone is free....

Thus the doctrine of Christian Liberty appears, to close the sequence and to complement the insistence upon struggle and discipline in the earlier passages.

In Comus Milton does not repudiate the order of nature; he does not deny an area common to nature and grace, or the ascent through it from natural wisdom to divine; he does not seek to divorce the two orders. But he believes that experience on the level of grace will cast a light back upon nature and enable one to realize its true significance.[6]

There can be no doubt that the frame of reference delineated by Woodhouse is a true and convincing one, though the bald summary here given robs it of its tone of humane persuasion and its supporting references to Spenser and to other works of Milton.

There remains, however, the chorus of misgiving about Comus, from which we might now isolate a few more individual voices. D. C. Allen argues that Comus is not a masque: it is too long, the cast is too small, the locale too precise, the plot too tense, the theme too serious; humour is wanting, there is emphasis on drama rather than on spectacle, dance, costume, and singing. The plot is implausible:

6. Woodhouse, "Argument of Milton's Comus," 70, 71.

Comus never brings his mother's traditional devices of glass and wand explicitly into play but uses magic dust and a chair. He tries to argue the Lady into drinking the cup only when she is in his palace, thoroughly aroused and suspicious. Seduction never develops into a real possibility. The ideology is obscurely embodied: some of the lady's strength is her own, some the Attendant Spirit's, some the Brothers'. Her own strength is in part conscience, in part the guardianship of heaven, and in part invulnerable chastity.

In the background is the classic complaint of Dr. Johnson in the "Life" that the action of *Comus* is improbable and that Comus himself does not seem corrupt, though alleged to be. The speeches are declamations; "the auditor therefore listens as to a lecture, without passion, without anxiety." The language is poetical and the sentiments are generous, but there is something wanting to allure attention. The language is too luxuriant for dialogue. The songs are vigorous and full of imagery, but harsh in their diction and not very musical in their numbers. It is a drama in the epic style, inelegantly splendid and tediously instructive. It is apparent that Johnson is attracted and repelled by *Comus* in a fashion which prevents a resolution of his judgement. Macaulay's detection of incongruities suggests the same reaction: "It is when Milton escapes from the shackles of the dialogue, when he is discharged from the labour of uniting two incongruous styles, when he is at liberty to indulge his choral raptures without reserve, that he rises even above himself." The perception of an irreconcilable dichotomy is also implied in the views of Miss Welsford already quoted[7] and, indeed, she becomes quite explicit. *Comus* is founded upon an idea. "The real soul of the masque, however, was the rhythmic movement of living bodies."[8]

Such reactions, the recognition of Milton's genius, the real delight both in the content and in the style of the piece, the conviction that it nevertheless fails to be what it sets out to be and that it achieves its success to the accompaniment of grievous breakdowns of the dramatic vehicle—these are elements hard to reconcile. It seems doubtful whether the scheme of nature and grace, perceived as the basis of Milton's exhortation, will nullify the strictures we have recounted.

In search of a fresh approach we might accept without dismay

7. See above, p. 21.
8. Welsford, *The Court Masque*, 330.

Milton's simultaneous employment of two kinds of dramatic architecture, that of the masque and that of the play. *Comus* was produced and published as a masque and all the elements of the masque are present, if we allow that the chief characters double as masquers. It would even appear that the detail and spirit of masque was dear to some side of Milton's spirit. "The gilded car of day" may be a transmogrification of the painted cart which brought Italian masquers to the scene; if so, the elevation of the image is quite in his manner. More to the point is his creation by verbal means of a rich mythical and pastoral scenery. In the spirit of masque, too, if we look at it rightly, is the enormous courtly compliment paid to the members of the Bridgewater family. At the same time, the conventions of a play are produced: situation, contrasting characters, involvement, reversals, climax, denouement. In whatever terms we wish to express it, the machinery is there. And the two constructs are irreconcilable. Perhaps this is an entrée to some private struggle of Milton's, only released for our observation because Lawes, in need of words for his projected masque, importuned his friend to provide them.

> Eheu! quid volui misero mihi! floribus austrum
> Perditus—

was affixed to Lawes's dedication and may mirror Milton's own mood. If the two genres Milton is harnessing refuse to pull together, it may be that a like recalcitrance afflicts his characters. They have an extraordinary reluctance to communicate with one another. The Spirit must elaborately bridge the gap between himself and the Brothers before he can explain matters and get the urgent search under way. To the Lady he never speaks till about to lead her offstage. Only to Sabrina, a fellow spirit, can he communicate comfortably and even so it is in an incantation. Comus speaks only to the Lady but notes her "different pace," and from the stichomythic and argumentative nature of their dialogue forms they appear to be on opposed sides of the stage. To her Brothers, to the Spirit, and to Sabrina the Lady never speaks. The Brothers, in turn, never speak to her, or to Comus, or to Sabrina. We are told that they rush in upon Comus, wresting the glass out of his hand and driving his rout in. It is unconvincing, so much so that when Arthur Rackham came to depict this scene as an illustration, he represented the Brothers by two brandished swords at the margin of the picture. In Blake's illustration, the two Brothers and Comus resemble three friends dancing while the Lady looks on.

We can find the difficulty of communication among the characters plausible if we regard each of them as strongly related to a powerful idea of Milton's, passionately conceived but not resolved into a spectrum of concepts. It is convenient, indeed, to pursue the idea that each character may inhabit his own space and that these spaces are not brought into a common perspective. The Spirit resides before the threshold of Jove's court, in a region of Platonic ideals. He descends directly from it upon the forest near Ludlow and he returns a little obliquely, but intelligibly, via the ocean and the Gardens of Hesperus in the west. Above his Platonic habitation is another region, which is Jove's court itself, where Cupid and Psyche are. Comus, in a quite different and earthbound space, inhabits the navel of a hideous wood which has some form of reality different from the world of Ludlow. His palace is not destroyed, as readers of Spenser might hope it would be. The Lady and her Brothers are told to leave its vicinity quickly for fear of further harm. The Earl of Bridgewater's "new entrusted sceptre" may bear sway in Ludlow but his writ, it appears, does not run in the forest. Both the Lady and her Brothers are seen against the pastoral backdrop which Milton has so lavishly decorated but they achieve no kind of relation to it or to each other; their irrational parting when the Brothers had "stept as they said to the next Thicket side" is plausible because we can hardly visualize them as a trio. (Let us think, for a helpful contrast, of the way in which Shakespeare's Arden received and amalgamated its discrepant residents and visitors.) Finally, we search for Sabrina's living space and find it under water in a world of magic different from the Spirit's world of ideals. That the total space implied is parcelled into cartouches which inhibit transit becomes apparent as we follow the plot. The Spirit apparently does not enter the heaven of Jove. His own Platonic world is not, within the play, specifically entered by anyone else. He is for some reason in the Hesperides where the terrestrial Venus sits by Adonis. Her son, however, who is the celestial, not the terrestrial, Eros, inhabits the very court of Jove. As for the Heaven of the Christian God, which will stoop to help feeble Virtue, that is something again which the imagination does not readily identify with any of the other regions mentioned.

If we are willing to look in a humble way at what the plot offers by way of a sequence of related events we may be surprised at the oddness of the succession. The Spirit has been sent by Jove to save the Lady and has come "Swift as the Sparkle of a glancing Star" to perform his task but stops to address ninety lines of blank verse to the audience. He is naturally too late. Comus comes on and makes a speech demonstrating his own moral corruption but the fall of the verse does nothing to convince us of his obliquity. These are the climactic lines:

> Hail Goddess of Nocturnal sport,
> Dark veil'd Cotytto, t' whom the secret flame
> Of midnight Torches burns; mysterious Dame,
> That ne'er art call'd but when the Dragon womb
> Of Stygian darkness spits her thickest gloom,
> And makes one blot of all the air,
> Stay thy cloudy Ebon chair
> Wherein thou rid'st with Hecat', and befriend
> Us thy vow'd Priests....

It is worth feeling the dulcet fall of this passage because in other instances such as the description of defeated deities in the Nativity Hymn or the Mulciber passage at the end of Book I of *Paradise Lost* we know and feel why Milton contradicts sound and sense. Here some different explanation must be sought. It would appear that the golden world of the pastoral which the masque form has invited to descend and occupy the stage is really inviolable, even to Milton's strictures. If it were to prove vulnerable, as it should, surely this is the moment, when the orgies of the Thracian goddess Cotytto are invoked by the enchanter. We are told by the foot-note that these were lewd and vicious; we find it difficult to believe.[9]

Enter the Lady with a burst of unprovoked censoriousness which instantly puts us off: "ill-manag'd Merriment," "loose unletter'd Hinds," "rudeness and swill'd insolence"; the petulance of these phrases chills our sympathy. And when she continues her soliloquy and puts her trust in Faith, Hope, and Chastity, the accusation already reviewed—that she shows a self-righteousness devoid of both charity and humility—is impossible to resist. By contrast Comus now exhibits

9. How carefully Milton avoided language that would convey a sense of lewdness is shown by the emendation which produced the line, "Us thy vowed priests till utmost end." In the Milton MS. it read, "And favour our close jocondrie."

a sensitiveness to beauty which charms us: "smoothing the Raven down / Of darkness till it smil'd," "sober certainty of waking bliss"— the words of an epicure perhaps but not, surely, of a sensualist. "I'll speak to her / And she shall be my Queen." This is Pluto and Proserpine but without violence.

The conflict between Lady and Enchanter fails for a number of reasons to induce genuine dramatic tension. He begins by the equivalent of tying her up, surely a poor preface to a speech of amorous persuasion. His argumentative method is that of crude logic embroidered with poetic images. He is an epicurean who would savour the sensuous pleasures of life and persuade others to do so. His argument that "Beauty is nature's coin, must not be hoarded" is unanswerable, for were it hoarded mankind would become extinct. The Lady's arguments take quite another course. When she scornfully asserts, "Thou hast nor Ear nor Soul to apprehend / The sublime notion and high mystery," she speaks the truth, yet if Comus cannot understand her the argument is no argument and the speech becomes a soliloquy addressed to the audience. The discrepancy between the pagan milieu, ideas, and language of Comus and those of the Lady, which are Platonic and Christian, is so great as to make real argument impossible. The reader or spectator, however willing, cannot for a moment suspend his disbelief and imagine that either Comus or the Lady could affect the ideas or the conduct of the other. The result is simple paralysis, for the Enchanter is as decisively immobilized as the Lady. There is nothing further that he can do, for he is clearly incapable of simple assault. And the Lady, for all her boast that she is able to bring down the palace—"shatter'd into heaps o'er thy false head"—cannot in fact release herself from the chair (and had better not have continued, with the words "Shall I go on?", into this and other hyperbolic statements which neither the Milton MS. nor the Bridgewater MS. include but which must have been added later). The sad thing about the Lady is that neither from the point of view of nature nor that of grace is she a sympathetic figure. Her priggish, self-righteous egotism unfits her for the pastoral world; her total lack of charity, humility, or a sense of sin disqualify her for the world of Christian character.

The Brothers are almost equally unappealing. Having lost their Sister by sheer neglect, they seek to persuade themselves (or rather the younger lets the elder persuade him) that she can come to no harm. But if so, why are they alarmed? If, in honest fact, a thousand angels hedge her about she is indeed immune, but even as he argues this, the Elder Brother is shifting his ground from a personal conviction that chastity repels all asaults upon it, through appeals to hearsay and classical antiquity, to a purely subjective view of chastity as that which purifies the soul. His vehemence cannot conceal the incongruity of his arguments. The Spirit now appears and although, as a denizen of a Platonic region of pure ideas he might be supposed to give them full credit for protective power, he proves full of alarm. His "O poor hapless Nightingale" communicates its tremor to the reader, who cannot now take seriously the rodomontade of the Elder Brother: "Virtue may be assail'd but never hurt...."

And now the full force of the incongruity begins to be felt. The strident claims made for chastity by the Brother prove largely without foundation. This is never admitted but becomes apparent when we consider that the Lady is understood to be in real danger and the Brothers (who presumably have also the sun-clad power of chastity) are quite unable to face the Enchanter. The Spirit comes to their support with the herb Haemony, the significance of which is extremely obscure. It is something magic. If we take it to be divine grace or redeeming power we are at a loss to know why its influence is so limited. If it is something in the realm of natural wisdom or goodness or subtlety, we cannot fathom why the Spirit or the Brothers or the Lady should not already possess this quality.

We move now to the climactic scene of the Lady's deliverance, pursued by an increasing group of incongruities. Not her own chastity, not guardian angels, not the Spirit sent by Jove, not even the virtue of the magic herb are employed to rid the Lady of the hateful presence of the Enchanter. A small application of physical force is all that is needed and Comus vanishes into the wood. Yet, so easily disposed of, he leaves behind an influence that needs a recourse to still another power—Sabrina. She has been said to typify divine grace. If so, we can only wonder why Milton must point in every direction but heavenward. She is in myth the illegitimate daughter of Locrine, done to death on the banks of the Severn. In Milton's version she is a girl with a difficult past—not a martyr, only an intended victim—who, after drowning in the Severn, has become a nature spirit, a water fairy. She is invoked in the names of Neptune, and his attendants, and the Sirens. Now "green ey'd Neptune," raving in defiance of heaven, is an old Miltonic equivalent for Satan and the Sirens are deceivers and destroyers of men no less than Circe. It is improbable to the verge of the impossible that Milton, if he wished us to accept Sabrina as the vehicle of a crowning act of divine grace, would invoke her in this fashion. Can we envisage the embodiment of divine grace descending, after her mission is complete, to perform a handmaiden's duties in the bower of Neptune's consort?

In any case Sabrina's magic does its work. Oddly applied to the Lady's finger and lip (as though she had actually tasted Comus' cup) and to the chair "Smear'd with gums of glutinous heat" (surely too adhesive an image), her chaste palms, moist and cold, release the spell.

And so the Lady is saved. But as a kind of anticlimax. Her intolerable pride and self-sufficiency disqualified her from the dignity of a willing martyr and now, having been awkwardly rescued by a mixture of force and natural magic, she shows neither gratitude nor humility. Stepping from the cartouche of majestic innocence and chastity, she dwindles into a little girl who has got out of a nasty situation in the woods and had better hurry home. The Spirit's tone is almost avuncular. The space into which her deliverance takes place contracts while we look on and becomes no bigger than the hall in Ludlow Castle.

The poet may have felt this for he added the mysterious dozen lines ("Waxing well of his deep wound" to "Youth and Joy; so Jove hath sworn") which do not appear in either the Milton MS. or the Bridgewater MS. These expand the epilogue into a vista of considerable but limited depth into which we should now direct our gaze. The Spirit first invites us to follow his flight to the Hesperides where nature blooms in unfading loveliness; there Venus watches by Adonis as he recovers from the castration wound. But why "eternal Summer" should be associated with this Adonis story of cyclical death and rebirth it is indeed difficult to say. To put it another way, how can the spruce and jocund Spring, the Graces and rosy-bosom'd Hours consort cheerfully with the Assyrian Queen as she "Sadly sits" by the couch of the still unawakened Adonis?

Far above this scene, presumably in heaven itself, we see the celestial form of Cupid embracing Psyche, from which embrace Youth and Joy are to be born. It is into this region that virtue can climb or, if too feeble, be raised by heaven's assistance. Yet if virtue is to be equated to the sage and serious doctrine of virginity it is hard to envisage it welcomed into this highly erotic, if transcendental atmosphere. Neither the Elder Brother nor the Lady has given us any intimation that the virgin soul is to achieve some kind of consummation in the arms of heavenly love. Once more the space into which the vista of deliverance admits us is inadequate. Even the union of celestial Cupid with Psyche gives rise to no more than Youth and Joy, which surely nature itself gives freely to mankind, without such high striving.

It is tempting to go on and ask why Milton did not include in his image of heaven stooping over wearied virtue the other image, which Spenser did not omit from the *Hymnes*, the image of heaven redeeming sinful man. Humility, here as elsewhere in the poem, is painfully absent. But to borrow a masterly phrase of Wittkower's, "Language and patience have limits when describing a Mannerist structure."

That *Comus* deserves to be examined in the context of Mannerist conventions we may now confidently urge. There is first the firm reliance upon traditional stylistic elements. There is nothing in the poem for which Christian or classical sources cannot be cited. The general contour or stance of the piece is such that we read it as an expression of Christian humanism of the Renaissance. But there are odd discrepancies, sheerings off at an angle, changes of direction, failures to fulfil normal expectations. Familiar elements are reconstituted, familiar effects rearranged. There is a deliberate willingness to provoke re-examination. The well-known marks of Mannerism abound. The style is elegant, precise, and refined; the action is strangely limited and the situations static. An intense self-consciousness shows in every character (and Milton has introduced both himself, qua poet, as a certain Shepherd Lad, and his *anima* in the form of the Lady). We feel "excess within rigid boundaries" and when there is release "the layer of opened-up space is shallow and clearly confined in depth." Nothing works out as it should. Yet few readers will agree that Milton was unable to pacify by a higher compromise the conflicts in *Comus* and that "for this reason the poem fails and we are baffled."[10] Most will feel with Lawes that they receive intense satisfaction from this piece, "so lovely and so much desired."

Comus is a great, a memorable, and a much loved work not because

10. D. C. Allen, *The Harmonious Vision*, 29.

it has no discrepancies and failures of resolution, and not (as is frequently implied) because its other merits outweigh these deficiencies,
but because the lapses and dislocations are such as to evoke an
aesthetic response of a new and intensely gratifying kind, even as
the Medici Chapel and the Laurentian Library, filled with violations
of the rules, nevertheless ravish the beholder. Our senses are charmed,
our emotions exalted, and our minds clarified.

Mannerist practice is dependent upon the existence of an anterior
body of work in which the conventions of classical and Christian
humanism are simply obeyed. It must be against the known pattern of
convention that the revealing strangeness is permitted to develop.
Comus is in a sense impossible without The Faerie Queene and
indeed the masterly delineation by Woodhouse of a progression in
Comus from nature to grace is accompanied by a parallel range of
references to the text of Spenser.

In support of the plea for a sympathetic view of dislocations in
Comus it can be pointed out that in the years since the appearance of
Grierson's edition of Donne we have slowly been taught that seventeenth-century imagery may be ambiguous; it is even claimed that
ambiguity is the chief virtue of an image. There is as yet scant
willingness to admit ambiguity in larger structures—unless in some
immensely self-evident instances like Hamlet or Don Quixote—though
surely it would be strange if seventeenth-century poets used
ambiguous imagery to decorate logically explicit structures and did
not extend their predilection for "significant darkness" to the larger
units of form. The problem will seldom arise in connexion with the
Metaphysicals, who excel in brief poems where a short line of argument is threaded through a few large and coruscating images. Milton,
however, is first and last structural.

Let us consider what lovers of Comus in the past (and let us not
think ourselves superior to them) may have experienced as they
traversed its terrain, full of geological faults, on which the pastoral
landscape spread its familiar charm. We know they sensed the fissures
and shifts of level but we know they achieved, as we can, an abiding
sense of satisfaction from the journey. The peaks of Christian doctrine
and the foothills of Spenserian allegory were always in view, as Woodhouse reminds us, to impart a sure sense of orientation.

The Attendant Spirit, lifting the mind to an initial vantage point from which the whole moral axis of the universe can be perceived, sets the pattern of ascent and descent upon that Jacob's ladder. The "due steps" of the righteous move surely up its Platonic gradations and "Swift as the Sparkle of a glancing Star" guardian spirits descend. Aspiration without strain; angelic protection swift and certain for the "favoured" ones who aspire. Comus the sensuous enchanter seems scarcely to be feared in such a cosmic scheme. The Spirit, for the better protection of his charges, will adopt a pastoral guise.

Now Comus himself enters. About him, as about the Spirit, a cosmology rapidly delineates itself in lucid poetic phrases. It is smaller than the Spirit's, reaching only to the stars, sun, and moon. Comus, much like his father, with blithe looks and curling locks, invites us to a revel, a debauch. Yet in Milton's range of experience there have been no riotous orgies and the frenzies and horrors of debauchery he knows nothing about. But how revealing, how true, how charming this innocence is, as charming as the inability of Sir Walter Scott to create a wicked character.

But innocent as Milton may be, he understands perfectly by a sort of divination (as indeed the least experienced Puritan always understands) the difference between moving toward the light and away from it. The Lady appears, counterpart of himself, the "Lady of Christ's." She is pure aspiration without compromise and can only look up. She is confused, in a touching and convincing way, about the safeguards which assure her vocation. She has a good conscience. God would send a guardian angel "if need were" to save her life and honour. In the meantime she would very much like to see her Brothers.

Comus, hearing and seeing her, falls in love with her beauty and through his appreciative senses we feel this beauty bodied forth. "And she shall be my Queen." How well their diverse temperaments would complement one another. How badly each needs the other. Such thoughts are not allowed to form. We are hurried away to find the Brothers. They take up and debate the theme of chastity in a timeless, unlocated fashion wrapped in the cocoon of night. Under the apparent classical lucidity of their debate the structure of their argument is frozen into a set of vectors pointing various ways, but all trying to aspire. Their Sister is perhaps in great peril. No, she is safe, guarded by the light within her own clear breast. But, though firm of purpose, she is in danger of rape and murder. But, no, she is guarded by chastity, which some people say gives physical protection and indeed the myths of the ancients seem to say so and truly a thousand angels (the inflation from the Lady's one angel is interesting) will guard her—but perhaps it is her thoughts that will be guarded, not her physical security. Perhaps, after all, as the Elder Brother says soon after to the Spirit, virtue may be surprised by unjust force but not enthralled yet still need to be rescued by prompt action and a strong arm.

The explanation for this backing and filling is that neither the Brothers, nor their Sister, nor Milton are willing to commit themselves to the Christian concept of martyrdom. The martyr hopes by the grace of God to prove invulnerable to spiritual assault. He does not expect to be protected from physical assault, any more than were Christ and the apostles. He has faith that after the wicked have done their worst, his soul will be received into the heavenly region of God's love, there to be safe, there to be rewarded. But in *Comus* there is a strong desire to make the Lady doubly invulnerable and give Comus no more than a very limited power over her or over the Brothers. If they have haemony (moly and Christ's thorn combined) they may safely invade his hall and with a fine show of brandished blades seize his glass and wand. This absence of an ideal of martyrdom troubles few readers. The expectation that the Lady will be able to out-argue and outface the Enchanter and that, having done this, she will be sure to escape his physical menace is so delightfully true to life as to disarm criticism. What youthful devoted poet could feel otherwise? Or what reader who put himself in the poet's place?

How emphatically the theme of martyrdom is avoided, the Lady's climactic speech to Comus clearly reveals. The sage and serious doctrine of virginity is approached but before the thought of the virgin martyrs and their cruel deaths and their rewards in heaven can be unfolded the Lady draws back with the excuse that Comus would not understand this high doctrine. The vision of the white-robed host in heaven who have sealed their faith with their blood is avoided. The layer of space actually opened up is not the great vault into which the flame of sacred vehemence promises to mount, but a smaller, flatter dome, more intimate and accessible in the form of a welcome to her father's great hall.

And since the deliverance is from rather than through tribulation, the means must be correspondingly in the earthly rather than the heavenly plane, though this must be a covert rather than a palpable shift. The symbolism of haemony and of the nymph Sabrina and indeed of the guardian Spirit himself is in each instance theologically vague and poetically deeply satisfying. The uncertainty and helplessness manifest in *Lycidas* are not allowed to appear. Instead there are the soaring idealism and dedication of spirit of a young poet who will pursue his course undeterred by temptations and menaces, but is not by any means a Douai Jesuit courting bright martyrdom.

But neither is he a dullard or sluggard. The vast view of a heaven of saints and martyrs has never opened up, but a vista now discloses itself carrying the eye to the Hesperides, the garden of Adonis, and Cupid and Psyche in the heavens. And this vista, not immediate to the theme of sensual temptation, contains images which could be called erotic if the word could be made to denote only love and fulfilment in their most ideal and ravishing sense. Even this vista ends with Youth and Joy and will not penetrate the holy of holies or the intense inane.

No one experiencing the abundant and profound delight which every new reading of *Comus* can give will disparage the poem because certain expectations implicit in its *dehors* have not been fulfilled. In their place we have what the equally unfulfilled architectural motifs of the Laurentian Library bestow, the sense of being actually within the aura of a great creative mind as it reshapes the known conventions to conform to the strict shape of its own inner necessities.

Comus reveals the struggles of a soul both Puritan and proud (a genus we recognize as having many species) to free itself from the temptations of beauty and the snares of passion, to dedicate itself to God unreservedly. All the while still young, without experience, without satiety, without the burning forehead and the parching tongue, or the sword that outwears its sheath—and without humility. There are alternate flashes of the ethical and the mystical, of will and imagination. We feel (to use a phrase that has been applied to Donne) "a shifting tension between outside possibilities." Yet all the while, obscurely, a coherent message makes its way to the heart. What is this final communication? That there is a ladder from earth to heaven down which come impulses and intuitions for our direction when in this world we move suddenly into the range of allurements of sense, and sensuousness and sensuality. Our self-centred ideals may fail to guard us and yet if we put up a good fight there is indeed a release from temptation, though our own tactless, inadequate posture of defence never manages to achieve it. The Platonic mind dedicating itself to the service of the Christian God, but without humility (either natural or by grace or from experience) is trapped, for all its protestations, and has awkwardly to be saved by the intervention of divine grace through unexpectedly natural channels of beauty, magic, and incantation. Release and relief from the clash between the sensuous world and the world of straining idealism comes from unconscious sources, from underneath the waters, from the flowery banks, from music and poetry and memory, all the deep wells of nature's purity and innocence. And so one is led home, silent and glad to get free. Yet there is no final resolution or compromise or closure achieved in this acquiescence. The impulse is still there, and will be again awakened, to seek a ladder to heaven and climb it stage by stage to the highest kind of love and union and happiness and now there is the knowledge that in spite of one's weakness there will be sufficient aid in times of trial. In the meantime Cupid and Psyche have bestowed upon us youth and joy.

In leaving *Comus* we might note that the ambiguous means of deliverance granted by Sabrina enables Milton to avoid at least two other solutions more in tradition. His theme could logically end in the vision of the fourteenth chapter of the Book of Revelation: "These are they which were not defiled with women; for they are virgins. These are they which follow the Lamb whithersoever he goeth." Another possibility, as Wilson Knight has suggested, would have been to reverse and deprive of its evil force the phallic rod of Comus as the Attendant Spirit wished to do. Either of these would have been a firm, explicit, and complete resolution of the problem, and this it is the business of a Mannerist sensibility and style to evade.

Lycidas

If we wish to look at *Lycidas* from the standpoint of classical or neo-classical correctness we need travel no farther than to the familiar dicta of Johnson in his "Life" of Milton. He finds the diction of

Lycidas harsh, the rhymes uncertain, the numbers unpleasing, and the passion affected. "In this poem there is no nature, for there is no truth; there is no art for there is nothing new. Its form is that of a pastoral, easy, vulgar, and therefore disgusting." Johnson is also, as a good churchman, disturbed by Milton's handling of Christian doctrine in conjunction with the conventional names and situations of pastoral: "With these trifling fictions are mingled the most awful and sacred truths, such as ought never to be polluted with such irreverent combinations." He concludes, apropos of *Lycidas*, as many spectators have concluded concerning the Laurentian Library ante-room, "surely no man could have fancied that he read with pleasure, had he not known its author."

This is the response toward Mannerist forms typical of a mind in which classical conventions predominate. The conventions employed set up certain expectations but these are disappointed by a new handling of the understood tradition. Bad taste, the intrusion of precious and affected tones into the expression of high religious aspiration, a pervasive dislocation and wilful avoidance of classical decorum: these are the perceived and castigated sins, as the classicist sees them.

It is not necessary to recapitulate here the evidence that Milton's employment of pastoral elegy reveals a dependence upon tradition probably unequalled in any other English poem. This, though of no particular value as evidence in itself, is what we should expect of a Mannerist poem,[11] and it is the precise handling of this convention that is crucial.

An immediate discovery is the ambiguity of the central figure.[12] It is nominally Edward King but, as Johnson has said, the poem reveals no convincing grief. Instead, Milton draws our attention quickly to himself. It may be replied that to pass from the fate of one's friend to one's own fate is normal in pastoral elegy—we think of Shelley, Tennyson, and Arnold. But in *Lycidas* the move is made with what seems inexcusably indecent haste. By the twentieth line Milton is engrossed with himself. Yet this very haste reveals the poignancy of the poet's concern for his own fame; here is a true passion if not the one Johnson

11. Cf. E. K. Waterhouse, *Baroque Painting in Rome*.
12. One is reminded of the ambiguous position of the central figure in such a Mannerist masterpiece as Tintoretto's picture of the Virgin going up to the Temple, in Venice.

Laurentian Library, Florence, staircase

St. Peter's, façade and piazza

St. Peter's, the baldacchino and the cathedra

S. Carlo alle Quattro Fontane, Rome, façade

S. Carlo alle Quattro Fontane, Rome, interior of the dome

S. Andrea al Quirinale, Rome, façade

S. Andrea al Quirinale, Rome, interior

The Grand Canal and S. Maria della Salute, Venice

wanted. And yet, though he shoves away the worthy bidden guest, the poet does not, so to speak, face the reader or take the centre of the stage. Other figures, more tremendous, intermittently do that. And in spite of them and of the reappearance of both King and Milton at the end, there is a substantial doubt, as in *Paradise Lost*, as to who may be the true centre of the poem. The *obiter dictum* of Frye comes at last to carry conviction. "Christ does not enter the poem as a character, but he pervades every line of it so completely that the poem, so to speak, enters him."[13]

Leaving aside, with the hope of returning to it, this tremendous possibility let us consider how and whence and to what end the various figures do actually appear in *Lycidas*. The Muses are briefly invoked and immediately disappear. An even briefer passage introduces old Damaetas, never positively identified as Joseph Mede. The nymphs are visualized on the hills, or on Mona's shaggy top, or by Deva's stream but only as not being there. And suddenly in the midst of these pale conventions we encounter in an altogether different plane, and with a frightful compressed intensity that in four lines changes the whole tone of the verse—the gory visage of Orpheus sent down the current of Hebrus. With what stabbing force this image came to the poet is revealed in the Milton MS. at Trinity College where the cancelled lines of the first draft read: "when she beheld (the gods farre sighted bee) / his goarie scalpe rowle downe the Thracian lee." The window onto this vision of ghastly dismemberment instantly shuts. A meditation on Fame ensues. This is all the more strange because we know from other evidence how fully the Orpheus myth had established itself in Milton's consciousness. In *Ad Patrem*, in *L'Allegro* and *Il Penseroso* we have already been told of Orpheus who gained fame by his song that made the ghosts of the dead weep and charmed Pluto to release Eurydice. In Book VII of *Paradise Lost* the image of Orpheus drowned out by savage clamour will still be fresh in Milton's mind and add urgency to his prayer to Urania for protection. But in none of these passages has the verse the same unbearable shock; in none does the bloody image of that head appear so fleetingly before disappearing down and under the stream.

13. N. Frye, *Anatomy of Criticism*, 121–2.

But now the poet is meditating on Fame and is once more fully self-centred. The erotic shapes of Amaryllis and Neaera, unlike Spenser's maidens in the fountain, are no more than glimpsed. The thought of sensuous love is crowded out by the thought of death, death nominally at the hands of Fate (who does no more than fulfil the destiny of any man) but actually inflicted by a blind Fury (as though to punish crime), and where this extreme tension of thought would lead cannot be guessed, for Phoebus intervenes, and again the tone changes. Phoebus opens to the eye a larger but still limited space, a pagan heaven where Jove judges all justly. And this vista is quietly faded out so that the pastoral may resume.

These manipulations of space are of the greatest importance in the identification of Mannerist effects.[14] There is no ordered landscape in which everything is made to achieve congruity, the kind of total organized space which in their quite different fashions both *The Faerie Queene* and *Paradise Lost* provide (or for that matter both *Epithalamion* and *L'Allegro*). Each figure tends to bring his own space with him and these neither combine into a totality of perspective nor separate into planes having some relation. We have no sooner re-entered the pastoral world (with the line "But now my oat proceeds") and discovered that a trial or rather a hearing of witnesses is proceeding, than the slow entry of Camus is followed by a wrathful irruption by St. Peter whose own space, including the gates of Heaven and Hell, is violently superimposed upon the pastoral scene. In this tremendous world the grim wolf and the two-handed engine start up before us.

Scores of suggestions have been made to elucidate this last image.[15] It is surely reasonable to suggest that it may refer to the sword of Michael. The thirty-three lines which Milton interpolated at this point, as he revised, bring the reader back to Michael as one might expect of an interpolation. In *Paradise Lost* (VI, 251 and 318) we behold Michael and Satan in combat. The "two-handed" sword of the angel is lifted to deliver a blow

> That might determine, and not need repeat,
> As not of power, at once....

14. See, in addition, Friedländer's comment on this subject in *Mannerism and Anti-Mannerism*, 8–9.

15. See W. A. Turner, "Milton's Two-handed Engine," *Journal of English and Germanic Philology*, XLIX, 562–5.

In *Lycidas* Michael and his sword are seen on the guarded mount, at England's gateway, opposite the menacing shores of Spain. The two-handed engine at the door would seem to be reasonably identified. And Peter, who invokes it, has already in Gethesmane had recourse to the sword. If Michael can be seen clearly in this traditional role, which the text seems to warrant, then we may further observe that no sooner is this stance achieved than the other and opposite quality appears as the angel is exhorted to look homeward and melt into tears. If this seems like over-reading, we may recall that in the eleventh book of *Paradise Lost* Michael, armed with this sword "Satan's dire dread," "gently" speaks to Adam and at the sight of Abel done to death is "also mov'd." But whereas in the epic changes come slowly and with due preparation, the references in *Lycidas* are hasty, angular, and individually coruscating. In brief, the tremendous ambiguous invocation of the sword, followed by a catalogue of flowers, followed in turn by the "great vision of the guarded mount," whose guardian is now invited to turn from his watch abroad and give himself up to tears—this is the kind of rapid shifting and refusal to satisfy expectation of which Mannerism is characteristically the source.

The way in which characters appear, the spatial relations implicit in each appearance, and the pace and manner of shifting the scene—all these are handled in Mannerist fashion. The same may be said of the versification, the complexity of which has been made intelligible by Prince,[16] whose argument must be followed in some detail. Milton, it appears, based the versification of *Lycidas* upon the Italian canzone but with an eclecticism all his own. The technical advances of the practice of late fifteenth-century Italian poets he freely appropriated but his seriousness is that of the High Renaissance and its classical antecedents. And he owes something to the high seriousness of Spenser's pastorals. The canzone on which Milton modelled the divisions of *Lycidas* was built of two sections linked by a key line. Each of the two parts might be subdivided (into smaller parts called *piedi* or *versi*) but in practice it was generally one or the other, seldom both. The first part of a divided canzone was linked to the second by a line rhyming with the last line of the first. When subdivision occurred these might also be similarly linked.

Prince now draws a comparison which, to anyone familiar with the

16. F. T. Prince, *The Italian Element in Milton's Verse*, 71–88.

history of the English sonnet, will be immediately clear and will clarify Milton's use of the canzone.

Just as in the original use of the sonnet the divisions and subdivisions between quatrains and tercets were observed by the diction and only transgressed for some special purpose, these divisions in the canzone were present to the writer and the reader and gave a distinctive emphasis and movement to the different parts of the stanza. And just as with the divisions of the sonnet, the divisions of the canzone were often deliberately overridden by sixteenth-century poets, but only because, even when the diction did not follow them, they remained in mind, and the effect was one of counterpoint between the rhyme pattern and the diction, such as Milton reproduces in his sonnets.

If this were all, we should not have a Mannerist technique. Counterpoint between rhyme and sentence structure is a commonplace (Byron comes first to mind) in English versification. But the process goes further.

Milton is using the principle of articulation of the canzone; and he has liberated it from its association with repeated *piedi* or *versi* within his paragraphs. This principle of articulation is therefore free to affect any part of his paragraphs....

Let us look at some familiar lines.

> "Fame is no plant that grows on mortal soil,
> Nor in the glistering foil
> Set off to th'world, nor in broad rumor lies,
> But lives and spreads aloft by those pure eyes
> And perfect witness of all-judging Jove...."

Here the principle of the rhyming line serving as a link is not only employed without a division of the passage into *piedi* or *versi* but is also reinforced by the shortening of the linking line to three feet so that after this failure of expectation the next line springs forward, the argument itself being thus opened out. The handling in the Laurentian Library of frames and mouldings so as to rupture enclosures which the eye expects to be completed and so as to contradict the consistency of planes is analogous.

It seems reasonable to regard such devices in *Lycidas* as Mannerist. They are based on profound understanding and very skilful application of the devices of the Italian Renaissance. They achieve their surprise by unobtrusive refusals to obey the rules. The effect upon the sensibility is emphatic but mysterious; with reason it exasperates the classically trained observer. This may help to explain why Johnson's complaint that the diction of *Lycidas* is harsh, the rhymes uncertain, the numbers unpleasing, and the passion affected can never be dismissed. There is, from one point of view, so much truth in it that it tends to become a starting point for any discussion of the poem.

A strange fact about the versification of *Lycidas* is its failure to affect the tradition of the English ode. It has not been possible to imitate Milton's springing movement, the devices by which the thrust and check of the verse suggest immensely powerful forces working within severe restrictions. And this cannot have been for want of a desire to emulate Milton, as the enormous output of Miltonic blank verse demonstrates. It is rather that, while Baroque practices are easily imitated, Mannerist techniques are, from their very nature, too demanding and too elusive to invite wide repetition in following generations. Bernini's saints set a standard and started a fashion the results of which are visible throughout Italy, but who has chosen to work in the spirit of his early subtle statue of Aeneas? It could be added, perhaps, that the pure Mannerism of certain poems by Donne and Marvell, for instance "The Bait" and "Daphnis and Chloe," has proved inimitable.

In our consideration of *Comus* it was of great value to have Woodhouse's exposition of nature and grace at hand. Only in the context of such an intention, only if such a scheme in all its completeness were somewhere available, could the Mannerist deviations, shifts of tone and changes of pattern, take on meaning. It is similarly salutary to an understanding of *Lycidas* if a logical pattern to which it appears to conform, and without which its nonconformity would not be recognized, can be adduced. Such a pattern—unfortunately sketched very briefly in the course of an article on a different subject—has been supplied by Arthur Barker[17] who argues that the poem consists of three movements practically equal in length and precisely parallel in pattern. These are rounded out by a pastoral introduction and conclusion. The first movement is concerned with the poet-shepherd and is resolved by the assurance "of so much fame in heaven expect thy

17. Barker, "The Pattern of Milton's Nativity Ode," *University of Toronto Quarterly*, X, 167–81. (See pp. 171–2.)

meed." The second laments the priest-shepherd and is resolved by the "two-handed engine" of divine retribution. The third sees the apotheosis of the poet-priest-shepherd who now worships the Lamb with the saints.

It is the cumulative effect of its three parallel movements which makes *Lycidas* impressive; the return to the pastoral at the beginning of each makes possible three successive and perfectly controlled crescendoes. The gathering up of the first two in the last gives the conclusion its calm finality; and the balanced unity of the design appropriately represents the calm achieved through the resolution of emotional conflicts.

With such an epitome of what the poem, as pastoral elegy, should be doing, we may well look again at the text.

The preciousness and self-consciousness of Milton's introduction were, of course, an obvious target for Johnson. The first forty-nine lines have the effect of bringing the reader into a closed world of pastoral forms and of shutting the door, just as, in entering the Medici Chapel or Laurentian Library, we find the door closing inconspicuously behind us so that a new and managed experience of space may take place. The contrast is very striking between this opening passage and the corresponding passages in *Adonais* or *Thyrsis*.

The traditional questioning of the spectators now begins but is broken into by Milton himself and it is not until thirty-four lines later that the Herald of the Sea goes on with the evidence. This breach of convention is a violent one. The nymphs, ready to testify, are pushed aside as having not been present. The brief vision of Orpheus' gory head is seen as by a telescopic lens. Then the poet strides up and down exclaiming that though he has passed Amaryllis by to devote himself to poetry the blind Fury sits ready to cut off his life. So intensely is the scene enacted that we shift suddenly from meditation to drama; Phoebus descends ex machina and speaks his comfort. Yet although there has been such an outburst, such excess of emotion within rigid boundaries, there is neither adequate resolution of forces nor adequate release of energy. Phoebus (who flayed Marsyas) is not presented as an embodiment of the powers of a risen Christ. The final couplet (a true couplet and not one of the linkings referred to above) rings somewhat hollow:

> As he pronounces lastly on each deed,
> Of so much fame in Heav'n expect thy meed.

It is far inferior in resonance to the passage of complaint which leads up to it. It is weak because what is in question is the pulse of dedication, while the reward is for achievement duly surveyed and registered.[18]

It is not to be supposed that this refusal to promulgate a resounding resolution is an artistic flaw, any more than the restless, unstable figures flanking the Medici sarcophagi are to be regarded as Michelangelo's mistakes.

Acknowledging that he has disturbed the expected flow of pastoral by introducing a higher mood, Milton proceeds with the judicial hearing. This in turn is broken into by the tremendous wrathful figure of St. Peter. He is nominally an appropriate witness, being Bishop of Rome in whose cathedral is the injunction "Pesce oves meas," but he comes with the keys of heaven and hell and in an attitude of strong perturbation, shaking his mitred locks. The violence of his speech increases to the culminating invocation of the two-handed engine at the door. This use of Peter as invoker of vengeance appears more incongruous when we recollect that the pastoralist, and particularly the Christian pastor, is in the nature of things non-violent and that Peter was told long before by Jesus, "Put up thy sword into the sheath." Once again the tensions set up are disproportionate to the area in which they can act and the result achieved by their operation is ambiguous.[19]

Milton now returns once more to the pastoral scene, acknowledging by "Return Alpheus, the dread voice is past" that the convention has been broken in upon. There follows the catalogue of flowers. Something a little precious about it is in keeping with the Arcadian images at the very beginning of the poem, for this literary Arcadia with its chime of classical overtones is not and is not intended to be assimilated to the Christian pastoral of the hireling shepherds and St. Peter. The two worlds represented are related, not by any adjustment of their space to a common perspective, still less by one being simply subsumed as an allegory of the other. What unites them is the swell of emotion which transverses their apparent boundaries.

18. That there is a false climax here has been noted by David Daiches in his *Milton* (p. 84).
19. G. Wilson Knight, seeking to explain *Lycidas* as a product of forced unification, described the poem as "an effort to bind and clamp together a universe trying to fly off into separate bits; it is an accumulation of magnificent fragments" (*The Burning Oracle*, 67).

Now as we come to the end of the poem vistas of brief duration and limited depth open and close. The Orpheus theme of dismemberment and death by water reappears though not explicitly. There is no attempt to develop Orpheus' gift of song to the Lesbians, his safe arrival in Elysium, the vengeance taken for his death by Bacchus.[20] But the subdued presence of Orpheus, "the hapless youth," pervades the lines. For brief moments we see the long stormy reaches of ocean as far as the Hebrides, then the Celtic underwater world of sea-monsters, lastly and at greater length the Cornish coast, the Spanish shore toward Cape Finisterre and St. Michael's Mount. Pastoral has given way to geographical actuality. And suddenly Christ, who has never been explicitly adduced until this moment, appears as "him that walked the waves" and this link between earth and heaven raises the dead Lycidas into the heavenly kingdom. Now indeed the full Baroque space of celestial joy and beatitude would seem to open above us. But as we look up it narrows strangely into a sight of the dead shepherd washing his locks in nectar. Thus purified he is surrounded by troops of saints singing the unexpressive nuptial song. The vision approaches mystical insight and it has often been wondered why it is in fact so much less satisfying than Dante's heavenly rose and eternal fountain, why it suggests, though it vastly transcends, the heaven of "The Blessed Damosel." The answer lies, I think, in a number of particulars all of which illustrate the same principle. The imagery is in part ("oozy Locks") dream-like and peripheral. The song and processional are not directed explicitly to or about the presence of God. The "nuptial Song" does not unite the soul of the dead shepherd to the love of the Great Shepherd—and one has only to put the words down to see why this cannot be. A complete Christian apotheosis in which the soul of Edward King was identified with the Bride of Christ would shatter the whole poem. Questions of fame as a poet would disappear. Questions of vengeance on Laud's clergy would be irrelevant. Even sorrow for the loss of Lycidas from among the shepherds would seem artificial. Once again Johnson is obscurely on the right track in his strictures: the "awful and sacred truths" do not mix well with the "trifling fictions." What is remarkable, however, is Milton's skill in avoiding by exquisite devices just this difficulty. Not least among these devices is the swift return of Lycidas to the

20. See Caroline W. Mayerson, "The Orpheus Image in *Lycidas,*" *Publications of the Modern Language Association,* LXIV, 189–207.

pastoral realm as Genius of the shore, unchristian if we recall "The parting genius is with sighing sent," and yet indubitably right in this context.

The heavenly vision, while achieved, obeys neither the absoluteness or ecstasy of Christian faith nor the empyrean opulence of Baroque painting. It is in accordance only with the demands of the poem and these are, as we have tried to show, compatible with the principles of Mannerism rather than with any other of the comprehensive art forms to which we might be tempted to assign the poem.

We must never lose sight of Wittkower's aphorism, "Language and patience have limits when describing a Mannerist structure." Aspects of *Lycidas* which this thought forbids us to enter upon may however be mentioned briefly. Mannerism is historically related to two impulses which seem scarcely complementary. One is an intense personal striving toward a spiritual ideal. There is no difficulty in conceding that Milton, as he depicted in *Comus* the triumph of the soul over private temptations or as in *Lycidas* he recorded a confronting of the disordered world of action, was in fact recording true experience of a piercing and personal kind. This experience included a sense of deep uncertainty and helplessness, it is apparent from both poems. Concurrently, if incongruously from a naive point of view, he was being most precious, aristocratic, learned, and mannered. "Never," wrote Phillips, "was the loss of friend so elegantly lamented." If we allow that his characters move in "a very narrow space, embarrassing the movements of the actors,"[21] that in these poems "the strongest psychological impulses meet insuperable pressure and resistance—they are denied space in which to expand," and that "their powerful expansiveness points toward liberation only in a transcendental and divine space,"[22] we may see these technical qualities of the poems as direct counterparts of their author's inner experience. In the process the very conventions of pastoral have been reworked as it were from the inside and we seem to have lost sight altogether of Arcadians described by Polybius as a virtuous people who practised music to offset their days of hard labour and their cold and overcast climate. They have long been vanishing down the corridors of pastoral practice and now are gone. It is an equal distance from the "Madonna del Collo Lungo" to the story in the Gospels.

21. T. H. Fokker, *Roman Baroque Art*, I, 255.
22. Friedländer, *Mannerism and Anti-Mannerism*, 15.

This intense reworking from the inside so as to leave the *dehors* undisturbed yet satisfy the emotional necessities of the artist extends to the shaping of characters and of single lines or phrases. Phoebus, St. Peter, Edward King all become something other than their normal selves in obedience to Milton's needs. Camus, if looked at steadily, resolves into the sluggish river, its "mantle" of water plants, its sedges by the bank, and above these the wild hyacinth or bluebell growing.[23] Individual words invite the attention of the analysts of ambiguity: sleek Panope, enamelled eyes that suck the showers, the oozy locks washed in nectar, the monstrous world under water, "when they list" with its overtones of "listlessness" and "lust." In a full consideration of the subject all these and their kind would deserve attention, like Parmigianino's elegant angel with oval jar in any consideration of his canvas.

We have paid no attention to the ottava rima with which *Lycidas* concludes. Deliberately split off from the poem proper by its versification, which with its regular lines and rhymes seems somewhat stilted, it nevertheless obeys the inner logic of the construction. Going unwillingly into his task, the poet must be glad to have accomplished it. The dragging reluctance of the opening lines is in contrast to the briskness and objectivity of the ottava rima. What the poet, objectively viewed as the Swain, now says is nevertheless odd. He tells us his time is up and he has finished his task in accordance with the best models, the Doric Theocritus and Virgil whose conclusion to a lament for Gallus is echoed in this coda. He has done a good job and tomorrow will start off to accomplish something new. That this resolution is out of key with the composition as a whole has often been noted. It implies perhaps that the questions raised in the poem have been laid to rest or at least suspended. Biographically it may point to Milton's Italian journey. It is certainly more than a final bit of pastoral to remind us of the form of the elegy. But the self-conscious concern with a completed formal task is hard to assess until we recall that Mannerists in general were greatly concerned with the practical (though less with the theoretical) side of their own techniques and very much concerned to justify their practices.[24] In *Comus* the poet

23. W. Tuckwell, *Lycidas*.
24. See C. de Tolnay, *The Medici Chapel*, and Wittkower, "Michelangelo's Biblioteca Laurenziana," *Art Bulletin*, XVI (2), 123–218.

had alluded to himself as a Shepherd Lad well skilled in every virtuous plant and healing herb, able to name and make use of the properties of the thousand things in his *materia medica*. It is hard to think of a better figure of speech for the combination of a well-stocked mind and poetic skill which Milton prided himself upon.

Lycidas in achieving its place as the most effective lyric utterance in the English language has relied heavily upon its Mannerist method. It is unmatched primarily because its technique is now inimitable. Its problems seem timeless because each is clothed in a conventional figure which has nevertheless been reconstructed from within to satisfy the exact needs of the poem. Its problems appear overwhelming because each twists its limbs and torso *contrapposto* to reveal every muscle. Its solutions never seem facile because each withdraws from a romantic expansion and is content to indicate rather than occupy the space in which liberation is fully achieved.

The crowning achievement of *Lycidas* lies in the enormously ramified complex of reactions, conscious and unconscious, which it provokes. These are not in the nature of sequences of ideas merely or numbers of identifiable references or rows of problems solved. They are rather in the nature of innumerable conflicting forces. These the poem reduces to a small number of intelligible vectors, to a further resolution of which it points the way. Greater works Milton may have composed but none more perfectly achieving what it attempts.

It follows from the complexity and ambiguity of Mannerism that one is constantly impelled to realign one's own evaluations. An identification of Mannerist traits in a given work and a close look at their precise effect may throw out of focus the larger view of the relative success of the whole piece as compared to other works. *Comus*, it must at some point be admitted, is by any standards inferior to *Lycidas*.

The superiority of *Lycidas* derives from its being the revelation of a Milton more mature, more perceptive, and more comprehensive than the Milton of *Comus*, though the chronological and biographical aspects of this change need not concern us here. We have shown that the dislocations of *Comus* rewardingly reveal the efforts of an idealizing mind to find assurance. But it can be argued that Milton failed to rework from within the traditional concepts of Christian humility,

Christian charity, Christian sanctification of natural beauty and natural affection. There are real omissions and evasions. The Mannerist approach is not pushed far enough or with sufficient vigour. To the Milton of *Lycidas*, on the other hand, no transformation seems too difficult. St. Peter, clad in the garments of apostolic pastoralism and the panoply of the Roman tradition, shaking his locks with the passionate effort of his own renewal, calls down destruction on the enemies of Milton and the English nation.

4. BAROQUE

IT IS CUSTOMARY to start any discussion of Baroque with a definition of the term and some account of the ramifications of its use in criticism. This, while inevitable and necessary at some point in the discussion, has often the effect of creating an initial bewilderment in the reader. We shall therefore begin in a simpler if more hazardous manner by adopting a limited concept of Baroque, as close to the historical centre of the phenomenon as possible. It is neatly contained in the opening sentences of the definition given in *A Dictionary of Art and Artists*:

BAROQUE. This is the style that succeeded MANNERISM and lasted, though with profound modifications, until well into the 18th c. The style is seen at its purest in the so-called "High Baroque", which is virtually confined to Italy (to Rome even) and to the period covered by the years *c.* 1630–80, that is, roughly the maturity of its greatest exponent, BERNINI.[1]

The chronological view taken by Wittkower is very similar. From *c.* 1625 to *c.* 1675 he regards as the age of High Baroque.

The period receives its imprint from the overpowering figure of Bernini, who for more than half a century dominated Italian artistic life at the focal point, Rome.

The works without peer are Bernini's statuary, Cortona's architecture and decoration, and Borromini's buildings as well as those by Guarini, Juvarra, and Vittone. But it was Bernini, the greatest artist of the period, who with his poetical and visionary masterpieces created perhaps the most sublime realization of the longings of his age. . . . I consider the Roman

1. Peter and Linda Murray, *A Dictionary of Art and Artists* (Penguin).

High Baroque of Bernini, Borromini, and Pietro da Cortona the most exciting years of the century and a half under review [1600–1750] and one of the most creative periods of the whole history of Italian art.[2]

Similar views are expressed by Pevsner, who argues that Baroque appeared as a reaction against Mannerism and that "the style thus introduced culminated in Rome between 1630 and 1670. . . . Maderna was the leading architect of his generation in Rome. He died in 1629. His successors in fame were Gianlorenzo Bernini (1598–1680), Francesco Borromini (1599–1667), and Pietro da Cortona (1596–1669)."[3]

Before going further, we should remind ourselves of some of the landmarks of the exploration of Baroque. Jakob Burckhardt's *Die Kultur der Renaissance* projected a view which met the needs of the reader of 1860. The group of painters now referred to as the Mannerists were, as one would expect, quite distressing to Burckhardt's sensibilities. In the next generation Heinrich Wölfflin gathered the results of a quarter-century of research in Renaissance and Baroque art into his *Kunstgeschichtliche Grundbegriffe*, which appeared in 1915. This book, the source of the famous five categories, was again timely and appealed to a generation of readers who had learned to accept, say, Monet. Wölfflin's theory of style changes in the seventeenth century has been modified, particulary by reassignment into the category of Mannerism of many phenomena which he had denominated Baroque, but no one interested in the field can fail to render him both homage and gratitude.

The employment of the term Baroque in literary criticism, which came about after Wölfflin's concepts had become established, is briefly reviewed later in these pages. If at the moment we try to simplify rather than complicate our concept, by limiting it to Rome and the second and third quarters of the seventeenth century, it is not difficult to accept the dictum that architecture, sculpture, and painting are the arts most worthy of attention and that their importance is in the order given. Fokker, in connexion with the critical recognition now accorded to Bernini, Borromini, and Cortona, remarks that "a hasty inference (which, as it happens, is perfectly right) may be drawn; as the three most important men of the Baroque were

2. R. Wittkower, *Art and Architecture in Italy, 1600 to 1750*, 89 and xxi-xxii.
3. N. Pevsner, *An Outline of European Architecture*, 175–6.

architects, architecture was by far the most prominent of the arts concerned, and as the most famous of the three architects was, at the same time, the greatest sculptor, and the least known of them the best painter, contemporary painting was the least important of the three."[4]

Roman Baroque was dependent on political and ecclesiastical patronage. Its course was influenced by the Council of Trent, by the Jesuits, and by individual popes (five of whom gladly employed Bernini). The opportunity to create works of a public kind, in obedience to a new dynamic yet for patrons who were of necessity traditionalists, led to the formation of an habitual motive expressing itself in an habitual movement of the creative mind. The artists typical of the period accepted authority, whether the spiritual authority of the Church or the authority which the Renaissance had given to the art-forms of Rome and Greece. Yet this fidelity to tradition was accompanied by a desire to reconstitute the elements, rearrange and recombine them, so as to achieve new effects. In compassing these new effects, the artists of this age displayed technical virtuosity, dexterity, and resource to an unparalleled degree.

The nature of the new forms may still be usefully surveyed under the five heads proposed by Wölfflin. The transition from Renaissance to Baroque is marked by a change from the perception of an object by outline and surfaces to a perception with less tangible design; there is development from the linear and from stress upon limits toward an apprehension of the world as shifting semblance. Instead of employing a plane or parallel planes in design, the new technique lays emphasis on depth, recession, and diagonal penetration of space. There is also a movement from closed to open composition, from a stable equilibrium dominated by vertical and horizontal axes to a looser form, frequently spiral in its movement and suggesting by its sweep a completion beyond its own mechanical limits. In similar fashion, the Renaissance use of multiplicity in design, relying upon the union of independent parts in harmony with one another, gives way to a unity achieved by means of a single theme or by the subordination to one dominant element of all the others; that is, to fusion instead of co-ordination. Finally, there is a change from absolute clarity, in which explicitness is the chief aim, to relative clarity, in which light

4. T. H. Fokker, *Roman Baroque Art*, I, 8.

and colour have their own life and beauty is perceived in the very darkness which modifies form. Baroque, in the formal sense, represents a perpetuation of the traditional forms accompanied by a reaction against them, the two being compatible in that the reaction amounts to √ intensifying or accentuating certain elements already present, dislocating or deliberately "deforming" recognized shapes in the interests of greater expressiveness, and achieving, on the familiar stage, a new and striking effect informed by a sense of splendour and actuated by a fresh interest in movement.

It is probably possible to isolate one central motive leading to this vast and complex change in sensibility and creative urge. With a due regard for the fragile and tentative nature of all abstract terminology one would venture to assume that it is a desire for power, an intense desire to assert the predominance of the will. It is not difficult to discover that a good deal of reputable critical opinion points in that direction.

Friedrich[5] regards as "perhaps the age's most revealing phrase" the well-known comment of Hobbes, "So that, in the first place, I put for a general inclination of all mankind, a perpetual and restless desire of Power, after Power, that ceaseth only in Death." "Riches, Knowledge and Honour are but several sorts of power." Stechow regards "the interpretation of this Baroque epoch as one revealing a basically new and optimistic equilibrium of religious and secular forces."

This era tended to harmonize the humanistic, the religious, and the scientific realms into one integrated whole, deliberately, yet often with a passsionate zeal and dynamic power of which the Renaissance had not been capable, and its new equilibrium was possible of attainment only thanks to the progressive revolution of the Reformation on one hand and the conservative revolution of the Counter-Reformation on the other.[6]

Mâle has shown that the iconography of the Counter-Reformation reflected struggle and affirmation, enthusiasm and the power to unite heaven and earth: "il exalte l'âme et lui montre le ciel s'ouvrant, dès ce monde, à l'amour."[7] The "enormous energy and exceeding fervour" of Baroque is noticed by Fokker.

5. C. J. Friedrich, *The Age of the Baroque, 1610–1660*, 45.
6. W. Stechow, "Definitions of the Baroque in the Visual Arts," *Journal of Aesthetics and Art Criticism*, V (2), 114.
7. E. Mâle, *L'Art religieux après le Concile de Trente*, 512.

Baroque art is a style, the first since antiquity, which was created on the soil of Rome and its immediate neighbourhood. It embraced the largest and most important part of the artistic activity in Rome during that period of modern history which saw the rise, the climax, and the decline of a Papacy which had ceased to uphold its pretentions to be the equal of mighty European monarchies, but on the other hand strove to be a power which controlled European politics as well as European religious life.[8]

What furnishes the connexion, it has been asked, between religious or political absolutism and stylistic coherence? It is not difficult to give a tentative answer. Whether we turn to the dynastic art of Egypt or to the Baroque styles enforced by Colbert in France we find a system of structures or accessories on which the ideal of the monarch as embodiment of the total life of the country leaves its shaping pressure. Absolutism supposes omniscience, omnipotence, and omnipresence which compel subordination or provoke decorous resistance within the accepted modes. All members of the structure, down to decorative elements, are oriented toward the source of authority and preserve a prescribed manner, itself a powerful quiet agent in the securing of a unified effect. It has been remarked regarding French literature of this period, "The keynote of the century is authority and the word which occurs perhaps more frequently than any other is les règles." "Authority is not accepted passively. It is accepted—and resisted, and it is this that gives the literature its life, its high degree of emotional vitality combined with a high degree of order."[9]

There is room for much variety in the working out of a grand style and particularly in the explicitness with which concepts are expressed. To the verbally minded critic there is something distressing in the thought that an affirmation is being made or an argument pursued by piling up blocks of limestone. But we are gradually becoming aware that when Borromini or Cortona takes hold of a piece of undifferentiated space and turns it into a single unified field of force, vibrant with energies transmitted by new arrangements of columns, pilasters, cornice, and dome, new versions of nave, transept, and choir, this assertion of familiarity with the traditions of the faith, of power to express them with fresh logic and clarified rhetoric, of ability to seize the intellect and the emotions of the worshipper

8. Fokker, *Roman Baroque Art*, I, 18.
9. Turnell, *The Classical Moment*, 7 and 15.

simultaneously—that this exhibition of sheer mastery is at least as explicit, as effective, and as intelligible as if he had written a book. And beside these displays are others more simply communicative. The reorganization of the interior and environment of St. Peter's so as to assure a single impression of dominant papal power is one of Bernini's greatest achievements as it is one of the best observed artistic phenomena of Rome. At Versailles there is nothing, from the long axial vistas of the park which imply regal omniscience to the details of décor whose Roman motifs suggest the imperium, that does not assert the sun-king's majesty.

It should not, of course, be assumed that affirmations of power always coincide with its possession or exercise. In writing of Bernini, Wittkower adds the salutary reminder that "while this cycle of monumental works seemed to propound Rome's final victory, the authority of the Holy See had already begun to wane."[10] *Paradise Lost* appeared after the Restoration; Blenheim was completed when the next English general to count on the Continent would be Wellington.

It was natural for artists to find in the exalted patronage of the period opportunities for high spiritual endeavour, or high artistic creation (and Bernini was possessed by both). It became possible to create worlds of intelligible authority and sensuous splendor, of complex yet not dispersed meaning. Space and mass were handled with an imaginative freedom only equalled by technical resource. Within boundaries which are in sober fact regular and rigorously defined areas, spaces are nevertheless made to seem immense and indeterminate. Enormous and solid masses are curved, broken into, and masked so as to simulate movement and depth. Domes are decorated to suggest an opening into infinity. Statues simulate dynamic or dramatic action. Contrasting qualities, such as movement and mass, limitation and indeterminate space, are made simultaneously realizable. Fusion or flow are everywhere preferred to static separation or mere linkage of serial parts.

In returning to the use of the term Baroque in literary criticism we find that it is customary, though not particularly useful, to say something about the derivation of the word. The origin of the word "Baroque" is obscure. It is said to have been a jeweller's term, derived

10. Wittkower, *Art and Architecture in Italy*, 94.

from Latin *verruca* or Arabic *burag*. A baroque pearl was not spherical but of a strange shape. Littré gives *baroco*, a mnemonic word from scholastic Latin (on a model familiar to readers of *Le Bourgeois Gentilhomme*), as the undoubted source of Baroque,[11] though the Oxford Dictionary is only willing to concede that form-association between the two may have influenced later English and French use. Either way, the suggestion is of something *outré* and irregular: "la armada del Occidente con las maderas, perlas, margaritas y barruecos" or else (to quote the report of a learned dispute) "It is neither in mode nor figure. . . . It is in Baroco."

More important than the derivation of the word is its semantic development. Beginning as a jeweller's or an academician's term, it has extended itself to embrace the whole culture of the seventeenth century. It has been suggested that Cellini and his fellow craftsmen may have carried the word from goldsmith's work to architecture. In any case, it was early applied to works of art other than jewellery. It long remained a term of disapproval, the art to which it was applied being viewed with contempt. Colen Campbell in *Vitruvius Britannicus* observes: "How affected and licentious are the works of Bernini and Fontana? How wildly extravagant are the designs of Borromini, who has endeavour'd to debauch mankind with his odd and chimerical Beauties, where the Parts are without Proportion, Solids without their true Bearing, Heaps of Materials without Strength, excessive Ornament without Grace, and the Whole without Symmetry?" Nineteenth-century references to Baroque are in much the same vein, the word being coupled with adjectives such as "absurd" or "frantic."

The English reader could see, early in the present century, signs that the tide was beginning to turn. M. S. Briggs, in *Baroque Architecture* (1913) and in other studies, made an eloquent plea for recognition of the merits of Baroque. The well-known works of Sacheverell Sitwell, beginning with *Southern Baroque Art* (1924), were testimony to increased interest in and a change of attitude toward the subject.

The application of the term Baroque to literature began in Germany. Fritz Strich as early as 1916 was referring to the body of

---

11. See R. Wellek, "The Concept of Baroque in Literary Scholarship," *Journal of Aesthetics and Art Criticism*, V (2), 77.

poetry between Fischart and Gunther as "Barocklyrik."[12] The use of Baroque as a term to describe works of English literature was also, to begin with, German, although one should note an early, deservedly well-known work in Italian, the *Secentismo e marinismo in Inghilterra* of Mario Praz in 1925 which dealt with two of the leading Metaphysicals, Donne and Crashaw, as Baroque.

In spite of doubts and some ridicule, the application of the term has continuously expanded and in more than one way. All the arts have been brought in and it is possible now to perceive the outlines of a huge and comprehensive total art form of the seventeenth century as Baroque. The style problem extends, indeed, somewhat further. Before the concept of Mannerism formed itself to contain many techniques and attitudes which were subsequent to and opposed to the High Renaissance, it was possible for some critics to regard even euphuism as a Baroque style.[13] In the other chronological direction, a variety of Baroque forms were correctly perceived in the arts of the eighteenth century. The Grand Style, once established, proved persistent and Baroque design might support Rococo ornament. The application of the term spread geographically. The princes and bishops of the Rhine and Danube valleys had delighted in deploying across the landscape their own version of Italian splendour and this movement the critics easily designated as distinctive German variants of Baroque (and Rococo). In Spain and Portugal and their colonies the style was suitable for both sacred and secular building. Criticism has not been slow to subdue all this terrain of forms and fashions to fundamental concept. More important: it has been gradually conceded and is now fully recognized that the art which Colbert encouraged to the glory of Louis XIV was, for all its anti-Italian bias, a genuine manifestation of Baroque principles. Another application of the term, again, is to the arts (generally the plastic arts) of times remote from the seventeenth century. The Athenian Erechtheum and the Temple of Venus at Baalbec have features which may reasonably be called Baroque.[14]

12. F. Strich, "Der lyrische Stil des 17 Jahrhunderts" in *Abhandlungen zur deutschen Literaturgeschichte.* And for an account of early uses of the word Baroque in literary criticism, see Wellek, "The Concept of Baroque in Literary Scholarship." 79.

13. F. Pützer, *Prediger des englischen Barock,* 12.

14. J. Lees-Milne, *Baroque in Italy,* chapter 2.

And, in fact, if we accept Spengler's theory of cyclic cultures which repeat the same succession of developments before dying out, the case for a Baroque phase in any richly creative culture seems a strong one.

The student who now inquires what signalizes a Baroque style, where it was practised, when, and in what branches of which of the arts, is inviting a great number of complex and sometimes incongruous answers. It might be better to skirt around the edge and endeavour to isolate certain salient ideas before attacking the main issue.

One such salience is the fact that Baroque is now an indispensable term and is not likely, under any kind of neglect or onslaught, to go out of use. Those who neglect the concept now do so at the peril of being left with inadequate historical concepts. The use of the term is defended effectively by Wittkower in the Foreword to his *Art and Architecture in Italy, 1600–1750*:

For the main divisions of the whole period, I have used the terms, by now well established, of Early, High and Late Baroque. Only recently have we been reminded that such terminological barricades contain fallacies apt to mislead the author as well as his public. Yet no historical narrative is possible without some form of organization, and though the traditional terminology may have—and indeed has—serious shortcomings, it conveniently and sensibly suggests chronological caesuras during one hundred and fifty years of history. If we accept "Baroque"—like "Gothic" and "Renaissance"—as a generic term and take it to cover the most diverse tendencies between roughly 1600 and 1750, it will yet be seen in the text of the book that the sub-divisions "Early", "High" and "Late" indicate real historical caesuras; but it becomes necessary to expand the "primary" terminology by such terms as "transitional style", "High" and "Late Baroque classicism", "archaizing classicism", "crypto-romanticism", "Italian Rococo", and "classicist Rococo", all of which will be explained in their proper place.

This kind of vigorously practical approach on the part of a critic very fully equipped with the historical facts of the period under review makes short work of a merely negative attitude to the type of criticism proposed and implies that the terminology is no more than a set of tools, not to be judged in themselves but in relation to the workmanship of which they prove capable.

The question may still be asked, however, as to what preliminary commitment to the use of such terms is expected of a critic whose studies have not obligated him to consider the graphic or plastic arts or what willingness to accept "Baroque" into his vocabulary may be expected of the reader who has a generalized rather than specialized sense of the problem. To this question an answer blessed with common sense has been supplied in the correspondence columns of the *Times Literary Supplement* (1945, page 391) by Ralph Edwards, who so to speak descends to do something for the layman:

Baroque relates in the first place to the architectures associated with the counter-Reformation—Bernini and Borromini are among its most illustrious exponents—and implies composition in mass with a thorough exploitation of plastic values, a dynamic sense of movement, and a bold, scenic use of light and shade. Along with these essential properties goes a considerable element of the whimsical and grotesque. Baroque as a descriptive term has been extended to painting and minor decorative arts which are informed by something of the same spirit. It thus covers a great variety of phenomena ranging from Ruben's pictures, with their ample, vehement rhythms, to the carved and gilt side-tables designed by Kent. And so employed, for most people acquainted with the terminology of art a common factor will be readily apprehended which seems to render the description intelligible.

This firm establishment of the term, like the just-quoted plea for its common-sense use, relates primarily to non-verbal arts but both are relevant to literature nevertheless. Experience has shown that in proportion as such terms achieve clarity and usefulness in one art a kind of osmosis carries them over to the others.

One can sympathize with the reader who sees in criticism based on the concept of Baroque only a confused clash of opinion in the midst of ever widening efforts to apply the term. "He sees not the firm root, out of which we all grow, though into branches" and there is some excuse for this; the branches have proliferated all too luxuriantly. In English literature alone the range of application of the term is startling: Shakespeare's tragic heroes, the preachers from Latimer to Jeremy Taylor, Donne and other Metaphysicals (especially Crashaw), dramatists from Jonson, Beaumont and Fletcher to Otway and Lee, Dryden both as dramatist and as poet, Milton. At the same time there has been no clear and basic concept of English literary Baroque as a whole. How matters stood in the middle forties has been summed up by Wellek in his indispensable article, "The Concept of Baroque in Literary Scholarship," published in 1946 in the *Journal of Aesthetics and Art Criticism*. Having dealt with the French rejection of the concept, he continues:

In England, the reluctance to adopt the term has somewhat similar reasons: the memory of Ruskin's denunciations of baroque seems to be lingering in English minds, and this distaste cannot be corrected by the sight of any considerable baroque architecture in England. The term "metaphysical" is too well established (though admittedly misleading), and today too honorific to be felt in any serious need of replacement. As for Milton, he seems too individual and Protestant to be easily assimilated to baroque, still associated in most minds with Jesuits and the Counter-Reformation. Besides, the English seventeenth century does not impress the historian as a unity: its earlier part up to the closing of the theatres in 1642 is constantly assimilated to the Elizabethan Age; its later part from 1660 on has been annexed by the eighteenth century.

Wellek then proceeds to show the difficulties of assessing and defining a Baroque style in literature either as a complex of stylistic devices or as an expression of the Baroque "mind" or "soul." He comes to the conclusion that neither will do by itself but that "the two may be combined to show how certain stylistic devices express a definite view of the world."

Wellek's survey has never to my knowledge been superseded but the *Journal of Aesthetics and Art Criticism* nine years later devoted a second issue to articles on Baroque style in the arts,[15] from which it is possible to assess changes and developments in the use of the term. While not spectacular, these are encouraging, in that they record an irreversible tide of recognition that the term is useful, a continuous process of clarification achieved by the division of ideas and works of art themselves into manageable groups, and a not unfruitful search for simpler descriptions of Baroque's dynamic impulse.

Friedrich, writing in this issue, makes the point that "a polar interpretation is to be preferred to a unitary one. For example, the baroque is not only Catholic, but also Protestant...." Far from being invariably associated with monarchical absolutism, it may be used as a

15. C. J. Friedrich, "Style as the Principle of Historical Interpretation"; M. F. Bukofzer, "The Baroque in Music History"; H. Hatzfeld, "The Baroque from the Viewpoint of the Literary Historian"; J. R. Martin, "The Baroque from the Point of View of the Art Historian"; W. Stechow, "The Baroque: A Critical Summary."

style by those who passionately reject the court. The decisive experience for Baroque is that of man's power in the face of the world. The struggle for power is never-ending because of man's inherent limitations and also because "every conquest of power produces a new rival."

Hatzfeld, writing as a literary historian, recognizes the usefulness of the concept of Mannerism as representing a transition between the two great styles of Renaissance and Baroque. Baroque itself he regards as indissolubly based upon Italian beginnings: "The whole theory of a Baroque period style must inevitably collapse if the principle of a derivation of Baroque from the style of the Italian Renaissance is not maintained." "The tenets of the counter-reformation gave content and impulse to the budding Baroque forms." "The Protestant North can only have been modified by it in the course of an indirect evolutive influence." French classicism has a strong element of Baroque which "is triumphant where a grandiose dignity seems to hide the serious tensions of the *condition humaine*, but reveals these tensions at closer inspection, all the better."

Martin, limiting his scope to painting and sculpture, recognizes as Hatzfeld does the usefulness of the concept of Mannerism: "the contrast between baroque and mannerism is more striking and illuminating than that between baroque and high renaissance." The problem of Baroque, he suggests, will not be satisfactorily solved "until we have developed new techniques of scholarship which, by transcending individual areas of specialization (the history of art, of literature, music, philosophy, etc.), will provide us with a more reliable and valid set of criteria than we possess at present." Provisionally he indicates some leading characteristics of the style. The first is naturalism, that respect for visible, material realism which we expect from an age that gave birth to the physical sciences. Naturalism is bound up with "an equally innate tendency to allegory." This equilibrium "echoes a comparable duality of naturalism and metaphysics in baroque science and philosophy." A further characteristic is a deep interest in psychology, particularly in the psychology of ecstasy, trance, and the extreme states of feeling associated with death and martyrdom, but also in humour which is allowed to mix with dignified traditions. Finally, a sense of the infinite, manifesting itself as an exhilaration in contemplating the continuity of space, in the use of obscurity to suggest limitlessness, in the employment of effects of light to dissolve limits. Closely allied to this concern with space and light is a preoccupation with time.

Stechow, in offering a critical summary of the essays by Hatzfeld and Martin (together with an essay on the Baroque in music history by Bukofzer), points out that in spite of some disparities, for example regarding the scope and importance of Mannerism, there is substantial agreement. His concluding sentences emphasize the special use made by Baroque artists of the search for power and of the equilibrium between religious and secular forces. Their consciousness of style and their consequent ability, as well as willingness, to express these dynamics to the full range of human experience set them apart from their predecessors.

5. PARADISE LOST:
Unity, Power, and Will

THAT MILTON'S THEOLOGY as delivered in *De Doctrina Christiana* is virtually identical with the theology implied in *Paradise Lost* has been conclusively shown.[1] It is reasonable therefore to suppose that any special personal accentuations of doctrine in the former will be of help in a criticism of the latter.

The opening words of *The Christian Doctrine* are appropriate to the creed of any Christian communion: "The Christian Doctrine is that divine revelation disclosed to all ages by Christ (though he was not known under that name in the beginning) concerning the nature and worship of the Deity, for the promotion of the glory of God, and the salvation of mankind." But it soon becomes apparent that Milton's approach to God has the immediacy and directness we have learned to associate with Puritanism. "This doctrine, therefore, is to be obtained, not from the schools of the philosophers, nor from the laws of man, but from the Holy Scriptures alone, under the guidance of the Holy Spirit." At one stroke the individual seeker, with the Bible in his hand, is placed in direct contact with his Maker and is ready to receive the full blessing of salvation and subsequent guidance without benefit of clergy or other intermediary. Not only is there no question of sacerdotal, angelic, or saintly mediation; the second and third Persons of the Trinity themselves direct the soul to the Father, the office of the Son being that of revelation and mediation and that of the Holy Spirit interpretation and inner witness. The Puritan mind is pervaded

1. See Maurice Kelley, *This Great Argument.*

by this conviction, which appears in its formal statements of principle and in the symbolic situations it conceives. (Robinson Crusoe, that secularized Puritan of the generation after Milton's, is shown under deep conviction of sin in the complete isolation of his island, but through reading a Bible found in his sea-chest is immediately and effectually enlightened and experiences the full sense of God's saving grace.)

With the source and channel of truth thus established, Milton proceeds as it were to assure himself that the line is clear of all interference and that the message is not tampered with in the course of transmission. The actuality of God is to be brought as close as possible to the comprehension of man.

Our safest way is to form in our minds such a conception of God, as shall correspond with his own delineation and representation of himself in the sacred writings. For granting that both in the literal and figurative descriptions of God, he is exhibited not as he really is, but in such a manner as may be within the scope of our comprehensions, yet we ought to entertain such a conception of him, as he, in condescending to accommodate himself to our capacities, has shewn that he desires we should conceive. For it is on this very account that he has lowered himself to our level, lest in our flights above the reach of human understanding, and beyond the written word of Scripture, we should be tempted to indulge in vague cogitations and subtleties.

Having made this statement of faith in the direct and unambiguous revelation of the divine mind to the human mind, Milton approaches the nature of the divine mind itself.

The attributes of God are discussed seriatim. First, Truth; second, subsistence as a Spirit; third, Immensity and Infinity; fourth, Eternity; fifth, Immutability; sixth, Incorruptibility; seventh, Omnipresence; eighth, Omnipotence. The ninth and last attribute, treated at greatest length, is for Milton climactic: "All the preceding attributes may be regarded as necessary causes of the ninth attribute, the Unity of God; of which, however, other proofs are not wanting."

Three more attributes, forming a separate and emphatic final sequence, are now examined: Vitality, Intelligence, Will. Of these will is treated at greatest length and indeed a whole sequence of fresh attributes is adduced to body forth the concept of divine volition. "With reference to the Will," Milton tells us, "God is infinitely pure and holy, he is most gracious, he is true and faithful, he is just." He then concludes, "From all these attributes springs that infinite excellence of God which constitutes his true perfection, and causes him to abound in glory, and to be most deservedly and justly the supreme Lord of all things, according to the qualities so frequently ascribed to him."

The effect is, then, that a group of eight attributes of God is reviewed. They are then gathered into the ninth—unity. These are evidently felt to be in some sense static qualities "which describe the nature of God, partly in an affirmative sense, partly negatively." The succeeding group of three, in contrast, are viewed as active, "such as show his divine power and excellence." Of these will is final and climactic.

As a kind of afterthought and out of either sequence, Milton adds, "God must be styled by us Wonderful and Incomprehensible." It is a feeble concession, after so much confidence in the rational understanding of the divine will.

Milton has been interpreted so variously and assimilated to the ideologies of such diverse critics that it is perhaps permissible to labour the point that pre-eminent among his ideas is this concept of unity and will. He shows, of course, no originality, in the sense of introducing fresh theological concepts. He does, however, re-order and re-emphasize common beliefs to produce new effects and new responses.

It is no exaggeration to say that Milton re-cast Christian doctrine in his own terms. This may not be entirely apparent so long as *De Doctrina Christiana* is read as a series of clauses, most of them looking like simple statements of orthodoxy. It is when we get into the sweep of his contention concerning the omnipotence of God as the central fact of all being and when we move into the argument that guards the person of God from all attempts to impose a trinitarian concept, that the controlling passions—they are far more than concepts—of Milton's own thought are revealed. Let anyone read over the great historical creeds, the Old Roman creed, the creeds of Antioch, of Eusebius, of the Nicene Council, of Athanasius, and go on to the Augsburg Confession, the articles of Zürich, the Scots Confession of 1560, and the Book of Common Prayer, and let him then turn to Milton's *Christian Doctrine* where the old familiar files suddenly form up to produce an entirely new intellectual tactic.

If we look at the text of *Paradise Lost* with no other idea in mind than to discover what part is being played by embodiments of power and volition, the findings are not without interest.

There is no doubt that, in the first book of *Paradise Lost*, Satan's discussion centres upon power and will. All is lost but "the unconquerable Will." God, Satan now concedes, is the Almighty, for only he could have overcome "such force as ours." To be weak is miserable and the sole pleasure of Satan and his host will be to oppose "his high will / Whom we resist." Such cogitations of revenge by the defeated are only possible by "the will / And high permission of all-ruling Heaven." Even if all resistance to God appears crushed, the mind has its own power of resistance "and in itself / Can make a Heav'n of Hell, a Hell of Heav'n." The devils march past in a great display of power and loyalty to Satan. Pandemonium, as its name indicates, is a symbol of their unity of purpose. Throughout this episode evil is seen simply as opposition to the will of God and good as simply submission to his will.

Book II pursues the same theme. The "immortal vigor" of the fallen spirits is praised in Satan's speech from the throne. They possess, he says, "union and firm faith, and firm accord / More than can be in Heav'n." He is followed by Moloch, the worshipper of power, who thought himself equal in strength to God and "rather than be less / Car'd not to be at all." Belial then counsels a temporizing, cautious policy but this is weakness in the eyes of his compeers and even in the eyes of Milton who forsakes his proper role to exclaim on Belial's "ignoble ease, and peaceful sloth." Beelzebub counters with the proposal to "build up here / A growing Empire," and to promote this rebellious enterprise against God the "sole King" by an active incursion into Man's universe. Satan then picks up this theme, unfolds his plan, and "with thoughts inflam'd of highest design" speeds toward the gates of hell. After a gigantic confrontation of opposing wills at the closed portal, Satan proceeds toward his objective: "he with difficulty and labor hard / Mov'd on, with difficulty and labor hee."

Book III reveals God contemplating, from the vantage-point of divine omniscience and omnipotence, what goes on below. His words to the Son concern his own will and free will in angels and men, who must give proof "Of true allegiance, constant Faith or Love" and must do so with freedom of "Will and Reason (Reason also is choice)." Will determines the future of mankind, for God "ordain'd / Their freedom" and "they themselves ordain'd their fall." The theme is developed, but only as amplification of this simple principle. The whole revealed plan, God affirms, is "As my Eternal purpose hath decreed." Salvation is the will of God giving, and the will of man receiving: "sav'd who will / Yet not of will in him, but grace in me." Among the saved are an especially favoured group, God declares, chosen by grace, "Elect above the rest; so is my will." The rest of the saved shall be enlightened as they show a willingness to progress "And to the end persisting, safe arrive." Freely given grace and freely exercised human will are declared essential to salvation. Then God's mercy having been shown as an act of will and of unity of purpose between Father and Son, and man's acceptance of salvation as an act of will, the sacrifice of the Son is shown as a voluntary self-abasement from which the Son knows that he shall rise victorious, and subdue his vanquisher. "I through the ample Air in Triumph high / Shall lead Hell Captive."

Now occurs an extraordinary and deeply significant comment:

> His words here ended, but his meek aspect
> Silent yet spake, and breath'd immortal love
> To mortal men, above which only shone
> Filial obedience: as a sacrifice
> Glad to be offer'd, he attends the will
> Of his great Father.

The love of Christ for mankind which could have been developed into an evangelical theme or into the mystical apprehension that "God is love" remains firmly contained within a concept of filial obedience and subject to the primacy of will.

God now concludes by promising that since the Son has been "Good" and in him "Love hath abounded more than Glory abounds" he shall be "Anointed universal King," all power shall be given him, all knees shall bow to him, he shall judge the wicked. The last judgement past, Messiah shall lay by his regal sceptre and "God shall be All in All." While it paraphrases Paul's statement to the Corinthians, the passage under Milton's handling loses the exigent, apocalyptic tone of the apostle to the Gentiles and becomes a formal and splendid reaffirmation of the primacy of unity in the divine order of ideas.

When, as the next book opens, Satan alights on Mount Niphates, his mind is filled with the same concepts, though inverted or degraded, as fill the heavenly scene we have considered. He has rebelled against heaven's "matchless King," though this was needless and of his own volition for he had "the same free Will and Power to stand" as the hosts who kept their loyalty. Now he will, by choice, continue in the path of evil; "by thee at least / Divided Empire with Heav'n's King I hold."

The universality of the power and will exercised by God, and unavailingly opposed by Satan's perverted will and power, extends over Eden. Adam tells Eve of "the Power that made us" and that requires simple obedience, "Among so many signs of power and rule / Conferr'd upon us, and Dominion giv'n / Over all other Creatures." Adam's one weakness, indeed, is not to exercise the power he possesses over his wife.

The visit of Raphael to Eden, extending over almost four books of the epic, is firmly contained within the same framework of active authority and its gift of volition. As he departs on his terrestrial mission, Raphael is carefully briefed about his purpose. Man is to be reminded that there is "Happiness in his power left free to will" and is to be warned against transgressing the divine command. The preliminary exchanges between Adam and his guest are filled with recognitions of the gifts "That one Celestial Father gives to all" and of the chain of being which unites, not by ramifications but by gradations, the whole created universe. The existing chain of being is, indeed, extrapolated into a possible future:

> time may come when men
> With Angels may participate, and find
> No inconvenient Diet, nor too light Fare:
> And from these corporal nutriments perhaps
> Your bodies may at last turn all to spirit,
> Improv'd by tract of time, and wing'd ascend
> Ethereal, as wee, or may at choice
> Here or in Heav'nly Paradises dwell;
> If ye be found obedient, and retain
> Unalterably firm his love entire
> Whose progeny you are.

The Platonic ascent is made contingent upon a continuous act of obedience to the Maker of all things.

As Raphael departs he impressively repeats his commissioned message:

> Be strong, live happy, and love, but first of all
> Him whom to love is to obey, and keep
> His great command; take heed lest Passion sway
> Thy Judgment to do aught, which else free Will
> Would not admit....

Raphael has supplied Adam and the reader with a wealth of information imparted with consummate tact and skill. His primary purpose, however, in which he has failed, has been by using these stories as exempla to persuade Adam to keep his will, which lies in his own power, united with the will of God.

Raphael's disclosures of divine plans and purposes are themselves full of co-ordinated energy. The war in heaven, it is really worth noting in some detail, is an affair of disrupted unity and is conducted almost without benefit of diplomacy, strategy, tactics, or plan of campaign but with the continuous and utmost display of incredible force, on both sides and on every hand. The will power of the combatants is everywhere absolute.

The initial speech of the Father to the assembled angels exacts of them complete unity under one head:

> United as one individual Soul
> For ever happy: him who disobeys
> Mee disobeys, breaks union....

Satan's rebellious dissent from acknowledging the lordship of the Son is denounced by Abdiel, who asserts that union is happiness: "Our happy state under one Head more near United."

When the loyal host marches to battle it is "in mighty Quadrate join'd / Of Union irresistible." It moves on "Indissolubly firm." The battle being joined, the irresistible power of the two hosts is kept within bounds only by absolute omnipotence of God himself: "th' Eternal King Omnipotent / From his stronghold of Heav'n high over-rul'd / And limited their might."

After the combat between Satan and Michael, both "Of Godlike Power," the rebels retreat and the secret of the loyal army's success is revealed:

> In Cubic Phalanx firm advanc'd entire,
> Invulnerable, impenetrably arm'd:

> Such high advantages their innocence
> Gave them above their foes, not to have sinn'd,
> Not to have disobey'd.

Unity among themselves, the fruit of their individual loyalty to the Almighty, is the source of their superior power and their loyalty is the fruit of their free will. Even when surprised, on the second day of battle, by the infernal device of cannon, the power of the loyal angels, undiminished, enables them to uproot whole mountains and overwhelm their adversaries.

God the Father now acts to bring the war to an end and simultaneously to fulfil "his great purpose" of transferring "All power" to the Son. From this point until the close of Raphael's military narrative the lines are filled with images of power and will and glory, as the "Sole Victor" fulfils his Father's command.

At the beginning of the seventh book Adam's thanks to Raphael show that he has grasped the purpose of the story of the war; it is God's warning to himself and Eve "to observe / Immutably his sovran will."

The discourse now moves on to the story of creation and as it does so care is taken to establish the familiar fundamentals. These are the omnipotence of the Father, the absolute and unquestionable nature of his will, and the consequent unity of the total scheme of things. This unity is polar, in that Satan "Fell with his flaming Legions through the Deep / Into his place," while as the Son returns with the victorious saints "th' Omnipotent / Eternal Father from his Throne beheld / Their multitude." Upon this axis, the poles of which are in heaven and hell, another world is about to be created and, lest it should seem a project separate from the organic life of heaven, there is the elaborated statement that if man conforms completely to the will of God, heaven and earth shall become one. Nothing could be clearer than this promise of a removal of the distinction between "there" and "here," providing that free will is well employed.

> ... a Race
> Of men innumerable, there to dwell,
> Not here, till by degrees of merit rais'd
> They open to themselves at length the way
> Up hither, under long obedience tri'd,
> And Earth be chang'd to Heav'n, and Heav'n to Earth,
> One Kingdom, Joy and Union without end.

Heaven, hell, and earth being now accounted for as integral parts of one universe, there remains the deep or chaos, which lies around and between. Of this vastness it is made clear (no matter how Saurat and those who oppose him have interpreted the passage) that God is cognizant of the totality of space and that if his goodness is not fully projected into every part of it this is of his own volition and for his own ends.

As the Father commissions Messiah to proceed upon the mission of creation there is careful insistence on the Father's controlling power. The Son is the Father's agent, gladly acknowledging "by thee this I perform." He goes forth,

> Girt with Omnipotence, with Radiance crown'd
> Of Majesty Divine, Sapience and Love
> Immense, and all his Father in him shone.

The Father himself in some sense proceeds forth also, for the gates of heaven open to the Trinity, "The King of Glory in his powerful Word / And Spirit coming to create new Worlds." Lest any doubt should linger about the role of the Father in the act of creation we are reminded of his presence at the phrase "Let us make now Man." Then when the great work is done it is explained, as the Father receives the Son back into heaven, that

>   he also went
> Invisible, yet stay'd (such privilege
> Hath Omnipresence) and the work ordain'd,
> Author and end of all things.

That these passages are not accidental but do indeed point to the primacy and pre-eminence of the Father becomes clear by the time chapter v of *The Christian Doctrine* is reached.

It is worth noting that Milton allots to this whole episode about five hundred lines, of which rather more than three hundred are a description of creation and the rest devoted to initial and closing ceremony including two triumphal processions, to and from the site of the new world. Milton has, of course, no sense of evolutionary pattern, no interest in biological relationships. His categories and descriptions are unimpressive. It is only when ideas of power enter that the story of creation takes on life:

> Part rise in crystal Wall, or ridge direct,
> For haste; such flight the great command impress'd

On the swift floods: as Armies at the call
Of Trumpet.

First in his East the glorious Lamp was seen,
Regent of Day, and all th' Horizon round
Invested with bright Rays.

      ...the Swan with Arched neck
Between her white wings mantling proudly, Rows
Her state with Oary feet.

      ...the swift Stag from under ground
Bore up his branching head.

Creation is conceived in images of court or camp, in terms of majesty, dominion, and splendour. To Adam is given rule over all created things because he is created in the image of God, yet this rule is conditional upon his being an obedient holder of his fief in Eden: "there to dwell / And worship him, and in reward to rule."

The angelic host rightly interprets creation as a stupendous tribute to the Father's unshakable power: "Who can impair thee, mighty King, or bound / Thy Empire"?

The eighth book, the most charming of the twelve, is replete with discussions of unity. Adam bears rule over all the beasts and speaks their language and Milton, following his source, implies that this is a tongue common to all of them. Adam nevertheless asks God for a partner, a consort with whom he can converse. God, in reply, instances his own singleness, "who am alone / From all Eternity, for none I know / Second to me or like, equal much less." Adam pleads that he himself is nevertheless "In unity defective, which requires / Collateral love." At the close of his discourse with Raphael Adam once more adverts to Eve and to their "Union of Mind, or in us both one Soul," and makes this the occasion to ask Raphael about love in heaven. There, says the angel, "if Spirits embrace, / Total they mix, Union of Pure with Pure." With a final warning that all love is subsumed under the will of God "whom to love is to obey," Raphael departs.

That Book IX is the story of severed union and misused free will need scarcely be pointed out. Adam urges that Eve remain with him. Her presence "Would utmost vigor raise, and rais'd unite." But Eve refuses: "from her Husband's hand her hand / Soft she withdrew." Her unsupported free will gives way before Satan's power as tempter.

Adam falls through his sense of union with Eve:

> Flesh of Flesh,
> Bone of my Bone thou art, and from thy State
> Mine never shall be parted, bliss or woe.

As his long sad speech to Eve concludes:

> Our state cannot be sever'd, we are one,
> One Flesh; to lose thee were to lose myself.

Eve replies in praise of "our Union," "one Heart, one Soul in both." This union in transgression is at once exposed for what it is first by their rapid descent into dissension, then, as the tenth book opens, by the contrast afforded by the glad voluntary submission of the Son in heaven to the Father's will. Adam and Eve, however, are soon reunited in repentance and in their two complementary apprehensions —the one rational, the other intuitive—of Michael's prophecy and admonition.

This great revelation provided by Michael ends with a double vision of unity. Messiah will

> dissolve
> Satan with his perverted World, then raise
> From the conflagrant mass, purg'd and refined,
> New Heavn's, new Earth.

In this hope, Adam may now possess a kingdom equal to "all the rule, one Empire" which he has lost—"A paradise within thee, happier far." In perfect mutual love and reconciled to God, Adam and Eve then leave the Garden.

Milton is concerned with the eternal desire of Christendom, the union of man with God, and true to the spirit of his age he conceives of its achievement as through the will of God and of man. "La perpetuelle aspiration de ce temps fut d'unir le ciel à la terre."[2]

In proportion as we pay attention to the continuous flow of Milton's narrative and discourse, it becomes clear that concepts of unity, power, and will provide the momentum of the great argument. These three, moreover, are best understood as forming a complex from which none of them is in any practical sense separable. Unity is conceived as imperium and as a guarantee that power will be absolute and volition dynamic. In this context will appears as conscious and purposeful

2. E. Mâle, L'Art religieux après le Concile de Trente, 301.

power. God's unity is tantamount to his omnipotence; this singleness of imperium is maintained by the use of power to crush rebellion and by the exercise of free will on the part of the loyal. Yet encompassing all is the larger consideration, beyond human comprehension, that as power and will have manifested themselves in angelic or human experience in emergence from the one eternal God—for even the most perverted power is subject to his permissive will—so will and power resolve themselves back into his unity. The Father pronounces to the Son, anticipating his final victory (III, 339–41):

> Then thou thy regal Sceptre shalt lay by,
> For regal Sceptre then no more shall need,
> God shall be All in All.

Not only is this great theme argued and demonstrated; there are in addition many symbols or symbolic instances of freely given obedience conducing to corporate power; for example, the angelic guard in Eden that "closing stood in squadron join'd / Awaiting next command" (IV, 863–4). Numerous episodes if closely examined reveal the same theme. The war chariot of Messiah, based on Jewish tradition, reveals the Son of God in his kingly power restoring unity to heaven.[3]

The steps by which God's purpose for the individual takes shape are realized in these same terms. Predestination is the act of God's sovereign will and if, as Milton acknowledges, it is related to God's foreknowledge this is the knowledge of which way man's free will is going to turn. Free will moreover is a kind of power given by God to men or angels as Satan realizes, asking himself, "Hadst thou the same free Will and Power to stand? / Thou hadst."

To the believer, whose act of faith has been foreseen and predestined, there comes the gift of Christian liberty which Milton, following Paul, designates as a release from the bondage of the law to serve God of one's own volition. At this point we must strive to recall that, although the Puritan revolution in the long run furthered the cause of democracy and the spirit of liberal individualism, it was not intended to do so by the generation which carried it out. Even Rainsborough is no democrat. Milton's *Ready and Easy Way* exhibits the greatest reluctance to put power into the hands of the people. As for Christian liberty being identical with "doing as one likes," it is

3. J. H. Adamson, "The War in Heaven: Milton's Version of the Merkabah," *Journal of English and German Philology*, LVII (4), 690–703.

Defoe in the generation following Milton who first presents us with the truncated Puritan ideology of a Robinson Crusoe, in which the upper range of dedication to God is almost muted and only the lower level of freely ranging activity is left. The effect of true Christian liberty, on the contrary, is simply to make the service of God an inward and voluntary matter, not a question of external authority and imposed discipline.

There is a crucial passage in the third book of *Paradise Lost* (165 ff.). Messiah has been pleading for man. The Father replies that man's salvation his own divine purpose has decreed. Of men, they shall be saved who will. Yet it is of divine grace. We are immediately reminded of the last line of *Comus*, "Heaven itself would stoop to her," and of the conclusion to the tractate on education, "If God have so decreed and this age have spirit and capacity enough to apprehend." There then follows a description of the elect, "Some I have chosen of peculiar grace / Elect above the rest; so is my will." These are not, it is clear, the elect in the Pauline sense of the word, constituting all the saved, but in some special Miltonic sense. Mankind is divided into three classes. First, the elect. Second, the general run of Christians who have limited enlightenment, "what may suffice," who heed the call to "Prayer, repentance and obedience," and who if they persist will arrive in heaven. Third, the reprobate, doomed to wrath. That this scheme is what Milton intends receives confirmation from *Samson Agonistes* (674 ff.), where we read of those "solemnly elected" by God, of the common rout of Israelites, and of the heathen and profane. In this passage the elect appear as filled with power and purpose, dedicated "To some great work, thy glory, / And people's safety."

If such is the constitution of Milton's moral universe, it follows that a special interest will attach to the quality of obedience which his omnipotent God can evoke. So exacting are his demands that we might expect rebellion, as in Satan, or an almost despairing acquiescence: "Doth God exact day labour, light denied?", falling into the real despair of Samson: "Just or unjust alike seem miserable." Or, as a third alternative, the mechanical round of reverential posture and lip service with which Satan falsely charged the loyal hosts. From these negative possibilities Milton rises into a positive flame of loyalty, love, and zeal, objectified most clearly in Abdiel. Obedience is linked with happiness, freedom, and power; it unites man's will with the divine will. Adam finds "Happiness in his power left free to will." Raphael's final injunction is,

> Be strong, live happy, and love, but first of all
> Him whom to love is to obey, and keep
> His great command.

It would be hard to imagine a concept of obedience more completely devoid of passivity and mere acquiescence than Milton's.

Will with Milton is paramount and holds a whip hand over reason and emotion. (In following the time-honoured division of man's faculties into feeling, thought, and will, we are not pretending to a scientific scheme but only to one which Milton, like other poets and like critics of poetry, has inevitably found convenient.)

Will is capable of acting when reason is disabled. Adam reassures Eve that what her will has resisted while reason was asleep, "Waking thou never wilt consent to do." God himself speaks of "Will and Reason (Reason also is choice)." And indeed reason only serves to confirm the rightness of God's will. If it does not it is not right reason.

Will similarly dominates emotion. God leaves Adam free to will his own happiness; Abdiel explains that the happiness of the angelic hosts holds while their obedience holds: "freely we serve, / Because we freely love, as in our will / To love or not." Love is a function of will, which takes first place: "His Loyalty he kept, his Love, his Zeal." What is still more interesting in this context is Milton's containing operation in Book III in which the whole discussion of Messiah's mercy and grace is bracketed within assertions of God's ordaining will and power to subdue his enemies. Most striking of all is the passage, already quoted, in which the love of Christ to fallen man is made a function of his obedience to the Father:

> his meek aspect
> Silent yet spake, and breath'd immortal love
> To mortal men, above which only shone
> Filial obedience: as a sacrifice
> Glad to be offer'd, he attends the will
> Of his great Father.

If feeling is, or should be, under the dominance of will and if reason is, in the last analysis, definable as agreement with the will of God, it remains to ask what is the prime mover behind acts of will. The answer would seem to be that there is none. Abdiel, reproaching

Satan, appeals to God's superior power, who as creator has "form'd the Pow'rs of Heav'n / Such as he pleas'd, and circumscrib'd their living." From a theological point of view this may be sound enough, since the very eternity and absoluteness of God make his decisions in a sense arbitrary and certainly unquestionable. Yet when Milton, who has undertaken to justify the ways of God to man, brings us into the presence of a God who is demanding "true allegiance, constant Faith or Love" from Adam, because he has created him, we are in the presence of a quite inexplicable absolute. Rebellion against such a God seems equally irrational. The origins of evil in Satan are as mysterious as the origins of good in his maker. His will to rebel, if we suppose him jealous of Messiah, springs from a pride for which we can discover no motive. What is more surprising is the inadequacy of motive in Eve and in Adam. If Eve is trivial, vain, and self-regarding, if Adam is uxorious, these are sinful long before the apple is taken and in any case Eve's hoped-for gains are so shadowy and their attainment so contrary to what we have learned of her intelligence that we cannot account for her act—still less for that of Adam to whom a moment's reflection would have suggested a talk with Raphael, or, failing Raphael, with Gabriel, before the rash step was taken. The fact is that Satan, Eve, and Adam alike rebelled against divine decree for the reason Hilary is said to have given for climbing Everest—it was there. Will, then, in Milton's view seems, not only in God but also in his creatures, to be a kind of absolute producing unfathomable, causeless, or mysteriously motivated acts. It is noteworthy that after his fall Satan can produce in his private thoughts no reason for not submitting to God but the irrational "Disdain forbids me and my dread of shame."

If we regard the smaller episodes of *Paradise Lost* as frequently designed to exhibit some great principle in miniature, like the medallions in Renaissance decoration which depict relevant or analogous mythical events, we may view in this way the speech by Raphael in the eighth book explaining why he did not witness Adam's creation. He had been sent with a full legion toward the gates of hell,

> To see that none thence issu'd forth a spy,
> Or enemy, while God was in his work,
> Lest hee incenst at such eruption bold,
> Destruction with Creation might have mixt.

> Not that they durst without his leave attempt,
> But us he sends upon his high behests
> For state, as Sovran King, and to ensure
> Our prompt obedience....

Most readers will feel that this parade of reasons ends in no reason at all. It is an odd, instructive passage, a microcosm of larger things, and God's reasons for forbidding the human pair the fruit of the tree form just such another.

A separate but related point which suggests that we are not mistaken in regarding acts of will in the poem as strongly irrational—beyond, above, or below reason—is the view of evil we get if we take the great sweep of the action and fix our attention on the broader masses of the design. We find evil represented as simple act of will. Satan desires to substitute his will for God's will but, with this in mind as an all-disqualifying proviso, we must concede that from a human point of view many of the activities of Satan and his followers seem laudable. They exhibit fortitude, loyalty, determination, management, constructive talent, inventiveness, powers of inquiry, and immense resource. Adam and Eve, apart from some sexual excess scarcely worth Dr. Kinsey's attention and some understandable domestic disagreement, seem little changed in character. Certainly they do nothing that loses them our sympathy. And in the long history of human error and sinfulness revealed to Adam by Michael, it is extraordinary to find that, apart from man's tyranny over man (i.e., the act by which he replaces God's ruling will by his own) and some brief and unspecific references to luxury and sensuality, there is nothing to rouse our natural horror or indignation. Milton's reluctance to move outward from the simple axis of man's rebellious will thrusting up against the will of God keeps him from doing more than suggest the existence of the complexities of moral degeneracy or the ramifications of spiritual wickedness. *This is a deeply revealing and endlessly significant fact.*

Yet let us not suppose that these considerations detract from praise of Milton as a poet. Causeless will may be a contradiction in terms to the nineteenth-century humanist but not to any reader who conceives of God as absolute (I am that I am) or of human volition as either unquestioningly submissive to the divine will or else (quite irrationally, for there can be no reason in disobeying God's command) without reason departing from it. And from the purely experiential view, it is hard to see why a twentieth-century reader should quarrel with the presentation of displays of supra- or infra-rational will.

But our real task is to discover what the power and will of the one God really meant to Milton and to his age, last of the ages of faith, when faith, becoming passionate and explicit and seeking rational justification, prepares to give way to reason and to sentiment.

Power and will, as establishing, preserving, or disrupting unity, pervade Milton's works. It is impossible, therefore, to isolate a discussion of this element in Milton and pass on to something different. In every situation the pulse of will beats. Bagehot remarked that every line in Milton "excites the idea of indefinite power."

External events favoured a display of the symbols of power in Milton's poetry. Charles the Martyr believed that his own powers were by divine right absolute. Cromwell's conviction was that God-given free will obliged him to bring the King to judgement. It has been said that the salient controversy of the age was between concepts of God's providence and man's volition as determinants of the destiny of the individual soul. In England the artistic expression of power was limited by special circumstances. The Stuarts were unable, for lack of money, to go on from the banqueting house in Whitehall to the erection of a great palace. Victory in the civil wars went to Puritans who took no stock of iconography. It is only with the campaigns of Marlborough that the arts, so to speak, catch up with concepts of glory and at long last realize themselves in the fabric and contents of Blenheim Palace. None of these limitations, of course, directly affects the poet.

But it is not only the external pressure of events that determines Milton's direction. Some deep and hidden predilection drives him toward the worship of absolute unity, goodness, and power. It has been pointed out that the kind of resolution and singleness of purpose which we associate with Cromwell and Puritans is but a link in a long tradition. The virtue of the Stoics made their ideal philosopher an equal of the gods. Stoicism became for the Romans an ingredient in their will to master themselves and their universe. Renaissance individualism, seizing upon this tradition as a means of justifying its own aspirations, projected two complementary ideals, that of the political men, the men of action, and that of the poets and scholars, the humanists. In the Elizabethan version of the Renaissance, Marlowe projects an ideal of resolution and will to power which becomes a landmark in the history of character types. When, therefore, Milton creates minds and wills to whom nothing is impossible he is clearly not fashioning them from the whole cloth of his own imagination.[4]

What is new in Milton's concept of virtue and resolution is his consistent desire, manifest in his earliest work and undeviating to the end, to identify the personal drive with the eternal will of a transcendent God. It impels him toward the achievement of the absolutes —so far as humanly possible—in his own thoughts and deeds. How powerful these urges are is well known to all readers of Milton. His feeling for unity impels him into Arianism. His concept of individual responsibility leads to an almost total neglect of the redemption, by the sacrifice of Christ, of sinful man. From a psycho-analytic standpoint Milton appears the perfect example of Adler's concept of personality. Assertion of the individual self and achievement of superiority over other selves mark Milton's God, as well as Milton's concept of himself and the misdirected struggle of Milton's Satan. The "will to power" (and for that matter "the masculine protest") are everywhere evident in *Paradise Lost*. It is also apparent that Jung's theory of the growth of the individual consciousness has a bearing upon Milton. "Individuation is an exceedingly difficult task: it always involves a conflict of duties, whose solution requires us to understand that our 'counter-will' is also an aspect of God's will."[5] Milton's understanding of the counter-will was profound, as his conception of Satan abundantly demonstrates, even though he denies, with protestations so vehement as to signalize a deep inner struggle, the right of Satan to do anything but acquiesce totally in the will of God.

One of the devices by which a sense of power and volition in the outer world is made one with the world of subjective desires and impulses is the primary axis which polarizes the universe of *Paradise Lost*. Milton transforms the chain of being, deriving from Plato, and referred to in Prolusion II as the golden chain which Jove suspended from heaven, into a compelling axis or vista or route down which energy flows, up which aspiration moves, uniting the mind of man with the mind of God; or along which the reprobating will of God passes to thrust Satan into hell. This axis unifies the universe, is a

4. H. Mutschmann, *Der andere Milton*, 79–81.
5. Jung, *Psychology and Religion*, 198.

positive drive-shaft for the transmission of will. Its action is compelling. Satan knows he is at the wrong end; there is no thought that he can be separate from God or judged by another standard, or quiescent as Belial advises. He can do nothing but press directly up against an axis that thrusts him directly down. There is no room for lateral movement; the lateral exploration of hell was a fiasco.

The axis in *Paradise Lost* differs from the chain of being in certain respects which will be considered later in these pages. Here we may say summarily that Milton's innovation lies in the avoidance or minimizing of gradations on the vertical shaft. The Persons of the Trinity, though not viewed by Milton as co-eternal, are not conceived as in a sequence, either. Milton's angels are not arranged in the customary hierarchies. The ladder from earth to heaven, though owing something to Plato and to Augustine and to Jacob's vision at Ebenezer, is not strongly or at all times graduated. Though Eve is in a sense beneath Adam, she receives direct warning, direct judgment, and direct revelation, from God. The animals, though heavily classified, do not appear in hierarchies. Every intelligence is related, by direct vertical axial influences, to God; vegetables and minerals are related directly to the sun, as the symbol of God.

A word should perhaps be said about Milton's capacity as an energizer of classical and biblical materials. In the account of Noah's ark in Genesis, the ark itself is described as a vast repository for animal life; the waters "bare up the ark, and it was lift up above the earth"; "the ark went upon the face of the waters"; in due course the ark "rested" upon Ararat. In *Paradise Lost* we see how Noah "from the Mountain hewing Timber tall, / Began to build a Vessel of huge bulk." Then amid the storm we descry the ark: "the floating Vessel swum / Uplifted; and secure with beaked prow / Rode tilting o'er the waves." The evoked image of Greek war vessel or armoured knight instantly gives power and purpose to the great act of rescue. Or, to take an example of a completely different sort, we may compare Virgil or Theocritus with the lines they inspire when Milton in *Lycidas* thinks of the death of Orpheus. Virgil's lines are (*Georgics* IV, 520 ff.):

> Spretae Ciconum quo munere matres
> inter sacra deum, nocturnisque orgia Bacchi
> discerptum laetos juvenem sparsere per agros.

and Theocritus writes (Idyll I, ll. 140–1):

> Δάφνις ἔβα ῥόον. ἔκλυσε δίνα τὸν Μοίσαις φίλον
>
> Daphnis went to the stream. The waters
> closed over him whom the Muses loved.

In *Lycidas* the Orpheus passage concludes:

> When by the rout that made the hideous roar,
> His gory visage down the stream was sent,
> Down the swift Hebrus to the Lesbian shore.

And this descriptive surge is at the same time the climax of an agonized question concerning God's justice. To read such lines of Milton's and then to walk in Rome from the static columns of even so massive a monument as the Coliseum up to Bernini's small church of S. Andrea al Quirinale there to encounter the never failing shock of its dynamism is to appreciate Milton, Bernini, and their age afresh.

It is perhaps not inappropriate here to give some thought to Milton's use of light in *Paradise Lost*. Though his handling of light has long been admired, some aspects of it still invite comment. Hell is represented as

> void of light,
> Save what the glimmering of these livid flames
> Casts pale and dreadful.

But this initial impression of "No light, but rather darkness visible" is gradually modified, as though our vision were accustoming itself to the scene. We see Satan no longer "Cloth'd with transcendent brightness" as in heaven and yet his form has not lost "All his Original brightness" but appears like the sun eclipsed. In the face of logic Milton achieves his desired effects of interpenetration, unity, and energy. Some remnants of heavenly glory persist in the fallen angels though their new medium is penal fire, a destructive flame, "hideous ruin and combustion." By subtle shifts the poet allows this fire of God's wrath to be neighboured by the fire of devilish rage and hatred. The very warriors who look like oaks and pines blasted by "Heaven's Fire" are themselves fiery, and we see

> Millions of flaming swords, drawn from the thighs
> Of mighty Cherubim; the sudden blaze
> Far round illumin'd hell.

This is an extraordinary passage. The infernal energy of the rebels can illuminate, if only fitfully, their prison-house. Illumination does not stream from Satan as the divine light streams from the throne in heaven. Even when he returns from earth in triumph to surprise his court, it is only by a "false glitter," a "sudden blaze" soon extinguished. But hell is full of purposeful lights and fires, defiant and revengeful. Fire forwards the smelting and casting of gold for Pandemonium, which is in due course lighted by "Starry Lamps and blazing Cressets." The final unification of the penal fires of hell with the fiery passions of its inmates comes in Moloch's words,

> let us rather choose,
> Arm'd with Hell flames and fury all at once
> O'er Heav'n's high Tow'rs to force resistless way,
> Turning our Tortures into horrid Arms
> Against the Torturer....

Milton has thus succeeded in the extremely difficult feat of making hell part of a unified cosmos in which God's will is everywhere in the ascendent, while at the same time establishing there a power totally opposed to heaven and yet not allowing the view of hell as prison-house to become independent of hell as Satan's kingdom.

What one would expect of a Baroque artist is that his handling of light should be simultaneously scenic, dynamic, and symbolic. In Bernini's Cornaro Chapel or S. Andrea al Quirinale the controlled influx of light is essential to the composition of the scene; it is the pathway up which the souls of the two saints aspire; it is also the complete and satisfying statement that God is Light. The long vista up into and down St. Peter's leads to a point of light which reveals itself as window with the figure of the Dove descending over the Cathedra of St. Peter. The down-streaming light provides the instantly accessible symbol of divine attestation and blessing.

The light emanating from Milton's heaven gives direction to movement in the universe and in the sphere of natural as distinct from spiritual life the sun easily becomes its vice-regent. It is typical of Milton's skill in subduing detail to controlling ideas that Satan on his way to earth should take his bearings by "the sacred influence of light" from the walls of heaven. To Adam and Eve the Sun, rather than the light of heaven, serves as a focal point yet he is clearly no more than part of creation. For a moment they seem like sun-worshippers;

at sight of his orb just clear of the horizon, "Lowly they bow'd adoring, and began / Their Orisons," but these are for God and the Sun falls into his place as fellow worshipper:

> Thou Sun, of this great World both Eye and Soul,
> Acknowledge him thy Greater, sound his praise
> In thy eternal course.

But the scenic use of light to establish centres and lines of direction (as when Uriel uses variously canted sun-rays to travel to and from earth), in both literal and figurative senses, is a means of imparting or awakening energy. Adam and Eve significantly begin their garden work with sunrise. God promises to put the light of conscience in his fallen human creatures:

> Light after light well us'd they shall attain
> And to the end persisting, safe arrive.

At the beginning of the famous invocation that opens the third book, Milton repeats the scriptural phrase, "God is light." The angels stand about him thick as stars receiving from their sight of the divine presence "Beatitude past utterance." (Raphael is later to explain to Adam that the stars are dependent upon the sun and "in their gold'n Urns draw Light.") The Son of God is the "radiant image of his Glory." This slight ambiguity is dispelled when we read a few lines later,

> in him all his Father shone
> Substantially express'd and in his face
> Divine compassion visibly appear'd.

The Son, it is once more made clear, shines by light which belongs essentially to the Father.

By the time Milton came to write *Paradise Lost*, commentators on the Scripture who were also neo-Platonists had made familiar the thought of God as source of light both physical and spiritual. Without effort the poet can pass from the praise of that natural light of which he is in his blindness now deprived to the inward light irradiating the mind which alone makes possible his poetry. He may have Augustine, Dante, Ficino, or Spenser in mind. They will all have drawn from the common source. His own modification, as one would expect, is to insist on the one source of light and to make light a source of energy and unity. If the sun impregnates the earth with fructifying beams it is because God has made the light and bestowed it upon this his luminary; it has no inherent powers of generation:

> Of Light by far the greater part he took,
> Transplanted from her cloudy Shrine, and plac'd
> In the Sun's Orb, made porous to receive
> And drink the liquid Light, firm to retain....

6. *PARADISE LOST:*
Space and Time

IT WOULD BE absurd to suppose that Milton consciously modelled the totality of space in *Paradise Lost* upon the manipulation of total space by the fabric of a High Baroque church. But it would be surprising if the concepts common to both were not subject to the great controlling ideas of form which imbued the collective mind of the period. That there are concepts common to both there can be little doubt. Each is the theatre of God's dealings with men. Each is conceived as both ideologically and architecturally total and complete. In each the purpose is to provide a means of progression onward and upward to a point beyond which no progression is possible because none is conceivable.

The High Baroque architects knew how to create the illusion of limitlessness within walls which were in fact the boundaries of an assigned space. Many devices were employed to this end.[1] Columns, pilasters, altars, balconies were used to conceal the mural nature of what lay behind them. Effects of plasticity under pressure were induced by curving the surfaces of walls or playing these against the mass of columns. Light was used to accentuate, to dissolve, or to make ambiguous the actual disposition of masses.

A controlling device was the combination of elements from differently conceived types of church plan. The Gothic desire to move down a long nave toward an altar was not necessarily suppressed by

1. T. H. Fokker, *Roman Baroque Art*, I, 143–4.

the Baroque architect but it could be combined with the Renaissance feeling for the centrality of dome rising over a square or circular space. With these could co-exist the suggestion of a cruciform plan, either Latin or Greek. The round dome might be modified into a Mannerist oval at the same time. Such a combination would be distinctively Baroque if it gave the impression of several distinct forms successfully unified by skilful devices and if it suggested some flow of space and movement of masses so that palpable strength and weight might co-exist with an impression of boundlessness.

The universe of *Paradise Lost*, if we are willing to look at it with a fresh eye, reveals a complex plan. It is axial in that heaven and hell are antipodal and no other polarity can compete with the dominance of this one. It is also cruciform, in a psychological rather than plani-metric fashion. When we are in heaven all is drawn up to God and there is little if any tendency to think laterally, as certainly no possi-bility of looking any way but down from the walls of heaven. Similarly hell draws all in it down so that lateral space outside its walls scarcely enters as a possibility. On the contrary when we are between heaven and hell chaos carries the mind right and left, so to speak, its property being to spread out formlessly. Superimposed upon these plans is the central space where the main action takes place, the theatre of Eden under the dome of the sky, from which the light descends. Such generalizations may appear vague until we look more closely into the parts or regions of Milton's universe.

There are, let us rather baldly put it, five locales to Milton's total space. Each is carefully described and situated with respect to the rest. Yet each is made to flow into the others both intellectually and dyna-mically; numerous cross-references connect each with all the others so that the mind never rests satisfied with a single spatial unit, and the action of the epic flows powerfully from one region into another. Furthermore, each region, although its plan has an air of being specific and precise, has in fact an essential ambiguity in its structure. All the regions, moreover, are vast, logical, sumptuous, and determined not by planimetric outline but by dynamic movement.

Heaven has a wall with battlements and towers yet a calculated ambiguity in the description keeps the fabric from becoming mun-dane. It is undetermined square or round; the materials opal and sapphire, suggest glancing, changing, and dissolving light. To the upward dimension of heaven we can feel no limit because the central mount, which is the throne of God, totally absorbs all speculation, all imagination, all aspiration. We may well imagine that had Satan's revolt not taken place our attention would never have been distracted from the centrality of heaven, to its having a North, to its being temporarily divisible into opposed regions. Strong emphasis is placed on the portal, and in true Baroque fashion, as the one accent in the wall, as proclaiming by its armorial bearings the quality of the occupant,

> With Frontispiece of Diamond and Gold
> Imbellisht; thick with sparkling orient Gems,

and as the focal point, from its position at the head of the stairway leading to earth, of the great processional acts of creation or errands of enlightenment to man. Heaven is vital, the wall rolling in to eject the rebellious angels. It is in physical substance all of a piece with the rest of the universe, like earth as Raphael explains, and it must be conceded like hell in that minerals lie under its soil. It should be observed that heaven not only dispenses spiritual influence; great and significant material movements take place which link it with the rest of the universe. The suffering bodies of the rebels in hell were formed in heaven; the redeemed bodies of the saints in heaven have been nurtured on earth.

Earth is not only like heaven; it is also "Not unconform to other shining globes" (V, 259). The ambiguity of Milton's presentation of earth is a piece of virtuosity which seldom receives the praise it deserves. It is always recognized that, in order to hold the balance level between what are (roughly) Copernican and Ptolemaic structures, Milton shifts ground continually. The famous "some say" and "some say" in Book X is only one of many similar shifts. What is not always perceived is that a far more difficult ambiguity is created by Michael when he takes Adam to the top of the specular mount. The whole passage deserves close examination. The hill is the highest in Paradise and permits the clearest possible view of the whole hemisphere of earth. Incredulity is instantly checked by the addition that from here we see no more (and by implication no less) than Satan showed to Christ from the mountain in the wilderness. This notion of being able to see all the kingdoms of the earth from one point has already been suggested to Adam by Raphael in Book V where the angel speaks of

> all the Earth,
> And all the Sea, from one entire globose
> Stretcht into Longitude.

From the mount in Paradise Adam is now shown, as Marvell would say, "cramped into a planisphere," the whole inhabited world. From east to west he views Asia and Europe and from Russia in the north he looks down to Angola "fardest South." This is the historical rather than the geographical world and one does not ask for Kamchatka, Japan, or the Cape. Then with the boldness of a conjuror Milton adds that "in Spirit perhaps he also saw" Mexico, Peru, and Guiana and instantly has Michael put drops into Adam's eyes and throw him into a trance. The showmanship, the dexterity, the sleight of hand are beyond praise. But what is the purpose? It is to produce a world picture which corresponds with the historical and religious interpretation of human events which follow.

Let us consider the alternatives to Milton's *tour de force*. If the earth is frankly and without compelling tension regarded as a globe to be explored, the mind takes in the Americas, Australia, and the oceans and poles. The view of earth as lying about Eden, which is directly under the gate of heaven and the eye of God, thus becomes diffused. Soon with Coleridge we find "the blue sky bends over all" and the intense axial organization of a moral universe begins to dissolve. This Milton resolutely forbids by a deliberate handling of perspectives both literal and psychological. On one of the ceilings of the Barberini Palace we find the painter Sacchi wrestling with the same problem. Celestial Wisdom points toward a globe. The axial emphasis thus set up and accentuated by the disposition of light within the composition throws Europe and part of Africa into relief. In Milton's century it was still possible to think of an earth of which the Mediterranean was the centre, to conceive without too much visualization that prayers went literally up to heaven, to subject, in other words, the implications of new science, discovery, and rational thinking to traditional images of an omnipotent, omniscient, and anthropomorphic God seated on his throne regarding the earth and its inhabitants beneath.

The preservation of this perspective in *Paradise Lost* is assisted by

the fact that the Bower, the Garden, Eden, and the earth are conceived concentrically about the single axis from the will of God to the
will of the human pair. A curious anomaly arises as a result. Eden's
gate must, like the gates of heaven and hell, receive a proper Baroque
emphasis. Set in a structure of alabaster, it is adorned with armorial
bearings (in the literal sense of a stand of arms) and with pillars
between which sits the captain of the guard. Yet it performs no
function. Milton's technical skill and powers of artistic accommodation and adjustment are miraculous and often we hardly perceive what
he is doing to our sensibilities. His occasional lapses therefore serve
to reveal his techniques. Here it would appear that the Puritan
demand for direct "vertical" communion with God has for once not
been harmonized with the Baroque layout which requires ceremonial
gates and stairways.

Earth is the centre of a universe apparently constructed upon
conventional lines. But the purpose of the traditional components is
changed to meet the needs of a new world view. The primum mobile is
arrested and becomes a fixed opaque shell hanging by a golden chain
from heaven. An opening like that in the dome of the Pantheon is
provided through which heavenly influences stream down. We have
thus, as in heaven and earth and the garden, the fulfilment of the
Baroque requirements of an apparently delimited enclosure with
a significant and accentuated portal. Above this opening are the
degrees of the ladder up to heaven, below it are the degrees of the
spheres forming a ladder down to earth. No use is made of either
structure because the dynamic of Baroque visitation and apotheosis
cannot tolerate any mediaeval movement from stair to stair.

In a number of ways the space contained within the shell of the
universe is ambiguous. Its function with its own bounding wall is
blurred by the mysterious crystalline sphere, which is in some sense
an ocean of waters above the earth. The whole system of concentric
spheres is ambiguous. They exist, they serve to carry round the
planets, yet they are permeable and, indeed, so impalpable that they
afford no impediment to vision and none to movement. Axial penetration of space is quite unhindered. Even more interesting is the
manipulation of focus and stress within the nominally spherical
totality of the universe. Satan, having surveyed it, with wonder, from
Libra to Aries and pole to pole, "Down right into the World's first

Region throws/His flight precipitant." Raphael and Messiah descend from heaven's gate in swift dynamic fashion. These axial movements capture the imagination and prevent the circle of the universe from suggesting the calm, symmetrical, unchanging completeness which it otherwise might. One diameter is heavily stressed, the others ignored. The effect is analogous to the deformation of the Renaissance circular plan for churches into the Baroque oval. This, to quote Pevsner, was

a less finite form, and a form that endows the centralized plan with longitudinal elements, i.e., elements suggestive of movement in space. An infinite number of variations on the theme of the oval was developed first by the architects of Italy and then by those of other countries. They constitute the most interesting development of Baroque church architecture, a development belonging in Italy chiefly to the second half of the 17th century.[2]

It may be objected that Eden being the centre of the universe the use of the word oval is unwarranted. But even if we take the word literally there is the curious supporting fact that Milton not only elongates the space of the universe by directional activity but also repeatedly (e.g., in IV, 592 ff.) suggests the sun as an alternative centre, and two foci are, in a geometrical sense, the essentials for realizing an oval.

The universe hangs in chaos and here Milton would at first sight seem to have abandoned Baroque principles. From its nature, chaos cannot be firmly bounded, nor can structure be achieved within it, nor can it project any constructive dynamism from itself into another region. It is a wild amoral ocean from which God has in some sense (though perhaps not in the sense argued by Saurat) retracted his controlling power. But in the face of this problem Milton's inexhaustible technical resource, as usual, throws up a solution. Formless in itself, chaos defines and accentuates form in other regions. Without chaos, the beauty and calming power of light from the heavenly battlements would receive no emphasis. Without chaos, the creative power of God who produces an ordered universe from disorderly elements and in the face of disorder would appear less striking. Without the voyage through chaos hell would seem less lost, less remote, and Satan's energies less directional, less heroic. Furthermore, it is notable that Milton has, so to speak, pulled in some of the

2. N. Pevsner, *An Outline of European Architecture*, 178.

slackness of chaos to create an organized space and a meaningful tension within it. Here, as nowhere else in the poem, allegorical figures are permitted to live and move and have their being. Sin and Death open the gate to chaos and actively work to construct a causeway across it. Chaos, Night, and Chance have here their thrones. Chaos speaks of the abridgement of his realm and its new limits which are now so straitened that the newly founded universe is "not far" from where he sits. This constriction, the references to the fall and pursuit of the rebellious hosts through space, and Satan's constant upward struggle all conduce to imposing upon chaos a pattern of stresses. Milton even persuades us that the Arch Fiend must struggle through a narrow passage like Jason or Ulysses (II, 1016–22). The allegorical figures placed in chaos like "elephants for want of towns," do their work and persuade us that even chaos is dynamically organized and is no "intense inane."

Beneath chaos is hell, a "dungeon stretching far and wide" from outside but from within a torture-chamber with gates and bars above but threatening downward lapses into bottomless abysses. By Satan's dynamic will-power this is turned into an empire, from being only "ravenous jaws" (X, 637). Its great gate, flanked by Sin and Death and impaled with circling fire for its armorial bearing, assumes Baroque importance, as the starting point of Satan's escape and of the construction of the causeway, and when shut for eternity as the sign of God's final, absolute, visible triumph over evil. Milton's enormously energetic handling of hell becomes logical when we recall that in a scheme of absolute power the dungeon is an important component.

> Such place Eternal Justice had prepar'd
> For those rebellious, here their Prison ordained.

Piranesi's Carceri series is only a late obsessional rendering of a theme familiar in drawings and prints of the period, the prison with its claustrophobic massiveness and its pulleys and wheels to suggest the strappado and worse tortures. From absolute power to rebellion to the punishment of rebels to all the apparatus of incarceration is a logical series in certain contexts.

The consideration of the various regions of Milton's cosmos may have suggested that the totality of extension as he presents it is not arrived at by the addition of parts, by an amassing or assembling of elements until all are accounted for. Pevsner has said of Borromini's churches that "space now seems hollowed out by the hand of a sculptor"[3] and the same is true of Milton, who we feel is not composing by an aggregation of determined areas or volumes but by indicating these within an already conceived total continuum, always existing in the mind of God. Only Pandemonium is composed of modules. It is probable that both for Milton and for his reader this sense of the omnipresent mind of God (viewed either as present in all places or as comprehending all possibilities of location) is the determining element in giving total space its feeling of indivisibility, but we should not neglect the formal devices by which the reader's imagination is helped to realize this unity. It has been shown that the regions within total space are all dynamic and generally ambiguously so. That is why diagrams representing the cosmos of *Paradise Lost*, particularly those drawn to scale ("thrice to the utmost pole," etc.) are never satisfactory. Cortona in the construction of the Church of SS. Martina e Luca "discarded the idea of a structure based on the relations between sets of values. He obviously relied on the impression of absolute space."[4] In practice it is the constant flow of force from one region to another that keeps up this impression in the reader's mind. Let us pass over the important but comparatively simple device of constant cross-reference; every reader of Milton feels the pressure of all other regions of the cosmos no matter in which region his attention may at the moment be centred. What is less obvious but more significant is the penetration of one region by energies originating in another. Heaven's influence penetrates hell negatively and earth positively. It penetrates chaos constructively at the time of creation. Hell's influence penetrates chaos and earth and would like to reach into heaven. What happens on earth stirs heaven and hell to action.

Gates as junctions, points of departure or return, and emphatic symbols of decision have already been mentioned. Even more important are vistas and processionals, which may be regarded as passive and active counterparts. Vistas permit the universe to compose itself from various vantage-points and give variety, all in conformity with the controlling omniscience of God. This absoluteness of God's vision

3. *Ibid.*, 182.
4. Fokker, *Roman Baroque Art*, I, 147.

is beautifully rendered in Book III. We commence with a simple looking-out from heaven as the Almighty Father bends down his eye to view his own works "and their works." Satan he sees flying toward earth and his vista at once enters the other dimension of time "Wherein past, present, future he beholds." When, therefore, a little later we find Satan who "Looks down with wonder at the sudden view / Of all this World at once" the relevance of this immense sight to the infinitely greater penetration of both space and time by the eye of God rushes into the mind.

The great apotheosis is that of Messiah after creation when "the bright Pomp ascended jubilant." The magnificence and majesty of this upward sweep giving the sense of a great cosmic *Treppenhaus* leading up to the gates of heaven from which point the royal procession moves to the throne—this is in the most straightforward way a product of High Baroque organization on the poet's part.

Two features of the cosmos that demand special notice are the "op'n Sky" or "Sublunar Vault" under which the terrestrial Paradise lies and the enigmatic causeway or bridge built by Sin and Death to connect the universe and hell. Each is recognizably Baroque in design. The use of the dome in church architecture to suggest heaven as well as the heavens has a long history.[5] The Baroque modification of the circular form—which to Renaissance minds had typified the oneness of God and the harmony of the whole universe—consisted in combining with it cruciform elements or devices to suggest axial movement. These of necessity set up tensions which the Baroque architect took pleasure in sustaining. The garden paradise of Adam and Eve is contained by a wall, within and above which can be seen "a circling row of goodliest Trees." While this circular place of worship is in one sense self-contained, it is also part of a larger whole which invites an axial vista: "Eden stretch'd her Line / From Auran Eastward to the Royal Tow'rs / Of Great Seleucia." Our first parents are therefore from one point of view in a state of perfect and stable felicity within the circle of the garden under the dome of heaven. If their "bodies may at last turn all to spirit, / Improv'd by tract of time" it will be a slow movement and even they may well prefer at times to inhabit their garden rather than the courts of heaven (V, 499–500). From another point of view, they live in Eden, which, as their "nether Empire," calls for

5. R. Wittkower, *Architectural Principles in the Age of Humanism*, 8–12.

penetration and into Eden and the wide world the future will take them. Certain it is that the image of self-containing security of tenure under the dome of heaven is from the beginning impinged upon by other special concepts. And indeed, as early as Book III we have seen Eden as a *rond-point* on that vision which from the "prospect high" of Omniscience reaches to the depths of hell and to the end of future time.

If the dome is a symbol of harmony, the causeway made by Sin and Death is a symbol of disharmony and disquiet, of equal force. It may be viewed in several ways, all of them causing intense mental discomfort. In the first place it is virtually impossible to visualize or sketch this structure. It is a paved causeway carried by a mole; it is an arched bridge, a "ridge of pendent Rock"; it is compared to Xerxes' bridge of boats between Asia and Europe. This arch, of which one haunch butts against the exterior wall of hell and the other against the outside of the primum mobile of our universe, must be roughly vertical for it follows the general course of Satan's voyage from hell toward the new universe hanging from heaven's gate and this voyage is, we know, a constant struggle upward. This arch, monstrous in its perverse orientation, is also illogically constructed. It is made of flotsam pushed together by Sin and Death, solidified by blows of Death's mace or (what would seem easier) petrified by his look. It is cemented with infernal asphalt. It is asymmetrical in the cosmos and presents a weighty, clogging lopsidedness. It is probable that the seventeenth-century reader, more alert than we to the symbolic and ceremonial significance of staircases, would feel more acutely than we do the peculiar hideousness of the infernal causeway. From earth to the primum mobile God provided the gradation of the spheres up which the mind of man may climb. From this landing, where Satan, it will be recalled, stood looking first upward to heaven then downward to earth, there rises the mysterious staircase to the celestial gate. Sin and Death then built another structure to this same landing,

> and now in little space
> The Confines met of Empyrean Heav'n
> And of this World, and on the left hand Hell.

In the so-called Imperial staircase, a plan invented in Italy but first realized in Spain, the initial flight of steps to the landing divided at that point into two, turned, and reascended. What Sin and Death have done is to produce a hideously mutilated version of the Imperial plan, in which, instead of ascending jointly with its partner, the left-hand flight is flung down in incongruous asymmetrical reversal forming a glissade to the dungeons beneath. However viewed, the work of Sin and Death is an architecturally deformed structure signalizing the moral deformity of its builders.

Such is the space Milton creates in *Paradise Lost*. New effects are achieved with traditional materials. In all-pervading continuity of space, structures may be vitally conceived and shaped; matter is brooded upon, "conglobed," "disparted," "spun out" until the fabric hangs in space "self-balanced" (VII, 234–42). There is likeness in kind among the various regions because of their common origins; as Raphael says, "things therein / Each to other like, more than on Earth is thought." The regions are linked by cross-reference, by

> some connatural force
> Powerful at greatest distance to unite
> With secret amity things of like kind
> By secretest conveyance.... (X, 246–9)

They are fused by the flow of influence and action, given perspective by piercing vistas and transfixing axes. Processions move from one focal point to another; manœuvres are carried out through vast distances: "Far on excursion toward the Gates of Hell; / Squar'd in full Legion (such command we had)" (VIII, 231–2). There is the full sweep of both apotheosis and katabasis. The surge of creative power is everywhere: mountains upheave their backs and waters precipitate themselves to shape the new earth; the new artillery lunges onto the battlefield; Pandemonium rises like an exhalation in massive gold; and in our world the swift stag from underground bears up his branching head.

Nice correspondences and contrasts invite attention. The laborious flight by Satan through chaos, the brief moonlit levitation of Eve's dream—these are the opposite of Raphael's swift angelic flight or Messiah's visit to Eden in viewless descent beyond human comprehension. Or let us note the process of bracketing by which Satan must explore hell, first on one side then on the other, or his similar movement in comprehending the universe from east to west, from top to bottom. These are in contrast to the omniscient view of the Father whose sight of all space and time carries no hint of effort.

It would of course be a mistake to assume that the spatial relations in High Baroque cannot be within a great poem transposed into models more subtle and more rewarding than these we have been considering. Confrontations, reversals, and contrasts may have architectural and verbal expressions which from their nature are not identical and yet spring from the same ideological or aesthetic impulses. Milton, however, deals with literal space so conscientiously and with such an abundance of identifiable devices that we can go a long way toward establishing his relation to Baroque by confining ourselves to these elements.

Milton handles time and space in much the same way and the two are often inseparable. Space is for action to roll out into and the first act of Messiah when creating the world is appropriately to delimit it with God's golden compass. The reader is in the time as well as the space of *Paradise Lost*. For various reasons he cannot get out of Milton's history of man any more than elect to escape from the universe. Michael's history of all time to come has syncopations but no lacunae. Divine purpose and human will are inextricably in the same continuum as space and time; there are no neutral zones accessible to the human mind. Milton's own desire to live "As ever in my great Taskmaster's eye" in fact applies to all mankind, obedient or otherwise.

In one sense, Milton has almost no latitude when it comes to laying down the highway of history. Creation, Fall of Man, Old Testament chronicle, the life of Christ, history of the Church, the seven churches of Asia as synoptic allegories of post-biblical events, Greece, Rome, Europe: all present themselves with the confidence that they are the actuality of man's corporate life from the first beginnings to the Last Judgement. Yet once again we see how a tradition may be accepted and its implications transformed.

The transformation is effected by intelligible devices. History is never, in *Paradise Lost*, related for its own sake. Nor is there any desire to produce a ribbon of chronicle unrolling smoothly from start to finish. Instead there is powerful accentuation aimed at specific effects, the interaction of distinct forms whose overlapping or superimposition produces a whole, the masking of a continuous process by concentrating weight on certain upstanding figures, the use of recapitulation and prophetic anticipation to achieve comprehensive and comprehensible unity, above all a sense of powerful movement overcoming the resis-

tance of weighty materials. Our plunge into hell at the commencement
of *Paradise Lost* exhibits the familiar pattern of *in medias res* but it is
more: this part of total history is given urgent initial attention so that
Satan may be erected into a possible, if not a fit, antagonist to God.
When Satan in Book X delivers his great apologia to the "Thrones,
Dominations, Princedoms, Virtues, Powers" light is not throw on the
events themselves but on his indomitable will. The pattern of things
viewed from hell is not the same as the pattern seen from heaven,
yet the events are the same and it must be admitted that the interpretations put on them are strangely similar. Satan on Mount Niphates
already knows himself doomed to "infinite wrath, and infinite despair."
God, though there is no admission of defeat, suffers the loss of many
angels and the greater part of mankind from his allegiance. At the end
of *Paradise Lost* it begins to look as though the rebellion of both
angels and men was somehow foreordained, in some sense inevitable.
Something quite extraordinary has happened. Jung might say that
Satan's role as a fourth in the cosmic mandala has been made clearer.
For our present purposes it is sufficient to say that two patterns
apparently discrete and irreconcilable have been made to adjust their
shapes so that an impression of a rich and complex order is produced.
The varied roles of Messiah throughout the long succession of events
are like a row of columns forming a single colonnade upon which
much structural weight can be sustained. Raphael and Michael, in
less impressive fashion, bear the past and future respectively upon their
shoulders. Their accounts are simultaneously to warn and comfort
Adam and to enlighten the reader by long vistas, full of alignments and
devices of perspective, back to eternity and forward to the same timeless absolute. What we are being given, all the time, is not only a tale or
a history but also a great demonstration and justification of divine
purpose, for the sake of which history exists.

That this is truly a Baroque artifice, full of power and purpose and
predetermination, is shown by Milton's unwillingness or inability to
produce any theory of history other than an apocalyptic one. Nothing
suggests that he has attentively read history dispassionately looking to
see what happens. Everything supports the belief that here is history
not only made subservient to the formal requirements of epic but also
totally subdued to one idea, the indisputable pre-eminence of the will
of God.

7. *PARADISE LOST:*
Personages and Plot

ALL PERSONS in the story of *Paradise Lost* are embodiments of absolutes. This single fact will take us a long way toward comprehending the Baroque quality of the piece.

We have seen, in reviewing Milton's concept of God the Father, that his absolute and undivided rule is scrupulously guarded, is protected from the smallest erosion. He limits the power of the combatants in heaven; he is himself the ultimate power in the creation of the universe; and, as Raphael explains to Adam, the secrets of the nature of things are best left, unexplored, to God's disposition and control.

When God is regarded not as a theological definition but as an actor in *Paradise Lost*, new problems at once appear. If to the requirements of Christian doctrine we add the demands of a Baroque concept of absolutism, the amalgam does not disintegrate of its own accord. But when God is made to act and the reader is asked to give whole-hearted assent to the divine rightness of these actions, disbelief refuses to be willingly suspended. Because God is righteous he is angry with Adam; because he is absolute in his demands for obedience his anger is a towering rage; because he is omniscient and ungoverned by time he gives vent to his anger before the trespass actually occurs. Except to a few minds like that of C. S. Lewis this is quite unacceptable, indeed unbearable, and, worst of all, not infrequently comical. If we confine our attention to Milton as a Baroque artist, neglecting all other implications of God's anger, a simple pattern appears. It is the familiar attributes of unity, power, and will that give rise to the dilemma.

Unity gives rise to God's absoluteness in all things. Power brings with it the necessity of divine control over the universe. Will ensures that this control shows itself in specific acts which can and must be justified. The problem attaches only to a Baroque God, not necessarily to a Christian God. The Old Testament presents a God consistent with primitive mystery and prophetic vision. The New Testament, proclaiming the marvel of incarnation and the efficacy of redemptive sacrifice, produces the one catalyst calculated to make all intellectual difficulties resolve themselves.

But clearly our argument is not complete. Bernini contrived—both in the intensely masculine disposition of forms in and before St. Peter's and in the feminine subjectivity of the Cornaro Chapel—to present the power and will of God in no uncertain terms and terms which have won wide aesthetic approval. The difference is that Bernini relied in St. Peter's upon a sacramental conception of truth and in his execution of the St. Theresa figure upon a mystical communion with the absolute. Milton's variety of Puritanism makes these approaches impossible. We seem then to be forced toward the conclusion that Milton's Baroque style and method are in important respects not compatible with the Baroque of the Counter-Reformation. This must be immediately and freely admitted, nor can the consequences be minimized. They form the subject of some pages further on in this discussion.

No personage in *Paradise Lost* has so many weighty and diverse roles as the Son, the Second Person of the Trinity. As embodying the executive side of divine will, he must necessarily act in many capacities: Son, King, Messiah, Captain of hosts, Judge, Intercessor, Mediator, Sacrificial Victim, Redeemer, Saviour, Bridegroom—no list can express the manifold richness of the theme. But how in the clear air of *Paradise Lost* is Milton to achieve psychological consistency between, say, the One whose regard is "full of wrath bent on his enemies" and the One who is "to death condemn'd / A shameful and accurst." Milton's solution, so stringent that it is generally denied by being ignored, is to throw back all motivation one stage, into the will of the Father. This can be done because the Son's status is less than that of the Father, Milton's Arianism here becoming explicit. Stress is taken off the role of Christ as Saviour of men and a correspondingly increased emphasis, far stronger than the generality of Christian belief demands, is laid upon direct submission of man's individual will to God. On the whole this solution works, though at some cost.

Milton is unquestionably heretical. The Jesus of John's Gospel is lost to him. *Paradise Lost* itself is rendered marmoreal, intractable, even brittle in places because the Son is denied his supreme due. When Messsiah is shown taking his orders from the Father before the final battle in heaven, he predicts victory and goes on to promise,

> Then shall thy Saints unmixt, and from th' impure
> Far separate, circling thy holy Mount
> Unfeigned Halleluiahs to thee sing,
> Hymns of high praise, and I among them chief.
> So said, he o'er his Sceptre bowing, rose
> From the right hand of Glory where he sat,
> And the third sacred Morn began to shine.

Something in this passage—perhaps its facility—disturbs the mind.

Milton's successful introduction of the Holy Spirit into the dramatis personae of *Paradise Lost* reveals both his beliefs and his poetic techniques. In Book VI he has taken great care to subordinate the Son to the Father. Now, at the beginning of Book VII, if the Holy Spirit were too overtly introduced as the object of his invocation the whole problem would be raised again. Not that Milton is averse to raising it in *De Doctrina* where the conditions of writing are totally different, but it is clear from the very firm, very cautious treatment he has given to the status of the Son that within the poetic framework such an operation is excessively difficult. Instead, therefore, of immediately claiming as his inspiring muse the Third Person of the Trinity, Milton works obliquely, alerting the reader at the outset ("by that name / if rightly thou art call'd") to the fact that he invokes not the abstract classical Urania, the heavenly Muse of the classical dictionaries who raises learned men to the skies, but the veritable Spirit of God. Then "Wisdom thy sister" becomes allegorical again. This is followed by the unmistakable clarity of "upled by thee." The reference to Bellerophon takes us back to allegory. Then comes the explicit "visit'st my slumbers Nightly." Then more allegory with Bacchus, and the clarifying final line "For thou art Heavn'ly, she an empty dream." The effect is not that of patchwork but completely single and consistent, thanks to Milton's confident rhetoric, and his use of a tried convention. The result is to suggest that the effectual grace ministered by the Holy Spirit is hidden and personal to the recipient, an effect produced throughout the New Testament in any case, and to give to Milton's poetry divine inspiration.

With regard to the Holy Spirit, as with regard to the Son, it is significant that Milton avoids, on the one hand, giving these persons of the Trinity a status equal with the Father and, on the other hand, subordinating them into a lower rank. What he does do is to make them willing agents of the Father's will so identified with him in purpose that questions of status are not readily raised. And the poet, we may be certain, is not anxious to have them raised.

Milton's characterization of the angels, fallen or unfallen, is extremely revealing, for here, in the paucity of direct scriptural reference to their nature and history, he can develop a concept which reflects his own inclinations. The archangels Michael, Gabriel, Raphael, and Uriel are particularly rich in implications of Milton's views. They are, beyond human imagination, splendid and powerful and are charged by the Almighty with commissions of great weight. Yet they accomplish nothing. Michael's strength, if we are to believe the text, is limited by God and at the decisive hour he stands obediently by and sees Messiah carry all before him. At creation the angels are spectators, not agents. Gabriel guards the walls of Eden with a considerable show of military efficiency but is not permitted to deal effectively with Satan. Raphael, the sociable archangel, transmits to Adam and to the reader a great deal of information but the warnings, for which his tales are parables, take no effect whatever. Raphael's treatment by Milton is exactly what Milton's predilections would lead us to expect. He is in Renaissance tradition the guardian angel par excellence, as Botticelli reminds us, and as Milton, who indeed makes reference to Tobias, is well aware. But he is resolutely prevented— in spite of his palpable interest in man and in spite of Adam's appeal that he "oft return"—from assuming in the slightest degree the guardian role. And this by now need not surprise us; Milton's determination to let nothing come between God and the soul of man is inexorable. We may add that Uriel's inefficiency as regent of the sun reaches comic dimensions, and that Michael's final task, while it includes a panoramic revelation to Adam and Eve, is primarily the negative one of expelling them.

Milton's reluctance to allow angels to get between God and man is instructive. Both Luther and Calvin had condemned devotion to guardian angels and Milton could never have brought Adam and Eve into the aura of the typical Counter-Reformation prayer, "Ange de Dieu, à qui j'ai été confié par la bonté céleste, illumine-moi aujourd'-

hui, garde-moi, dirige-moi, gouverne-moi." Raphael is sent to Adam
on an assignment, with terminus ad quem clearly laid down and he is
instructed to speak "as friend with friend." Michael makes a clean
break with Adam and Eve, taking his hands from theirs. No guardian
follows them into their new world. The angels of the Nativity Ode
do not mix with the shepherds but "sit in order serviceable." In *Comus*
the guardian Spirit scarcely speaks to the Lady. In *Paradise Regained*
angels attend the Son, but as his adoring servants. In *Paradise Lost*
the angels guarding Eden never speak to the human pair.

All this, far from appearing as negation or as impoverishment, has
a powerfully unifying and energizing effect upon the plot structure.
Man is at all times immediately responsible to God and, like the
twelve tribes of Israel, instantly serving him day and night. For the
same reason, hierarchy among the angelic ranks themselves is carefully made ambiguous. Ithuriel and Zephon are under Gabriel's command but when they encounter Satan direct aid is given them from
heaven: "awe from above had quell'd / His heart, not else dismay'd."
In the first stages of the war in heaven Abdiel, keeping faith, is
directly commended, not by his superior officer, but by God. Under
Milton's skilful and deliberate manipulation the nine ranks of
heavenly spirits are suggested but not allowed to become operative. If
we regard heaven as a court or a camp, these are all heroes and paladins. But the notion of hierarchy, which lay ready even to the
Puritan's hand in the nine names given in the New Testament, is
never permitted to develop. Union, obedience, and order are everywhere apparent but only because each feels himself as ever in his great
Taskmaster's eye.

But apart from this negative capacity of never obscuring the will of
God, the angels contribute positively and powerfully to the unity of
the poem. In every sense of the word they are a chorus, perpetually
hymning the praises of the Almighty and developing with unwearying
reiteration the central theme of his beneficent will. Occasionally this
choral function descants into unexpected effects. Eve reminds Adam
of their angelic guardians:

> . . . how often from the steep
> Of echoing Hill or Thicket have we heard
> Celestial voices to the midnight air,
> Sole, or responsive each to other's note

> Singing their great Creator: oft in bands
> While they keep watch, or nightly rounding walk,
> With Heav'nly touch of instrumental sounds
> In full harmonic number join'd their songs
> Divide the night, and lift our thoughts to Heaven.

Here are smoothly harmonized the military aspect of angelic service, its choral function, and the effectual unity between earth and heaven which angels provide. Biblical overtones sound in these lines, Jacob's ladder and the Psalmist's "songs in the night."

The angelic hosts beautifully link epic tradition with Christian doctrine by providing about the throne of God a choir, a court, an army, so that, whether we think of heaven as a place of spiritual harmony or as a regal palace or as a military camp, the imagination is satisfied. Uniting all these inevitably is the thought of heaven's King, supreme in power and splendour, which is central to Milton's imagination.

A further effect of unity provided by the principal angelic characters concerns their acting as exempla or icons, as formalized perfect examples of service, fortitude, vigour, obedience, and the like. Of such microcosmic embodiments of Milton's total theme, Abdiel is the most striking and most perfect. And since Abdiel is cut out of the whole cloth by Milton, as his own creation, we may be certain that in attributing this quality to the named angels we are making no mistake. Even Uriel has great amplitude and beside the disguised Satan is like Jove to Mercury.

What Milton might have done with archangels had he been a practitioner of earlier Renaissance techniques rather than of Baroque is apparent when we review the traditional list.[1] Michael is *victoriosus*, with palm and standard; Gabriel *nuncius* with lantern (or lily) and mirror; Raphael *medicus* with pyx; Uriel *fortis socius* with drawn sword and flame; Barachiel *adjutor* with white roses; Jehudiel *remunerator* with crown of gold and leash; Sealtiel *orator* in an attitude of prayer. The obvious use of this deeply significant rank of figures would be in emblematic or iconographic contexts but Milton, to a different end, makes use of only the four salient ones. Uriel's distinguishing badge of flame fits him to be the radiant guardian of the sun. Gabriel's light-bearing function similarly fits him to be guardian

1. See E. Mâle, *L'Art religieux après le Concile de Trente*, chapter VII.

of the alabaster gates of a pristine Eden. Michael's military quality is far more fully exploited, both in heaven and on earth. And Raphael's safeguarding and ministering function appears most extensively of all, his kindness to Tobias being also part of the understood background. Milton does not go against any part of the given list of attributes but boldly selects and simplifies, reforming the original file of angelic personages into a hand-picked guard of paladins each sent on a separate errand vital to the fulfilment of God's purposes. Their prompt and disciplined obedience is remarkable. Raphael and Michael act within strict limits of time; Gabriel desists instantly on a sign from heaven; even slow Uriel hastens back to his post.

Adam and Eve present a problem of characterization not posed by God or by angels. They are our first parents; their actions both determine and symbolize our own choice of action; in a very real sense they are ourselves. They are not great saints or great commanders; if they embody perfection it is not a perfection strenuously achieved but initially bestowed. How then can they be remoulded, from the substance of the biblical narrative, into Baroque figures, which Milton's type of epic demands? We have seen how the varied roles of Messiah are united by the insistence that all he undertakes is in willing fulfilment of the absolute will of the Father. Clearly Adam and Eve, though their obedience to God is always in view, are variable humans.

Foremost among the devices Milton does employ to secure unity and amplitude in his presentation of Adam and Eve is that of double or multiple function.[2] They are not allowed to develop like characters in a novel so as to present a gradually revealed or maturing psychological unity. They are always total and archetypal wherever we find them, yet constantly shifting in the nature of the absolute they embody. It is probably fair to say that just as no poet has been able to reproduce the effect of Lycidas because only Milton had the technical knowledge to unify its diverse ingredients, so nobody, for the same reason, has been able to present us with characters at once so statuesque and so immediate, so intellectually incongruous and yet so permanently convincing as Adam and Eve in Paradise Lost.

The most extensive double functioning performed is to fulfil simultaneous dramatic and epic roles. The evidence for Milton's dramatic intentions before or during the composition of Paradise Lost need not

2. For architectural analogues to double function, see below, chapter xi.

detain us now; the dramatic elements in the poem are patent. The hero falls from high estate, partly because of external pressure but partly because of a tragic flaw of character. Behind all this are mysterious workings of supernatural agencies. Foreshadowing, hubris, irony—all are present. A chorus attends and the appearance of *deus ex machina* closes the action.

That the poem is nevertheless fundamentally epic needs no argument. In addition to the abundant use of epic conventions and devices it exhibits in the fullest sense what might be called the epic topography. A known world is revealed, but set in the midst of boundlessness, between upper and lower gods. The cycle of events embraces the life and death of individuals and the rise and fall of kingdoms. It begins at a nadir of princely fortunes. There is eventually disclosed a consistent order in nature which the gods control and which will be extended to men if they accept it.

If we look at the central events of the poem as tragic drama, this in turn supplies a variety of function for its chief characters. It is a tragedy of wronged innocence, of ambition, of betrayed love and marital disaster, of loss of the king's favour, of disobedience to authority and rebellion against the royal power.

If we think of the poem as epic we find it both Christian and classical, not in the sense of new wine for old bottles, but two forms so superimposed that we can see either at will by adjusting our vision. It is also simultaneously a timeless religious epic and a national Puritan epic.

Adam himself is representative man in a state of perfection; his nativity, education, and marriage are deployed before us. Care is taken to present in synoptic form the familiar course of childhood and early experiences:

> As new wak't from soundest sleep
> Soft on the flow'ry herb I found me laid
> In Balmy Sweat, which with his Beams the Sun
> Soon dri'd....
> Myself I then perus'd, and Limb by Limb
> Survey'd, and sometimes went, and sometimes ran
> With supple joints, as lively vigor led:
> But who I was, or where, or from what cause,
> Knew not; to speak I tri'd, and forthwith spake,
> My Tongue obey'd and readily could name
> Whate'er I saw.

He is also a Renaissance man, a humanist filled with curiosity about the universe. Even though this intellectual urge to know seems to play no part in the fall, it is given great prominence in the pre-lapsarian books.

Adam is also the archetypal free agent, the test case for the operation of free will. So trivial is the offence of eating the apple in itself, and so careful is Milton not to load it with explicit symbolism, that it discloses its inner simplicity as a test, to obey or to disobey.

But Adam also exhibits, in the period following the fall, a perfect paradigm of processes of reconciliation. Within his personal psyche, in his relation with Eve, in his function as father of the human race, in his rapport with the cosmos and with God himself—everywhere reconciliation is effected. Nor does it follow that these are only different ways of saying the same thing. Adam might have made it up with Eve but have continued to evade God. Or he might have returned to his divine allegiance while hating the cursed earth and hoping for release from it. The reconciliations have to be separately, though harmoniously, effected.

Adam is, furthermore, the kingpin of what has been aptly called the paradox of the fortunate fall. When action, both dramatic and epic, has almost run its course, a glow appears in the moral firmament, the purposes of God are seen as richer, more mysterious, more beneficent than we had thought, and Adam, who has hitherto been nerving himself to endure his fate, exclaims, "O goodness infinite, goodness immense! / That all this good of evil shall produce / And evil turn to good." This is an illumination of such scope and profundity—far beyond the intimations at the end of *Macbeth* or *Hamlet* that Scotland or Denmark may now be better governed—that it breaks the normal bounds of epic or drama.

The perception of Adam's roles could be extended if those mentioned did not sufficiently illustrate his multiple character function. He is, for example, a pastoral figure in communion with the animals and enjoying the Arcadian delights of Eden.

We should remind ourselves that these varied roles in which Adam appears do not make for diversity. On the contrary his position on the axis of the universe which connects his will with God's will is always apparent. Before the fall there is a long conversation (VIII, 295-499) between this first man and his creator in what can be called without hesitation friendly terms. God smiles and has a little jest with Adam about finding a girl for him. Later he speaks face to face with Messiah and it is clear that he has often happily done so before. When he is spoken of as governing the animals there is an instantaneous reminder of the power of "God Supreme who made him chief / Of all his works" (VII, 515–16).

Eve, no less than Adam and in a far more delightful way, exercises a variety of separable functions. In the interests of unity under the divine will she is subordinated to Adam: "He for God only, she for God in him." The bonds of this unity are ruptured at the time of the fall, but at the close the accord of Eve with Adam and with the universe is carefully re-established and re-affirmed.

Eve is perfect womanhood, representative yet without fault. She is at the same moment a Grecian goddess. That she is naked (Milton insistently reiterates the word) only adds to the regal, statuesque, classical quality of her beauty. Yet she is simultaneously the archetypal temptress. (To say murderess is quite wrong for it dispels the mysterious, ineluctible, wayward nature of her impulses.) Yet, in apparent contradiction, she is also betrayed innocence surprised by the king of the underworld as she stands like Persephone half hidden in the flowers. And we have our choice whether to regard her fall as a piece of fairy-tale disobedience, with fairy-tale penalties, or as an invitation to examine the psychology of rebellion.

Eve, as Adam's lover, wife, helpmeet, is so convincingly portrayed that her role as mother of mankind may be neglected. But it is clearly adumbrated. From the time when, leaving Adam with the benevolent Raphael, she goes to visit her "Nursery" where the budding flowers "at her coming sprung / And toucht by her fair tendance gladlier grew," to the last passage where, having turned aside Adam's desire to remain childless, she rejoices in the hope of Messiah's birth, her role as mother of the race is apparent.

Milton employs a variety of stratagems to make us shift our focus and see a character first in one role then in another without either blurring the distinction between them or destroying the sense of an indivisible personage, and these devices are too numerous to examine in detail. In the passage just mentioned we move from the abstract qualities of Eve, "lowliness Majestic" and "Grace," to the veiled maternal references, then easily to the expected return to Adam's arms and "conjugal Caresses." Then, with some support from "Majestic," which has prepared the way, we rise above ordinary married life: "O when meet now / Such pairs, in Love and mutual Honor join'd?" And immediately we can see Eve in her classical dignity, "With Goddess-like demeanor," the Graces attending her as their Queen.

About the character of Satan it is now difficult to say anything fresh or even to take account of the variety of views expressed. Here we are concerned only with Satan as a creation in the Baroque manner. That he is at all points involved in a struggle to impose his own unity and power upon the true unity and power of God needs no demonstration. Werblowsky's comment in his *Lucifer and Prometheus* bears on this point: "The ideas of the Kingdom and the Power seem to me to be the centres of gravity of *Paradise Lost*. They correspond, in a way, to what Dr. Tillyard has called the theme of 'heroic energy.' Power and might are almost obsessions with Milton; his sensitivity to strength and energy burgeons out continually. Even his awareness of 'values' moral, aesthetic or religious, is determined by their power-aspect."[3] As Werblowsky goes on to demonstrate, the grandeur of Satan derives from Milton's having endowed him with Promethean qualities.

Satan, then, demonstrates to the fullest degree the trilogy of unity, power, and will, by his own positive exercise of these or his struggle to attain them or, conversely, because at all points his negative reveals the positive of God's true unity, beneficent power, and eternal will.

His multiple functions are immensely rich in implications; that he should be the incarnation of the principle of evil, and at the same time a kind of Prometheus struggling to change the nature of human life and to free himself and others from dependence on God, is a double role of immense suggestiveness.

Satan is at the bottom of the axis of will central to the universe, for his will is diametrically opposed to God's. Yet at intervals his pride looks along this axis as though he were on top. And we are continually encouraged to see in Satan the inverted simulacrum of divine power. He is

> Hell's dread Emperor with pomp Supreme,
> And God-like imitated State. (II, 510–11)

3. R. J. Z. Werblowsky, *Lucifer and Prometheus: A Study of Milton's Satan*, 68.

He rules hell, is acclaimed by his angels, sits on his royal throne in Pandemonium. His will, in an inverted fashion, resembles the divine will; his pride is, in the words of Coleridge, "The fearful resolve to find in itself alone the one absolute motive of action, under which all other motives from within and from without must be either subordinated or crushed." He "enlightens" man, "could love" man, has a place for all mankind in his abode.

Satan is simultaneously one of a dramatic trio with Adam and Eve, and one of an epic trio, pitted against God the Father and God the Son. He is not a hero in the eyes of God but to his own followers in hell and to some readers of *Paradise Lost* his heroism is real. He functions sometimes like a wrathful Achilles, then a cunning Ulysses; he is a refugee who founds a city, like Aeneas; he is girt round by his paladins like Arthur; he is off on a perilous journey like many heroes.

The mention of Satan inevitably recalls the distribution throughout *Paradise Lost* of the accent of heroism. The question, Who is the hero of the story? cannot be answered by a single nomination. Whose conduct is heroic, either in the old context of prowess in battle or Milton's preferred context of "better fortitude, heroic martyrdom"? Since all the decisions of God the Father are absolute, the effect of the action which he determines is rather majestic than heroic. The same is true of the much more overt acts of the Son, which are all traceable to the Father's will. An apparent exception is the offer of the Son to sacrifice himself for man. Yet this is muted partly by the revelation that it is after all in the will of the Father and partly by Milton's refusal to give any kind of warmth or fervour to the gospel story. Abdiel is indubitably heroic and, to a less striking degree, so are the other angels, but they are by definition subordinate actors. Adam is scarcely heroic in any conventional sense, for he succumbs, like Eve, without a struggle. It is true that at one point in their road to recovery both of them show what are by Milton's definition heroic traits. Adam "To better hopes his more attentive mind / Labouring had rais'd." He commends Eve in that her contempt of life and pleasure argues in her "something more sublime and excellent." But one is forced to conclude that their greatest effort is no more than an attempt to comprehend their new conditions and possibilities. Satan is, of course, filled with his own perverse heroism in Books I, II, V, and VI yet only by an irony (fully exploited by Saurat) can he be said to carry

Milton's theme of better fortitude. The true heroism, then, is in the tone of the poem, to which Milton's own voice as commentator makes the most effective contribution, urging us with the deepest moral conviction clothed in the most elaborate and telling rhetoric, to the heroism of the Christian view of life. At the beginning of Book IX he disclaims mediaeval military heroics as "Not that which justly gives / Heroic name to Person, or to Poem." Placed where they are, just before the account of mankind's feeebleness and folly, these phrases suggest he was aware that poem rather than characters would win the crown.

The distribution of heroic energy in *Paradise Lost* invites attention to another device of Milton's, that of sustaining the theme by releases of energy through the characters, so as to override weaknesses in the plot. It is a means of achieving unity by successive controlled demonstrations of power.

The plot of *Paradise Lost*, considered as a blueprint, is ramshackle. An all-wise, benevolent, and all-powerful God permits a rebellion to set heaven in an uproar and end with the loss of a third of his hosts. He creates an elaborate clock-work universe in the midst of which he places a garden; here a newly created man and woman live within reach of a tree whose fruit God forbids them to eat, knowing that they will not obey. He permits the leader of the defeated rebellion to visit the garden and the human pair fall easy prey to his wiles. The fruit being eaten, the whole constitution of the universe is changed for the worse. Although the Son of God promises to take on himself man's punishment, this only ensures that a small proportion of mankind will be forgiven. The rest, together with the rebellious angels, will finally be shut up in a place of torment while in a new earth and heaven hymns will ascend in praise of God's wisdom and goodness. If these are the bounding walls of Milton's structure, they must be reinforced by some other device for they will not of themselves carry the great dome of God's glory. Columns which successively release upstanding strength must bear the weight and must sustain a continuous frieze and cornice which emphasize a more complex and meaningful unity of design. The successive release of energies is indeed Milton's grand strategy of composition. It is no accident that when we think idly of *Paradise Lost* it is Satan rising from the burning lake, or Messiah driving upon the rebel hosts, or Michael seizing Adam and Eve by the hands that come first to mind.

All characters in the poem are imperious. This goes farther than the elevation and amplitude demanded by the epic form. It is inherent in their expressed status. The angels are "gods"; Adam is lord of Eden, his "empire"; Eve is conceived as queen, empress, goddess; Satan is the sultan of his dark divan; Ithuriel and Zephon, even they, are imperious as Satan and able to compel him. This intense feeling of lordship and individuality is not inconsistent with the single axis of God's will traversing all creation; it is rather a consequence of the direct mandate from God which each obeys (or in reverse defies). It goes without saying that this continues into Milton's concept of the individual Christian, who is an heir of God and one of his "kingdom of priests." And the concept squares perfectly with Christian liberty and Milton's part in the Great Rebellion.

By spaced releases of purposeful energy—from the great scale of "He on his impious foes right onward drove" to the intimate natural-ness of "to the field they haste"—Milton masks the limitation of his plot and sustains instead the unbroken grandeur of a dominant theme. As Borromini may acknowledge the traditional cruciform ecclesiastical plan before soaring into an encompassing oval dome, so Milton scrupulously acknowledges the *donné* of his plot and carefully adjusts the sutures between its parts. Eve's story is dovetailed into Adam's. Raphael, beginning his narrative as early as it is possible for the human mind to distinguish time from eternity, recites the history of the rebellion, omitting only the events in hell which we already know, and carries on into the story of creation, ending with the heavenly outburst of jubilation which, he reminds Adam, "thou remember'st, for thou heard'st." In Book X care is taken quickly to review the effects of the fall in heaven, in hell, in chaos, in the universe, on earth, so that nothing is left unaccounted for. Michael's narrative begins with a slow procession of Old Testament tableaux, then acce-lerates its pace to sweep in the whole of world history up to the last judgement and the resumption of an absorbent eternity. His survey of space employs the same tactic, which is designed to produce the illusion of absolute continuity and completeness.

But these gestures of preserving plot structure are not the substance of the poem. This is all the while being provided by astonishing emissions of primal energy expressed in acts of affirmation, investiture, jubilation, rebellion, armed insurrection, rhetorical defiance, formal combat, disordered violence, overwhelming onslaught, enforced flight, confrontation of the intolerable, immense fortitude, self-resuscitation, frantic loyalty, vigorous fabrication, deliberate plotting, cosmic jail-breaking, hazardous voyages, subtle intrigue, breach into God's fold, junction of earth and hell, disorder of the planetary system, judgement of all mankind, panoramic review of all time and space and purpose, provision for total deliverance, promise of divine incarnation, vision of utter destruction and heavenly renewal when God shall be all and in all. And in the eternity which embraces this vast temporal procession, other great events unknown to us but real and "durable" loom on the ultimate horizons of the mind.

As we have seen, these events are clustered like groups of columns to transmit only vertical forces. Each is either in specific fulfilment of the will of God or in specific opposition to it. The total effect, therefore, in spite of its apparent wild diversity of scale, intention, and locale, is completely and dynamically fused.

It will be asked whether the fall itself comes within the category of energetic affirmation. It is doubtless presumptuous to comment summarily upon a subject which has evoked so much learned discussion. But it does seem that Milton is here demonstrating the importance of will itself. The finger of a wilful child pulls the trigger of a forbidden firearm and the fatal shot which follows demonstrates the value of obedience.

This brings us to the central problem of the fall of man. In recounting this piece of biblical history, Milton has performed a miracle of virtuosity. In the Borghese Gallery may be seen several pieces of statuary embodying Bernini's subtlety in the handling of a similar problem. They represent Aeneas bearing Anchises out of Troy, Apollo laying his hand on Daphne, Pluto carrying Proserpine away, and David about to release the taut sling. Each is a moment of metamorphosis in which are contained a character and history past, together with a total change and a new destiny. Each (with the exception of the Aeneas, which has strong overtones of the Mannerism Bernini learned from his father) vibrates with tension between past and future, a past and a future which in each instance are already in the observer's mind. How Milton contrives this double effect of instantaneous change and yet of past and future not incongruous with metamorphosis is a sheer delight to observe.

From the very beginning of our acquaintance with Eve we have not only known from external sources that she will succumb to Satan; we have seen the tragic flaw which will lead to her fall extend itself more and more visibly. Her incipient vanity has revealed itself in her first act, admiration of her own face in the watery mirror. Her dependence upon Adam is a dangerous one, for she is not simply and self-sufficingly one degree below him on the scale of being, she is "th' inferior, in the mind / And inward Faculties, which most excel" (VIII, 541–2). It is worth noticing how this is put. It is not said that the archangels are inferior to Messiah in military skill, most needed at the height of the rebellion. On the contrary each angel, down to the rank and file, Ithuriel and Zephon, seems self-sufficient under the direct inspiration of God. Eve, however, suffers from a built-in disability peculiar to her station or more likely to her sex. It is difficult to say, for she is the only woman, other than allegorical figures, in the whole range of the cosmos. Though by definition unable to stand alone, she wishes to do so. It could be argued that she had feminine beauty, maternal expectations, and an intuitive reason not possessed by Adam: "the Soul / Reason receives, and reason is her being, / Discursive or Intuitive" (V, 486–8). But, although intuitive powers are nobly realized by Eve after the fall, culminating in the beautiful passage "For God is also in sleep, and Dreams advise...," her intuition before the fall seems to lead her anywhere but in the right direction. Her dream, literally inspired by Satan, giving a clear preview of her temptation and fall, appears to have awakened in her terrors but not salutary fears. Weak, credulous, vain, and becoming hungry, she stands ready to receive the fatal fruit. Milton then tells us that Eve is "yet sinless" (IX, 659), and, recalling suddenly the theological rigour of the plot, we know that it is so. We suddenly agree that this goddess, this helpmeet of Adam, this fairest of creation last and best, need not sin, that the decision to eat the fruit is in its entirety still suspended and the way wide open to resistance. In Bernini's Apollo and Daphne, bark is clinging about the body of the nymph, her fingers sprout leaves, roots from her toes already pierce the ground, but she is still the unravished, untransmuted, and adorable Daphne who, were the god but to withdraw his hand, would continue in her flight.

Milton preserves the autonomy of the instantaneous act, yet simultaneously makes it the centre of a tragedy. And this tragedy is also an epic story; the one being superimposed upon the other and fused into it without its essential shape being lost. And the epic ends by revealing behind its own formal pattern a vastly greater entity, the absoluteness of God's will. Milton achieved unity not by obliterating distinctions but by infinitely varied devices of subordination, superimposition, merging, interaction, and dynamic flow, all in obedience to the grand principle that no tradition must be distorted but all subsumed under the divine will.

8. PARADISE LOST:
Paradox and Ambiguity

AS CRITICS HAVE OFTEN remarked, the practitioners of the Baroque style attempt so much that effects of paradox and incongruity—for good or ill—appear almost as a matter of course. Milton's own concern with absolutes is an exhausting one. The "great argument" of things "unattempted yet" demands of the writer singular expertness in the properties of materials. The virtuosity employed is in danger of over-reaching itself. So much is attempted that success may take the final form of a great paradox.

Sometimes a small passage in Milton's enormous canvas seems to have the wrong tonality and by examining it very closely we see with what difficulty a transition has been effected between two forms. One such inconspicuous corner, which the reader may be willing to peer at for a moment, is the exploration of hell by its inhabitants after Satan has gone on his hazardous mission to earth. Up to the moment of his departure his presence has been absolutely dominant. His council "rejoicing in their matchless chief" disbands, but only "till this great Chief return." In this lacuna, however, none of the great unifying devices that Milton has developed for his epic is actually in operation. The axis of will between heaven and hell is carried by Satan himself. The calculated releases of enormous energy are not now available, for the devils will attempt nothing remarkable while Satan is away and God will not discharge any special vengeance their way in the absence of the arch-fiend. Still more important, the story line supplied by the Bible or by the main highway of Christian tradition, upon which Milton so heavily relies for continuity, is here suspended. This is an interlude between mighty actions and, in the tradition supplied by both *Iliad* and *Aeneid*, is accommodated with heroic games and contests. So far, so good. Even the presence in hell of fiery steeds and of chariots is made to seem consonant. Nor does the imagination refuse Milton's ingenious and characteristic enlargement of the scene to include music, heroic poetry, oratory, and philosophy. The Olympian games had been almost as comprehensive.

But when there is added to these classical competitions a Renaissance theme of geographical exploration, our suspension of disbelief becomes less willing. Incongruities multiply. Styx, Acheron, Cocytus are either real streams of water or allegorical streams of hatred, sorrow, and lamentation; in neither instance does poetic decorum allow them to flow, as in Milton's description, into a real and literal lake of fire. Crossing Lethe, the exploring devils reach a frozen continent. This too is a torment, one of extreme cold.

> Thither by harpy-footed Furies hal'd,
> At certain revolutions all the damn'd
> Are brought: and feel by turns the bitter change
> Of fierce extremes, extremes by change more fierce.

At this the imagination stops dead. The allegorical Furies, pale and ill-defined, are no match for Satan's warriors. Nothing gives them force or actuality. But worse is to come. In crossing Lethe—though in the narrative of exploration they have already voluntarily and safely crossed it—the devils, we are told, are in some kind of bondage and struggle in vain to drink its waters of forgetfulness. Then the bald statement which creates no image: "But Fate withstands." Then, following Homer's account of Ulysses in Hades, Milton adds, "Medusa with Gorgonian terror guards / The Ford, and of itself the water flies." Neither image has here any meaning, for if oblivion is desired by one in torment the Gorgonian threat becomes welcome and if the water flies from those who "ferry over," like the boatmen on Styx, a ludicrous picture is presented of the boat itself falling with the tide.

Weak as it is, we could not wish this passage of *Paradise Lost* away. It discloses by its ineptitude some of the secrets of Milton's general success. The concluding lines are especially revealing:

> A Universe of death, which God by curse
> Created evil, for evil only good,
> Where all life dies, death lives, and Nature breeds,

> Perverse, all monstrous, all prodigious things,
> Abominable, inutterable, and worse
> Than Fables yet have feign'd, or fear conceiv'd,
> Gorgons and Hydras, and Chimeras dire.

This kind of negative squalor Spenser does extremely well. But Milton, like Bunyan, once off the track has no sense of direction or knack of exploration. This limbo, peopled by exhausted allegories, cannot support the visitation by active, suffering, fallen angels whose energy, vigour, resource, "firm concord," and other residual virtues we have so recently seen displayed. Only the axis of will is meaningful and the far side of hell has no real relation to it. In support of this view, it may be observed that on the one other occasion when Milton let himself stray from the axis of will it was into that other limbo, the Paradise of Fools. Here we watch the confused, shapeless, meaningless procession of Embryos and Idiots, "All th' unaccomplisht works of Nature's hand, / Abortive, monstrous, or unkindly mixt"; here we see the fools too comical to be damned who "Fly o'er the backside of the World far off / Into a Limbo large and broad." But here the incongruities and stupidities are tributary to a great burst of sardonic, heavy-handed but effective humour. In hell this solution is, of course, impossible, as impossible as it would be in heaven.

From this small but instructive instance of incongruity provoked by the massive, pervasive unity which Milton constantly seeks we may turn to half a dozen types of a more extensive and revealing kind.

The bringing of heaven and earth into close relationship by an insistence on the goodness of matter leads to several strange impasses of a logical sort. The insistence that heaven is much like earth leads to wounded angels and spirits pent in their battered armour and provokes Pope's faintly derisive line in the mock-epic of Ariel's defence of Belinda, "But airy substance soon unites again." It leads to Raphael's difficulty in describing the love of angelic beings for one another. His situation when Adam puts the unexpected question is only incidentally comic; it contains a real dilemma, left unresolved by Raphael's hasty reply and immediate departure. Adam has been speaking of "procreation" as a purpose of "the genial Bed" and Raphael in his almost clinical reference to "membrane, joint, or limb, exclusive bars" seems to acknowledge that heavenly love is in a continuum with earthly love. If so, is there procreation in heaven? Neither scripture nor tradition permits it. In making heavenly love the same in kind though not in degree as earthly love Milton has risked a logical impasse, has moved momentarily off the axis of single devotion to God and has left Raphael little alternative to closing the conversation.

Still another difficulty develops from the same set of assumptions. Adam and Eve expect, even before the fall, to have children. If these grow to maturity and physical perfection and are arrested in their development at this point no reader beyond the age of twelve will suspend his disbelief. Raphael overcomes this difficulty by the promise that

> Your bodies may at last turn all to spirit,
> Improv'd by tract of time, and wing'd ascend
> Ethereal, as wee, or may at choice
> Here or in Heav'nly Paradises dwell.

Here the substantial sameness of earthly and heavenly bodies, already heavily emphasized by Raphael's willingness to eat and digest, is again in view. But what have the human pair to gain by this ascent? From Raphael's own words no place in heaven is so satisfactory that they might not choose rather to return to Eden. As regards their relation to each other, their heavenly embraces may be "total," but heaven by definition will not permit Eve to conceive a child or exercise her maternal affections. More serious still, there would appear to be no real gain in spirituality since as and where they are the human pair may adore God and love and obey him and "what can Heav'n show more?"

Through these odd cracks in the texture of the argument we may discern a familiar Baroque pattern. Some tremendous truth is struggling to express itself, the conventional modes of conveyance are being strained to the utmost, a breakdown in credibility or logic is barely avoided, yet somehow the very contortion of the operation permits a new form to be expressed, some new emphasis to be achieved, things unattempted yet.

Milton's other major devices to secure unity are equally productive of paradoxes. The drawing out of dramatic situations into the controlling epic situation leaves much unanswered. The sharp, agonizing, personal questioning, Why do the gods treat me so? "Phoebus, Lord, was all thy mind turned into darkness?" does not sort with epic amplitude. Many such questions are put as Adam and Eve are plunged

into the tragedy of their fall. By a device of rhetoric these appear to
receive answers but only such as shift the situation into another
dimension.

Adam replies to Eve's complaint, that he ought to have restrained
her from wandering,

> I warn'd thee, I admonish'd thee, foretold
> The danger, and the lurking Enemy
> That lay in wait; beyond this had been force,
> And force upon free Will hath here no place.

He has a point and he could have gone on to argue that he dealt with
Eve, in this matter, precisely as God had dealt with him.

The last third of the tenth book is one long act of recognition of
their fallen state on the part of the two transgressors. Adam ponders
and complains:

> As my Will
> Concurr'd not to my being, it were but right
> And equal to reduce me to my dust,
> Desirous to resign, and render back
> All I receiv'd, unable to perform
> Thy terms too hard, by which I was to hold
> The good I sought not. To the loss of that,
> Sufficient penalty, why hast thou added
> The sense of endless woes? inexplicable
> Thy Justice seems.

Again Adam has a point. He was constitutionally incapable of letting
Eve perish alone. Furthermore, his sin, unlike Satan's, appears to be
a finite one and yet he is threatened with "endless woes," an unexpected expansion of the original mysterious "surely die."

To this question, Adam makes his own reply which barely offers the
surface of credibility demanded by the theme. He should, he says,
have declined God's conditions when first he heard them, after his
creation. Had he done so we can imagine the anger and invective
with which both the poet and the God of *Paradise Lost* would have
received the renunciation; "ignoble ease and peaceful sloth" would
have been the least of Milton's accusations, had Adam elected to
return to oblivion.

Adam continues his self-condemnation by supposing that his own
son "Prove disobedient and, reprov'd, retort, / Wherefore didst thou

beget me?" One would suppose that were the reproof a sentence of death there might be some justification.

At last, however, Adam comes to the real point and at the same moment we find ourselves on familiar ground:

> God made thee of choice his own, and of his own
> To serve him, thy reward was of his grace,
> Thy punishment then justly is at his Will.

After all, both Adam and Milton admit, the justice of God's will springs from its being the will of God.

But now Adam's fears begin to explore two kinds of infinite suffering, first, that "in the Grave, / Or in some other dismal place, who knows / But I shall die a living Death?" and, second, that his descendants into an endless future shall on his account be condemned to die. With some reason he feels himself at this point "To Satan only like both crime and doom."

Eve then appears and, after a touching scene of reconciliation, she faces the prospect of bringing into the world a race of lost souls doomed to divine retribution. She makes what we (with Adam) can only regard, in view of the information she possesses, as heroic proposals. She suggests sexual continence as a means of forestalling the propagation of a sinful race or, if that is not feasible, suicide. Certainly if the prospect is that her descendants will suffer endless retributive wrath from the hand of God, the proposition she presents to Adam is reasonable as well as courageous and disinterested.

Adam's reply is indeed a curious one and worthy of close attention. God, he says, would not be outwitted by our suicide but would simply condemn us to eternal punishment: "rather such acts / Of contumacy will provoke the Highest / To make death in us live." Adam goes on to argue that the promised Seed may ensure for them a triumph over Satan. Furthermore, God's mildness to them after the fall suggests a not intolerable life under his direction. This life he begins, with a wealth of imagery, to forecast and by this device of keeping the argument in rhetorical motion Adam's despair is dissolved away. We are brought thus to the end of Book X where we are left poised until Michael appears to introduce the last two books. Adam is now drawn out of himself (while Eve is laid asleep) by a long monotonous historical forecast which becomes less pictorial, more generalized and conceptual, and less verbally exciting as it proceeds. Then climactically the paradox of the fortunate fall is put forward together with the ideal of a Paradise within. The will of God, the glory of God, the immense, mysterious, ultimate apocalyptic purposes of God fill the whole scene. A unified universe develops, its poles extending to the providential will of God and the private will of the individual Christian. It is justified by rough and ready reasoning and made compelling by rhetoric. This, once more, is Milton's triumph. It is also authentically Milton's vision because it covertly emphasizes the primacy in human affairs of individual will, devotion, and effort, and forms the image of an elect minority, as little concerned, each of them, that the unregenerate perish as Abdiel cared that his rebellious fellow angels were hurled into hell.

Michael has hurried Adam along, keeping the scene in continuous motion, shifting from Old Testament tableaux like small moralities to successive, accelerating, rapid surveys of man's departures from God and the attendant catastrophes. When the screen darkens and we resume our ordinary selves we are only too ready to leave with Adam and Eve, ushered swiftly out by the angel, whose projection is now complete. Not for a long time do we recall that Adam's questions were never answered. Why, since his will did not consent to his creation, should he be punished? Why the inexplicable sentence of wrath upon his innocent descendants? And as for the comforts offered by Michael—who but a solipsist or an egomaniac could enjoy a paradise within coupled with the knowledge that myriads of his children, including his firstborn, are doomed to everlasting pain? And if by some paradox of reasoning the fall is held to be fortunate, as Adam seems to believe—"Full of doubt I stand, / Whether I should repent me now of sin / By mee done and occasion'd, or rejoice"—then what are we to make of the original prohibition with all its threatenings and denunciations? Milton's driving desire to complete the justification of God's ways to men leaves the demonstration fractured in all directions and the "great Argument" wretchedly incapable of proof, we say to ourselves and then we add, such are the penalties of working in the grand style and with the Baroque mode. But by shifting our perspective, regrouping the structural elements into a fresh vista, we at once recover our sense of the fundamental greatness and integrity of the poem. Michael's effort at reintegration, the manner in which he distracts our attention from the smaller arena of Adam's personal and domestic tragedy to the larger issue of the fate of mankind is beyond praise. Epic enfolds and assuages the imperfectly healed wounds of the tragic conflict. To this enlargement Michael adds the further dual vision of a God who is all and in all, after the final judgement, and of a subjective totality of being, "a Paradise within thee." The outline of the epic structure itself wavers, reflected in this ocean of the absolute will of God, or this hidden pool of the absolute inner beatitude of man.

Any consideration of paradox in *Paradise Lost* leads to the question of Milton's humour. For some reason the majority of Milton's critics are disturbed by the thought that he could have been extensively and consciously humorous in so serious a work. The remarks that follow are therefore offered as an excursus without the hope that many readers will find them congenial.

Most readers of Milton have felt that his work deserves the remark made by the schoolboy about the work of Arnold: "Not the place you would go for a laugh." Johnson's "Life" has helped to fix in all minds the picture of Milton as stiff and unsmiling. We all know Johnson's phrases: "Such is the controversial merriment of Milton; his gloomy seriousness is yet more offensive. Such is his malignity, that hell grows darker at his frown...an envious hatred of greatness, and a sullen desire of independence; in petulance impatient of control, and pride disdainful of superiority." Johnson misunderstood not only the character of Milton but also the nature of the opportunities for formal gaiety which the conventions of Renaissance art permitted.

Actually as the unbiased reader moves through *Paradise Lost* at a reasonable pace, fast enough to catch the rhythm of successive episodes and the counterpoint of light and solemn themes, the smile of pleasure turns not infrequently to the smile of amusement and now and again to the laugh of pure fun. When this is pointed out, the usual reply is, "Yes, but did Milton intend it?" That Milton, writing a professedly sublime epic on a religious theme, could have been consciously amusing is thought incredible. But it is conceded readily enough that Donne or Herbert exhibits a gay humour, that in Herbert "all things are big with jest," that a seventeenth-century poem may at the same instant be deeply serious and crackling with wit. It is in this context of the so-called "metaphysical" style (in its expanded rather than in its condensed form) and within the ambit of the art-form known as Baroque that Milton's humour is at last finding recognition. Tillyard in his *Studies in Milton* has a number of perceptive remarks about humour in *Paradise Lost*. He does not care to exhaust the subject and he has left it to others to expand his suggestions.

Here let us limit our consideration. The sardonic side of Milton's humour, in which punitive ideas are expressed or implicit, has long been recognized—the violent cross-wind of the Paradise of Fools, Satan's mouth crammed with ashes, God the Father's smiling remark, "Nearly it now concerns us to be sure of our omnipotence." Let us confine ourselves, for the moment, to a more elusive, subtle, and wholly delightful form, springing from a sense of liberation. Such a consideration is in line with modern theories of humour; there is increasing recognition that laughter, in its biological origins, is genial and affirmative; the play theory which has arisen out of scientific observations of young children lends support; and laughter, it is worth remembering, has been held by a variety of critics, including Voltaire, to spring primarily from gaiety, happiness, or joy. The notion of Milton indulging in carefree humour is also in line with the practice of Baroque artists. Not infrequently in the history of Baroque art-forms we find that architect, sculptor, or painter has achieved such an easy mastery over the elements of his craft that the creative spirit is at liberty, smiling over its own dexterity. Bernini plants an Egyptian obelisk, replete with hieroglyphics, on the back of an elephant, exquisitely adjusting the apparently incongruous pedestal to its burden. Within the Baroque convention of heavy mass and lively movement, deliberate effects of legerdemain are natural. A flat painted ceiling simulates, to an observer entering the building, a vault with pillars and arches, although from a viewpoint a few yards distant the whole is utterly distorted and collapsing; an elaborate façade, leaping in redundant curves, may be quite separate in design from the interior it conceals; a stone ship, in the pool of a fountain, has streams of water doing duty for smoke from its cannon-mouths and cables from its hawse-holes. Fokker has remarked that "by the aggregation of contrasting bodies or by creating a decoration in a gigantic shape, the artist can achieve an effect of superb caprice."[1]

1. T. H. Fokker, *Roman Baroque Art*.

Let us ask at what point in *Paradise Lost* we should expect to find Milton liberated into the kind of exuberant freedom we have described. Not, certainly, when he is dealing with God in heaven or with Satan in hell, and not when he is occupied with those episodes where the primal sin casts its gloom over all. Rather when he is concerned with the human pair, as yet unfallen, and especially when he portrays the archangels, those magnificent creatures, so acclimatized to the pomp and ceremony of the Baroque world.

Uriel amuses even the superficial reader:

> His back was turned, but not his brightness hid;
> Of beaming sunny Rays, a golden tiar
> Circl'd his Head, nor less his Locks behind
> Illustrious on his Shoulders fledge with wings
> Lay waving round; on some great charge employ'd
> He seem'd, or fixt in cogitation deep.

Satan, disguised as a cherub, enters.

> He drew not nigh unheard; the Angel bright,
> Ere he drew nigh, his radiant visage turn'd,
> Admonisht by his ear, and straight was known
> Th' Arch-Angel Uriel—one of the sev'n
> Who in God's presence, nearest to his Throne
> Stand ready at command, and are his Eyes
> That run through all the Heav'ns.

He is one of God's "eyes" yet so unseeing that he must rely upon his "ear." His pompous, patronizing speech to the disguised fiend, ending, "Thy way thou canst not miss, me mine requires" is in contrast to his anxious haste soon after when, discovering his mistake, he shoots down to warn Gabriel:

> Thither came Uriel, gliding through the Even
> On a Sun-beam, swift as a shooting Star.

His approach and return have a switchback effect:

> Return'd on that bright beam, whose point now rais'd
> Bore him slope downward to the Sun, now fall'n
> Beneath th' Azores.

Uriel's switchback is one of several machines which Milton produces in the space between heaven and hell where he can, as it were, spread himself. They are devices of which Inigo Jones might well have been proud. As Tillyard has indicated, both the golden stair to heaven and the causeway to hell are sources of humour. In general, Milton's machines and stage-sets are in keeping with the deep love of Baroque artificers for turning life into stage-effects, with their delight in garden and city design, with their large-scale theatrical appliances at once rational and scenic.

The brightest coruscations of Milton's humour are to be found in the books dominated by the "sociable" Raphael, the most gay, talkative, and friendly of the archangels. Here Milton is recording a situation he knows with loving familiarity, the meeting of two friends for a free interchange of ideas. Raphael has the creation of a universe to recapitulate and a great epic conflict to delineate and decorate. His listener is a willing and responsive one, a man on his honeymoon, in the highest good humour. (The comedy of the situations and conversations between Adam and Eve, about which Tillyard has some good things to say, is perforce given no attention here.) Raphael and Adam have a whole afternoon before them, with no God to overawe or Satan to disturb; indeed, after a point, there is no Eve to distract their attention. It is Milton and Diodati, Milton and Lawrence, Milton and Skinner; perhaps even Milton and King or Manso or Marvell. Here is an academic exercise in debate, conducted, as Tillyard says in another connexion, with "baroque gravity like that of a good heroic play." They are having a wonderful time, revelling in "enormous bliss." Raphael is on holiday from heaven; strictly, on a half-holiday; Adam is determined to cram all he can into these few hours. From beneath the imperturbable gravity of Milton's high style and the elevated manner of Baroque rhetoric their joyful mood breaks irrepressibly forth. Adam, although he is all deferential politeness and is filled with real reverence for his guest, is simply bursting to hear all and tell all. Raphael is there to warn Adam of his danger, but he is drawn into (it is hard not to say jockeyed into) telling Adam what will satisfy his curiosity. The four books are a rippling stream of grace and gaiety.

Raphael, having eaten lunch "with keen dispatch/Of real hunger" and having assured Adam that he possesses an excellent digestive system, is ready to treat "Of things above his World, and of thir being / Who dwell in Heav'n." Adam, feeling increasingly at ease with this denizen of Zion, is inclined to pump him a little: "his wary speech /

Thus to th' Empyreal Minister he fram'd." He continues, in effect: It is indeed good of you to have a meal here when generally you have meals in heaven, and how are the two to be compared? Raphael replies with a discourse on spiritual natures and promises that Adam may attain to such "If ye be found obedient." Adam says: Your words delight me as music; I knew I was created free; I am sure we shall never disobey God; my only doubts are about the nature of this war in heaven you mention; tell me all; I will keep very quiet. Raphael, his monitory purpose deflected, pauses, as well he may. He then says, in sum: It is a hard task: some of the story may not be lawful to reveal.

The description of the war in heaven, into which Raphael now launches, suffers a skilful omission which is deliberate on Raphael's part but seems to escape Adam. Although Raphael is a participant, he says nothing of his own exploits, at the place where these would be appropriate he glides into easy generalities:

> Deeds of eternal fame
> Were done, but infinite: for wide was spread
> That War and various.

Humour of a different kind, and outside our immediate scope, is provided by the bravura of the epic battles; the heavy jesting over Satan's artillery is only the most obvious passage.

The description of creation provides less humour than might be expected. The true comedy scene of creation is to be found in Book IV and may be for convenience transplanted into this context. Adam and Eve sit down quietly in the early evening and watch a little circus performance:

> Sporting the Lion ramp'd, and in his paw
> Dandl'd the Kid; Bears, Tigers, Ounces, Pards
> Gamboll'd before them, th' unwieldly Elephant
> To make them mirth us'd all his might, and wreath'd
> His Lithe Proboscis.

Milton, resembling his own elephant by combination of massive strength and sly finesse, is telling us in solemn and imperturbable numbers that he can tie a knot in his trunk.

As the end of Book VII is reached, Adam has fallen into the glazed immobility common to all who listen attentively to long lectures.

> The Angel ended, and in Adam's Ear
> So Charming left his voice, that he a while
> Thought him still speaking, still stood fixt to hear;
> Then, as new wak't thus gratefully repli'd.

Thank you, thank you, "Divine Historian," he says, but could you tell me how this firmament, these planets, and so forth actually work? Once more it is fresh information he is seeking and the counterpoint continues of his desire to acquire knowledge and Raphael's commission to impress warnings on him.

Eve observes that Adam "by his count'nance seem'd / Ent'ring on studious thoughts abstruse." She wisely rises and leaves, while Milton solemnly assures us that the men would have preferred her to stay and that she delighted in such discourse. The conversation, nevertheless, becomes notably more free and easy thereafter. "And Raphael now to Adam's doubt propos'd / Benevolent and facile thus repli'd." His reply is a masterpiece of evasion. God, he says, has concealed the springs of the celestial machine; if men try to reason out the mechanics of the system, God will only be amused; there will be heard "His laughter at thir quaint Opinions wide." Whether the sun moves round the earth or the earth round the sun is not for you to trouble your head about, says Raphael.

Adam is visibly disappointed and gives up his attempt. There is gentle irony in his reply, beginning, "How fully hast thou satisfi'd me, pure / Intelligence of Heav'n, Angel serene."

He tries a new tack; nowhere is the comedy of his relation with Raphael better seen: "now hear mee relate / My Story, which perhaps thou hast not heard." This is too transparent and he adds hastily: You see I am merely enticing you to stay, for I love your company. Raphael plays up nobly:

> say, therefore on;
> For I that Day was absent, as befell,
> Bound on a voyage uncouth and obscure,
> Far on excursion toward the Gates of Hell.

At Adam's look of incredulity, which can hardly have failed at so palpable a fabrication, he goes on, hastily improvising.

> Squar'd in full Legion (such command we had)
> To see that none thence issu'd forth a spy,
> Or enemy, while God was in his work,

Lest hee incent at such eruption bold,
Destruction with Creation might have mixt.
Not that they durst without his leave attempt,
But us he sends upon his high behests
For state, as Sovran King, and to enure
Our prompt obedience.

And all this, like the painted ceiling in some church of the Asam
brothers, may be perfectly sound from one point of view and perfectly
preposterous from another.

Adam now tells his story, which brims with humour. Alone in
Eden, he asked God for a partner and God "with a smile more
bright'n'd" asked if the animals were not company enough; and Adam
ventured to say, No they were not; and God, "not displeas'd," said,
Well you see I live alone; and Adam said, Yes, but you are perfect
while I am imperfect and need companionship and God said, Well
argued, Adam, I'll give you just what you want. And He gave me
Eve, says Adam, in a burst of confidence, and Eve is simply marvellous:

what she wills to do or say,
Seems wisest, virtuousest, discreetest, best;
All higher knowledge in her presence falls
Degraded, Wisdom in discourse with her
Loses discount'nanc't, and like folly shows.

Raphael frowns.

To whom the Angel with contracted brow. . . .
In loving thou dost well, in passion not,
Wherein true Love consists not.

But Adam has been growing in confidence all along and is not quite
put down even by the archangelic rebuke:

To whom thus half abash't Adam repli'd. . . .
Bear with me then, if lawful what I ask;
Love not the heav'nly Spirits, and how their Love
Express they, by looks only, or do they mix
Irradiance, virtual or immediate touch?

At this direct request for the details of his sex-life, Raphael blushes,
babbles forth something, and says he really must go.

To whom the Angel with a smile that glow'd
Celestial rosy red, Love's proper hue,

Answer'd. Let it suffice thee that thou knows't
Us happy, and without Love no happiness. . . .
But I can now no more; the parting Sun
Beyond the Earth's green Cape and verdant Isles
Hesperian sets, my Signal to depart.

The pace has quickened from book to book and insensibly familiarity has mingled with awe in increasing proportions. Thus when at the close Adam scores heavily off Raphael, we are not surprised. But all this comedy—and here the Baroque sense of total structure is beautifully evident—is without damage to these books as structural members in the edifice of *Paradise Lost*. At the beginning of the next book we are told that Adam's talk has been "Venial discourse unblam'd."

Milton's humour, then, is far more varied than one would imagine. Not always sardonic; indeed, sometimes gay, but never artlessly so; the concept of formal gaiety is here required. What has been sadly neglected is a study of the artistic mode in which formal gaiety here operates—the world of Baroque. It involves a felt freedom on the part of the artist, based on complete familiarity with accepted forms (e.g., High Renaissance interpretations of classical originals) and on superb technical competence in handling them. The convention provides a firm frame, familiar elements, known rules. Within these, and with an air of high seriousness, the game is played. In the metaphysical conceit of the seventeenth century this process has long been understood and appreciated. Milton too is metaphysical but on a great scale and his conceits are displayed on a stage of grand proportions. The bliss he achieves in Eden is, even in its comedy, "enormous."

9. MILTON AND SPENSER

MILTON TOLD Dryden that he had taken Spenser for a model and his phrase "a better teacher than Aquinas" suggests the deep affinity of ideas which an examination of parallel passages confirms. Both poets are intensely doctrinal and didactic, consciously English and Puritan, and made free of the riches of the Renaissance. It is tempting to seek for some source of their divergence of form, when so much unites the content and intention of their works. One possibility lies within the categories of style change proposed by Wölfflin; though much modified in their application by subsequent criticism, they have never been superseded.

There are cathedrals, it is said, of which the total structure may be inferred from the cross-section of a single pillar, and a single stanza of *The Faerie Queene* tells us nearly as much about Spenser's architectonics. Nor need the stanza be hand-picked; the most ordinary examples will serve.

> Arrived there, the little house they fill,
> Ne looke for entertainment, where none was:
> Rest is their feast, and all things at their will;
> The noblest mind the best contentment has.
> With faire discourse the evening so they pas:
> For that old man of pleasing wordes had store,
> And well could file his tongue as smooth as glas;
> He told of Saintes and Popes, and evermore
> He strowd an Ave-Mary after and before.

This familiar stanza from the first canto of the first book is on the face of it both part of a sequence of events and a satisfying, self-contained picture. The same principle extends to the lines taken individually: the majority are end-stopped; rhyme as Spenser uses it creates an echoing relationship among lines, not a forward impetus; the final Alexandrine is not only complete in itself but by its extra amplitude seals off the stanza so that the reader must make a new beginning with the next. The thought corresponds to these forms: the self-containment of "The noblest mind the best contentment has" makes it aphoristic and timeless, and the line preceding it has, too, the air of being a perfect statement of an immemorial situation. Nothing from the earlier part of the plot enters pressingly into the stanza. It is consonant with what precedes but not urgently determined by it. And even though, in Spenser's world, entrance into the house of a Roman Catholic magician cannot bode any good, the fall of the final lines absolutely forbids any suspense or mystery. We can lay *The Faerie Queene* down at this point and go for a week's holiday.

These considerations may appear obvious and perhaps trivial, but they open a door to Spenser's total method of presentation. Cantos and books are also self-contained and, in the same balanced fashion, inter-related. The passivity of the links between books is shown by our almost complete lack of curiosity as to what the missing books would have been like and our complete inability to look on their absence as a truncation or mutilation of the poem.

Spenser's shorter works show these propensities with the utmost clarity. The four hymns in honour of love and beauty can be read separately without reference to each other and, although they represent planes of experience and although these planes are related, nothing goes compellingly across the boundaries. Even within the compass of a single hymn the fusion of powerful ideas is not remarkable. In the lines to Heavenly Beauty we are given the means of a Platonic approach to our Creator:

> The meanes therefore which unto us is lent,
> Him to behold, is on his workes to looke,
> Which he hath made in beauty excellent,
> And in the same, as in a brasen booke,
> To read enregistred in every nooke
> His goodnesse, which his beautie doth declare.
> For all thats good, is beautifull and faire.

> Thence gathering plumes of perfect speculation,
> To impe the wings of thy high flying mynd,
> Mount up aloft through heavenly contemplation,
> From this darke world, whose damps the soule do blynd,
> And like the native brood of Eagles kynd,
> On that bright Sunne of glorie fixe thine eyes,
> Clear'd from grosse mists of fraile infirmities.

This kind of neo-Platonism, belonging to the world of Bruno, Ficino, and Pico della Mirandola, is a commonplace of Renaissance thought. The speech of Bembo in the fourth book of *The Courtyer* comes to mind and so does Raphael's image of the successive spheres of created life,

> So from the root
> Springs lighter the green stalk, from thence the leaves
> More aery, last the bright consummate flow'r
> Spirits odorous breathes . . .
> Your bodies may at last turn all to spirit,
> Improv'd by tract of time, and wing'd ascend
> Ethereal.

But even as Milton's angel opens to Adam this prospect, he warns him against disobedience and we know that Satan is in the vicinity. It may be asked whether Spenser is not also aware of sin. The lines following immediately on the stanzas quoted above run as follows:

> Humbled with feare and awfull reverence,
> Before the footestoole of his Majestie,
> Throw thy selfe downe with trembling innocence,
> Ne dare looke up with corruptible eye
> On the dred face of that great Deity,
> For feare, lest if he chaunce to looke on thee,
> Thou turne to nought, and quite confounded be.

> But lowly fall before his mercie seate,
> Close covered with the Lambes integrity,
> From the just wrath of his avengefull threate,
> That sits upon the righteous throne on hy. . . .

Here is a Protestant feeling for individual sinfulness for which the remedy, immediate and without intermediaries, is the righteousness of the Lamb of God who has suffered for the sin of the world. It is placed beside the neo-Platonic ladder of contemplation, without a single line, a single word of mediation. Only because Spenser accustoms us to see his ideas related but not fully resolved is this manœuvre possible.

Spenser's use of linked rather than fused elements is associated with the chivalric form of his poem. It is not a question, with Spenser any more than with Morris or Tennyson, of the actuality of the true mediaeval world. The conventions of chivalry were a convenient guise for a good deal of Renaissance idealism and provided a model for splendour to mould itself upon. Tasso, Sidney, Shakespeare, Cervantes: the names will suggest to us the rise and decline of this ideal of the Renaissance knight. Milton's repudiation of chivalric tales strikes both at content and at form:

> Not sedulous by Nature to indite
> Wars, hitherto the only Argument
> Heroic deem'd chief maistry to dissect
> With long and tedious havoc fabl'd Knights
> In Battles feign'd; the better fortitude
> Of Patience and Heroic Martyrdom
> Unsung; or to describe Races and Games,
> Or tilting Furniture, emblazon'd Shields,
> Impreses quaint, Caparisons and Steeds;
> Bases and tinsel Trappings, gorgeous Knights
> At Joust and Tournament; then marshall'd Feast
> Serv'd up in Hall with Sewers, and Seneschals;
> The skill of Artifice or Office mean,
> Not that which justly gives Heroic name
> To Person or to Poem.

It is clear from the deliberate boredom inflicted by the catalogue that the poet is expressing his disgust with the interminable linked episodes and descriptions of the chivalric world. The objection sticks still deeper. Milton's antagonism is to the world of individual prowess unsubdued to one will. Loyola showed a similar impatience with the forms of mediaeval monasticism.

It is a perpetual source of delight to see a known poetic device respond first to Renaissance and then to Baroque needs. Spenser's sonnet form in the *Amoretti* reflects his desire for linkage of elements but not for fusion. He has adopted the Shakespearean form of the sonnet with one modification, the repetition of the second rhyme of the first quatrain as the first rhyme of the second quatrain, and similarly as between the second and third quatrains. This produces an effect similar to the linkings within the Spenserian stanza, though less sophisticated. The thought of Spenser's sonnets generally corresponds to the form.

> Lyke as a huntsman after weary chace,
> Seeing the game from him escapt away,
> Sits downe to rest him in some shady place
> With panting hounds beguiled of their pray:
> So after long pursuit and vaine assay,
> When I all weary had the chace forsooke,
> The gentle deare returned the selfe-same way,
> Thinking to quench her thirst at the next brooke.
> There she beholding me with mylder looke,
> Sought not to fly, but fearlesse still did bide:
> Till I in hand her yet halfe trembling tooke,
> And with her owne goodwill hir fyrmely tyde.
>   Strange thing me seem to see a beast so wyld,
>   So goodly wonne with her owne will beguyld.

The initial simile is related in only the simplest way to what follows; the hounds, for example, are decorative, having none of the force of symbolism possessed by Acteon's hounds. The mellifluousness of the verse, the charm of the diction, the tenderness and restraint of the sentiment should not, for the moment, conceal from us the simplicity of the story and the easy consecutiveness of the stages.

Let us, in contrast, hear Milton in the sonnet on the massacre in Piedmont, where two patterns are played one against another, the Petrarchan rhyme scheme and the run-on line pattern induced by the rhetoric. The rhymes themselves deserve attention. English rhymes are harder to find than Italian ones, for obvious reasons. In fact, what alternatives have we to "stones," "groans," and "moans," once "bones" is written? There are only one or two others that the context could tolerate. Milton must manage a tension between the desired sense and the available rhymes. All four of his rhymes—there are no more in the fourteen—are plangent and re-echoing and tend to end-stop their lines on that account. But resistlessly the rhetoric moves over them. At the end of the eighth line, where a Spenserian sonnet is coming quietly to rest, Milton starts a new outburst which runs through the ninth line and into the tenth. The density of the diction, the terror of the theme, the imprecatory violence of the sentiment with its fury of righteous indignation, the appeal to the absolute power of the one true God—

there is no mistaking the claim of this sonnet to take its place among the loci classici of Baroque. *Multum in parvo.* (Borromini's S. Carlo and Bernini's S. Andrea occupy minimal widths of frontage on the via Quirinale.)

> Avenge, O Lord, thy slaughter'd Saints whose bones
> Lie scatter'd on the Alpine mountains cold,
> Ev'n them who kept thy truth so pure of old
> When all our Fathers worship't Stocks and Stones,
> Forget not: in thy book record their groans
> Who were thy Sheep and in their ancient Fold
> Slain by the bloody Piemontese that roll'd
> Mother with Infant down the Rocks. Their moans
> The Vales redoubl'd to the Hills, and they
> To Heav'n. Their martyr'd blood and ashes sow
> O'er all th'Italian fields where still doth sway
> The triple Tyrant: that from these may grow
> A hundredfold, who having learnt thy way
> Early may fly the Babylonian woe.

Scarcely less remarkable is the diverse handling of pastoral motifs by the two poets. *Lycidas,* as we have seen, is a tightly woven pattern. The whole Mannerist effect depends upon close incorporation of resistant and incompatible elements. *The Shepheardes Calender,* on the contrary, disclaims any such intention. "A shepheards swaine saye did thee sing, / All as his straying flocke he fedde." By creating, on a French model, a calendar of twelve parts appropriate to the twelve months, Spenser sets his seal upon a method which will be expanded to suit all his subsequent poetic purposes and which he will never renounce. The twelve eclogues form a linked sequence marshalled into three ranks, the Plaintive, the Recreative, and the Moral.

In theme and form the various eclogues differ widely and the lack of anything resembling a close-knit structure extends to the internal organization of the separate pieces. The April Eclogue's song in praise of Elizabeth is rightly regarded as a thing of extraordinary beauty but its organization could scarcely be looser. Apart from the queen's first sitting down and later rising to depart there is hardly a suggestion of sequence. The thirteen stanzas permit themselves to be rearranged in several other ways without noticeable damage to the poem. And this does not mean that Spenser is careless but that he works in an Elizabethan mode.

If we look, not at the detailed manifestations of Spenser's technique but at *The Faerie Queene* as a whole, the contrasts with Milton's work are consistent and significant. It has been argued[1] with a considerable show of evidence that the plan now visible is the result of superimposing a second scheme upon an earlier and simpler one. According to this view, Spenser began with a plan of eight books of eight cantos apiece. The first seven books were to deal with the seven deadly sins and the eighth with Prince Arthur, under whose aegis the fight against them had been waged. The first four books dealt, conjecturally, with Despair, Avarice, Lechery, and Wrath. Then with the desire, it is supposed, of giving classical form to his poem, Spenser moved to the plan of twelve "Aristotelian" virtues: Liberality, Magnificence, Magnanimity, Mansuetude, Desire of Honour, Verity, Affability, Urbanity, Fortitude, Temperance, Justice, Prudence. Such a list is to be obtained from Lodowick Bryskett's *A Discourse of Civil Life* (1606).[2]

However one views Spenser's attempts to erect a consistent structure in *The Faerie Queene*, it is at least evident that he was influenced by the Renaissance concept of unity as the disposition, "with due decorum everywhere," of harmonious elements so that, without losing their individual integrity, they constitute a stable and balanced whole.[3] Hurd in his *Letters on Chivalry and Romance* (1742) compares the plan of *The Faerie Queene* to a garden where formal alleys diverge from a fixed centre. It is an apt comparison, in that it emphasizes the formal unity obtained by arranging commensurable components symmetrically without any attempt to achieve a dynamic interrelation.

Equally clear is Spenser's predilection for mediaeval materials. Though Gloriana sits at the centre of things and Arthur is in the literal sense peripheral, rounding off the knightly quests by his encouragement or intervention, yet Spenser's indebtedness to the Round Table is palpable enough. And in the course of the narrated knightly quests, though classical mythology adorns the episodes and Gloriana is the centre of power, the bestower of renown, and the ideal of beauty, yet none of the neo-Platonic or classical ingredients can disguise the fundamental similarities between Spenser's narratives

---

1. Janet Spens, *Spenser's Faerie Queene*.
2. In the dialogues of this discourse there is an inconclusive exchange between Bryskett and Spenser on the subject of the virtues. Bryskett then says that he himself has consulted Picolomini, from whom he quotes the list given.
3. H. Wölfflin, *Principles of Art History*, 15.

and Malory's. In taking account of the mediaeval strain in Spenser, we find that he borrows in order to adapt and, like Tasso, endows his armoured knights with Renaissance sentiments. (It is bad luck that Spenser's knights never found, as Rinaldo found in Tiepolo, the painter who would give an extra visual impetus to the character.) When he proclaims his indebtedness to Chaucer, we must recall that it is not our Chaucer but a more serious and religious writer, a poet of unhappy love and a beautifier of the English language whom Spenser, from his Renaissance standpoint, saw.[4]

Spenser's use of mediaeval elements should also remind us that national characteristics have a real influence on poetic practice. As in any consideration of Milton as Baroque we must allow for his experience of the English Puritan revolution, so in thinking of Spenser we must remember that he was a child of the Tudor Renaissance, that very late and intensely English movement. It is Wölfflin himself, the master of generalization and advocate of the European view, who has insisted upon the importance of national differences. "In spite of all deviations and individual movements, the development of style in later occidental art was homogeneous, just as European culture as a whole can be taken as homogeneous. But within this homogeneity, we must reckon with the permanent differences of national types. From the beginning we have made reference to the way in which the modes of vision are refracted by nationality."[5] One persistent feature of English literature is a desire continually to revivify and reinterpret the picture of days of old when knights were bold.

Approaching, in this spirit, the setting of *The Faerie Queene*, the great tapestry which the poet unrolls behind his characters, we find it, as we should expect, a composite fabric. In the simplest sense it is the great wild wood of Sacheverell Sitwell's Gothic North, which is the obscure origin of all those dreams and fairy-tales in which a wood-cutter's hut or a castle set above trees is the starting point for adventures that take us deeper into the forest. But once again old mediaeval materials are given the shaping pressure of Renaissance ideals, a thirst for fame, visions of Platonic beauty, a belief in the power of princes and the purpose of the state.[6] As the prologue to Book II tells us, Spenser's fairyland is in some sense his own England.

4. E. de Selincourt, Introduction to *The Poetical Works of Edmund Spenser*, xviii.
5. Wölfflin, *Principles of Art History*, 235.
6. Isabel E. Rathborne, *The Meaning of Spenser's Fairyland*.

The primary function of fairyland is to serve as the theatre for knightly action, not the instinctive and intuitive action to be found in Froissart or Malory, but highly idealized and self-conscious knight errantry. There is endless space for an infinite multiplicity of adventures, each of which contributes something to the clarification of the hero's character. But what will happen next, neither hero nor reader nor the poet himself can tell. In his letter to Raleigh, explaining his intentions in *The Faerie Queene*, Spenser briefly sketches the events of the third book, and adds, "But by occasion hereof, many other adventures are intermedled, but rather as Accidents, then intendments. As the love of Britomart, the overthrow of Marinell, the misery of Florimell, the vertuousness of Belphoebe, the lasciviousness of Hellenora, and many the like." Hurd's image referred to above is appropriate to both plot and setting. A number of avenues radiate from Gloriana's Cleopolis and each runs on unpredictably far into the glades of the forest where unknown enchantments wait. The contrast with Milton's masterful disposition of events within a preconceived totality of space, organized about one grand avenue of divine prescience and purpose, is complete.

Not only is Spenser's narrative without a cogent and controlled space; it is also in a time continuum of the vaguest kind. Presumably each of the twelve knights takes a year to complete his quest but Prince Arthur habitually (though not invariably) appears in the eighth canto of each tale and most readers feel they are in a timeless world.

This is not to imply that Spenser lacks principles of organization or devices for securing unity. He uses the principle of sequence with great effect. As the poem opens we see first the Knight, then the Lady, then her lamb, then the Dwarf. They immediately enter a forest in which we are shown, individually and without relation, the Pine, the Cedar, the Elm, the Poplar, the Oak, the Aspen, the Cypress, the Laurel, the Fir, the Willow, the Yew, the Birch, the Sallow, the Myrrh, the Beech, the Ash, the Olive, the Plantane, the Holme, the Maple. Of such a list, without climax, internal organization, or external point of reference, Milton is incapable. But its suitability and charm, or to use Spenser's word its decorum, in this world of fairyland are undeniable.

The use of clear and separable components, seen with linear distinctness and each meaningful in its own right, is Spenser's habitual method. As we approach the house of Pride, one of the many self-contained entities in his landscape, we have leisure to observe his descriptive devices. Of travellers who enter few if any return and they are totally debilitated. (In Bunyan, by contrast, all the pilgrims must traverse Vanity Fair.) Of the castle itself we see sequences of towers, galleries, windows, bowers; a clock tells the sequence of the hours. Lucifera sits on her throne, her court about her, a dragon at her feet, six wizards her councillors, and the picture is in the simplest sense all in one plane. One cannot avoid the contrast of Milton's Lucifer who "far within" is preparing to ruin mankind by one stroke to be delivered at a far-off point and moment in space and time.

The goddess ascends her coach but, unlike the tremendous processions and journeys of Milton's characters, hers is no more than a jaunt to take the air. The twenty stanzas which follow her ascent describe, one by one, her team and attendants. Here Spenser's method may be seen with great clarity. The third of the outriders is Lechery, mounted on a goat. The last two stanzas of his description are as follows:

> In a greene gowne he clothed was full faire,
> Which underneath did hide his filthinesse,
> And in his hand a burning hart he bare,
> Full of vaine follies, and new fanglenesse:
> For he was false, and fraught with ficklenesse,
> And learned had to love with secret lookes,
> And well could daunce, and sing with ruefulnesse,
> And fortunes tell, and read in loving bookes,
> And thousand other wayes, to bait his fleshly hookes.

> Inconstant man, that loved all he saw,
> And lusted after all, that he did love,
> Ne would his looser life be tide to law,
> But joyd weake wemens hearts to tempt and prove
> If from their loyall loves he might them move;
> Which lewdness fild him with reproachfull paine
> Of that fowle evill, which all men reprove,
> That rots the marrow, and consumes the braine:
> Such one was Lecherie, the third of all this traine.

The inevitable contrast is with Milton's Chariot of Paternal Deity,

> Flashing thick flames, Wheel within Wheel, undrawn,
> Itself instinct with Spirit, but convoy'd

> By four Cherubic shapes, four Faces each
> Had wondrous, as with Stars thir bodies all
> And Wings were set with Eyes, with Eyes the Wheels
> Of Beryl, and careering Fires between.

Spenser's desire for distinctness of parts goes beyond the structure of his poem or his verse into his habitual mode of vision. He sees Lechery in all his lineaments, motives, and actions, yet no complexity arises, no interrelation between this sin and any of the others, and no gesture that carries the eye outside the cartouche of words in which the poet has folded him. As for Lechery and his goat supplying any traction to Lucifera's coach, the idea does not bear examination. This is not to condemn Spenser but to observe that his linear distinctness of delineation precludes other effects. It is on a par with his handling of light. Even his most vigorous employment of it has a limited and static quality:

> And ye high heavens, the temple of the gods,
> In which a thousand torches flaming bright
> Doe burne, that to us wretched earthly clods,
> In dreadful darkness lend desired light....

For Spenser light is one among many phenomena which he may see clearly, record distinctly, and clothe with his own idealism. For Milton light means a vast variety of forms and ideas, from the "long levell'd rule of streaming light" that in imagination pierces a shrouded landscape to the perception and the doctrine that God is Light.

Spenser's singleness and distinctness of view have a decisive bearing upon his type of characterization. We see Milton's manifest identification of himself with his characters operating to strengthen debate, interchange, and dramatic tension among them. To take the simplest example: Raphael the willing teacher of mankind is palpably one side of Milton, while Adam, the eager recipient of knowledge, is another side. Yet this only makes for an admirable and fruitful tension between them. Spenser is so intimate with his heroes that we tend to see only what they see and to be circumscribed by the woods that enclose them. But we never discover in them anything like complexity; they never change; we see them always from the same viewpoint very close at hand. It is difficult to deny an analogy between the forms of classical, Renaissance, and Baroque statuary on the one hand and the character formation of classical epic, of Spenser, and of

Milton, on the other. Many classical bronzes and marbles were free-standing and permitted the viewer to take any of a number of views. Equally, Ulysses or Aeneas, in their massive roundness, permit a circulation of ideas and interpretations. Renaissance statuary offers one preferred viewpoint from which a highly specific effect can be obtained (Donatello's David). Tasso and Spenser similarly give the reader a viewpoint of each of their heroes from which it is not easy to depart. It is quite impossible to ask whether the Redcrosse Knight would not have been wiser to get on with his quest rather than turn aside to engage in a perilous fight with the dragon Error. Nor can the value of any of the knightly objectives be questioned. That Una's father cruelly and arbitrarily seized on Archimago, at the end of the first book—this and similar objections cannot be made; it is only with difficulty they can be thought of.

Baroque statuary and characterization differ from both the kinds we have just described. Bernini's statuary groups in the Borghese museum,[7] to which reference has already been made, are created to be seen primarily from one viewpoint. They are nevertheless conceived in depth and because of their complexity cannot but offer a variety of views. Of these views one, and the one Bernini indicated that he intended when he first placed these groups against a wall, is likely to establish itself as the spectator's own preference. In *Paradise Lost*, Adam as victim of Satan's guile, Adam betrayed by Eve, Adam accepting the paradox of the fortunate fall—all these are likely to resolve themselves back into Milton's primary Adam, the man who received and misused the gift of free will. Similarly, whatever admiration may be evoked by Satan's indomitable will, it is to the rightful predominance, in the universe, of God's will that Milton endeavours to conduct his readers.

Spenser's habit of making us give the whole of our attention to one item at a time in a series, together with what might be called a habit of linear portrayal (the images, the phrases, the metrical units all showing up with individual distinctness), is on a par with his use of separable planes of allegory. Too much was at one time made of the allegory, in Spenser criticism, and there is frequent doubt, on

---

7. In the same category are the angelic figures of the Ponte S. Angelo, primarily intended for the spectator approaching St. Peter's, and the marvellous Habakkuk statue, placed in a niche yet modelled in depth with projecting limbs.

the political plane, of Spenser's intentions. Allegory is nevertheless a major part of the poet's strategy and we are invited to read much of the first two books as romance or as moral allegory or as political allegory with topical reference to the Elizabethan scene. It has been suggested,[8] further, that Spenser's long review of history in canto x of the second book ending with Tanaquill (Elizabeth) is intended to show human life only from the viewpoint of Cleopolis, the city of Fame. Parallel accounts from the point of view of Jerusalem, the city of God, or Babylon, the city of Pride, supply two other planes of apprehension. Spenser and Milton diverge very sharply here, for nothing could be less like an exercise in relativity than Michael's account in the last two books of *Paradise Lost*.

Compared with Spenser, Milton is an adept at the fusion of materials. His congenital temperament, the ideological tensions of the age, and the available devices of the Baroque style are in the happiest state of interdependence and mutual support. The reader of *Paradise Lost* sees the elements of Renaissance idealism and order pass in review but they are armed with new weapons and proceeding to new and unexpected conquests. Milton's organizations of space and time, of plot and characterization, are overlapping webs of correspondences, causal relationships, and traditional affinities. The assumption of universal reason and the employment of a sustained rhetoric seem to make these merging superimpositions easy even when they are in fact most difficult. Milton's combination of Christian and classical worlds, his accommodation of monarchist and republican sentiment, his provision of stairs from nature to grace, from flesh to spirit, from ego to super-ego: each of these unifying manœuvres extends significantly beyond the simple junction of two elements or the simple mingling of two ingredients.

8. Rathborne, *The Meaning of Spenser's Fairyland*.

10. PURITANISM
AND BAROQUE

THERE IS NO direct path for criticism to follow between Italian architectural Baroque and the poetry of Milton. Hauser's *Social History of Art* significantly devotes its chapter on "The Baroque of the Protestant Bourgeoisie" to painting of the Dutch school, but Milton consorts poorly with Vermeer and Steen. If we are to account for Milton's subject and style by reference to the society in which he lived, to consider why the son of a scrivener should think in absolutes and write by preference in a rhetoric filled with exalted images, then "society" will mean more than one thing, as it would have to mean more than one thing in a consideration of Xavier or Loyola. The Puritan revolution was not only directed toward establishing a social system in which the middle class would be free from royal, aristocratic, or ecclesiastical control; it was equally the recognition of a society of the elect associated with "the sweet Societies" of *Lycidas*, of the utmost exaltation.

If we endeavour to relate *Paradise Lost* to the few manifestations of Baroque building and painting in England, the direct path is again non-existent. Whitehall, Blenheim Palace, Temple Bar, Castle Howard, St. Paul's and other of Wren's churches—nothing provides a useful link. Nor is this to be wondered at. These are expressions of the royal, aristocratic, or ecclesiastical forces to which Milton is a consistent enemy.

Milton's Baroque sensibility, anti-monarchical and anti-Catholic as it is, nevertheless springs directly from the concepts of absolute divine power and of regal splendour we have already discussed. This paradox is explained by two consistent transpositions of key. The first of these is the transposition of the whole scale of loyal, courtly, and adulatory sentiment from Charles I to God Himself, or if we prefer so to regard it, the rolling back of the powers of divine right descended from heaven upon the king, so that they return to their source and only safe base of action, the divine presence itself. This is Milton's major manœuvre in the realm of ideas. The second transposition is to shift all values away from institutional frameworks. Church, palace, monastery, law-court, university—all disappear. Academy and House of Parliament remain but these are no more than shells which barely contain the free, self-disciplining, eager service of God and man on the part of elect souls.

A point of the utmost importance is that in such a world the arts of architecture and mural painting are at a heavy disadvantage. But music and poetry, the least institutional of arts, reap a corresponding benefit. Poetry, moreover, because it is a verbal art, can be used to call up in the imagination the effects of architectural and pictorial splendour in an ideal or spiritual world. Milton's Baroque structures and compositions in chiaroscuro are vaster, more overwhelming, more sumptuous than anything the dealers in stone or paint or plaster could produce, and they subsist, immune from decay, in the regions of the mind.

By the oddest of paradoxes, therefore, it is in a society torn by civil strife, under a monarchy too harried, an aristocracy too poor, and a church too constricted to practise the expansive sumptuousness of the Baroque assertion of power, in a congeries of Puritans shot through with iconoclasm and deep suspicion of contrived aesthetic effects, that the supreme verbal embodiment of Baroque is achieved.

The resemblance of Milton's art to that of the Counter-Reformation lies in the fact that he too was concerned with unity, power, majesty, splendour, with the demonstration of divine invincibility and triumphant faith. Although it is the God of English Independents and not the Catholic Church which is his focal point, his parallelism with the Counter-Reformation remains.

It is generally conceded that the Counter-Reformation was an attempt to establish unity in Christendom. Some confusion exists as to the nature of the corresponding Protestant concept of unity. It has been labelled as a concept of universally acceptable science, the

science of reason and research. To this identification there are material
objections: it is more appropriate to the Royal Society, a consciously
non-religious foundation appearing too late to belong to the heyday
of Puritan vigour to which Milton's thought belongs. It is analogous
to confusing the Puritan's Christian liberty with later notions of
democracy. Above all, it neglects the feeling for unity which possessed
Puritan minds, then as now. This may be put succinctly as a belief
in the overriding power and purpose of God the Father, whether in
predestination or in the ordaining of free will; the Lordship one and
indivisible of Christ over the individual believer and over the Church;
the fellowship in the Spirit enjoyed by all believers. Under this aegis
the unity of reintegration after religious doubt and strife could be as
powerfully experienced by English Independents as by those who
looked to the Council of Trent.

How this Puritan spirit achieved expression in the form of the epic
Milton has revealed in the autobiographical section of *The Reason of
Church Government*. It is the conjunction of the most strenuous
possible endeavour, for God and one's country, and the most sublime
and comprehensive literary form known, the classical epic, the form
of "highest hope and hardest attempting."

Milton is, as his admirers claim, an apostle of liberty, but liberty as
he conceives it is the ability of the individual, without let or hindrance, to bring his will into conformity with the will of God. The
foundation of liberty is God's absolute and beneficent power. Human
will can achieve nothing good but in compliance with this will; both
the duty and the happiness of man are inseparable from active obedience to his Maker.

The unity, in doctrine and in practical life, which those obedient
to the will of God must necessarily exhibit seemed to Milton's age,
as to our own, sadly out of line with the disagreements among the
sects. This fact Milton faces in precisely the way that Nonconformists
face it today. His justification of diversity within unity, in the course
of the argument of *Areopagitica*, is well known. The time is come, he
says, when all the Lord's people are become prophets. Some inexperi-
enced souls are in agony "lest these divisions and subdivisions will
undo us." The adversary waits his hour.

Fool! he sees not the firm root, out of which we all grow, though into
branches; nor will beware until he sees our small divided maniples cutting

through at every angle of his ill-united and unwieldy brigade. And that we are to hope better of all these supposed sects and schisms, and that we shall not need that solicitude, honest perhaps, though over-timorous, of them that vex in this behalf, but shall laugh in the end at those malicious applauders of our differences, I have these reasons to persuade me.

The reasons are conveyed in a succession of famous images, embodying unity, purpose, vitality. These are, the besieged city confident of victory, the vigorous human constitution, the strong man waking refreshed, and the emblematic eagle renewing its youth.

Christian liberty to Milton is inseparable from this sense of oneness, of organic vitality, of dedication. This liberty which he enjoys determines his position in politics and in religion. He can obey neither king nor bishop, for his ideas of imperial power and splendour, of majestic will acting in accordance with its own royal nature, are removed from Charles I as sovereign and as head of the Church and return to God as sovereign of the universe and only object of reverence. But Christian liberty guards him equally, on the other side, from putting faith in egalitarian democracy, in individual licence, in "doing as one pleases," or in self-indulgence, or self-improvement without intense dedication. And as with individual men, so with nations, in Milton's book.

Christian liberty is the key to many of Milton's apparent ambiguities. It explains how he can be simultaneously the revolutionary, the lover of freedom, and the exponent of absolute rule. If the divine will is supreme then a sine qua non to obedience is freedom from every species of human domination. This explains why Milton pays only the most perfunctory attention to organization within Church or state. He is filled with the thought of the individual son of God, free, strong, divinely energized, guided, illuminated, and justified. Finally, the possession of Christian liberty enables Milton to conceive everywhere of order without the system of hierarchy imposed by autocratic forms of government or the ubiquitous bureaucracy inseparable from democratic systems.

This doctrine of Christian liberty was a constant element in Protestant thought and truly pervasive in Milton's thinking. It made him, in politics and religion, an Independent while preventing him from any advocacy of democratic equality. This is put with great clarity by one of the foremost critics of seventeenth-century thought.

Milton remains the chief exponent of Christian liberty, turning it to many uses and responding to its influence in his whole ethical and political thought; but the doctrine, or its variants, also appears in Robinson, Walwyn, Roger Williams, and the anonymous authors of the *Paraenetic* and *The Ancient Bounds*. It offers indeed a very striking example of the influence of Puritan dogma on Puritan thought first in relation to the church and later in relation to the state: it is a part of Protestant theology, the heritage of the Reformation; it is essentially individualistic, connoting the freedom of the believer achieved through personal faith in Christ; its place in the groundwork of the Puritan conception of liberty emphasizes one of the chief obstacles in the road from Puritanism to democracy, for liberty is assumed to be the special prerogative of the regenerate. A large number of the Puritans, and Milton among them, never pass securely beyond this assumption.[1]

Liberty is the special prerogative of the regenerate: to Milton nothing can be more indisputable, central, seminal. To pass beyond it would be to leave the centre of truth and move towards chaos and disintegration. There is no thought in his mind that freedom broadens slowly down from precedent to precedent. For him the fullness of Christian freedom is available without hindrance, from the throne of God itself, to the individual or to the nation obedient to the divine will and therefore fit to enjoy the glorious liberty of the children of God.

In considering Milton's variant of Puritanism it is illuminating to set beside him another Puritan of his period, John Bunyan. At first blush, Bunyan's education, experience, and outlook would seem to reduce comparison to unfruitful generalities but the case is far otherwise. We have endeavoured to show that Milton's world was penetrated by a constant axis between human and divine will. *The Pilgrim's Progress* is laid down on the same axis, though the form of the narrative makes of it a path from the City of Destruction to the Celestial City, not a nexus of will between man and God. The rigour with which Bunyan adheres to this controlling image exceeds even Milton's commitment to his. The pilgrim's progress in the first book is on a road which admits of no alternatives and from which the least deviation brings the most deadly penalties. Through the Valley of the Shadow of Death Christian scarcely knows how to place one foot in

1. A. S. P. Woodhouse, "Puritanism and Liberty," *University of Toronto Quarterly*, IV, 403.

front of the other, for fear of disaster; when with Hopeful he climbs a stile to walk on the grass, Giant Despair descends upon them; when in the second book Matthew so much as picks an apple off a branch leaning from outside over the path he is sick almost unto death. Such closely held symbolism is significant in the extreme; the relentless pursuit of the invariable image demonstrates the depth of Bunyan's conviction.

Like Milton's axis, Bunyan's straight and narrow path is emphatically not intended to traverse an area and open it to exploration. True it could be charted. From the Palace Beautiful it is possible to see the Delectable Mountains in Emmanuel's Land and from these, in turn, to see the gates of the Celestial City. The path runs south, presumably because Satan is traditionally in the north. For a moment, in a remark by the smallest of the children, it becomes vertical, like Milton's axis: "The way to heaven is as up a ladder, and the way to hell is as down a hill." It is a moral absolute at all times.

Unity, will, and power, exercised under the absolute rule of the King of Heaven and in "diametrical" opposition to Satan's Kingdom —these are as powerfully bodied forth in Bunyan as in Milton. Heaven and earth are brought in constant and close relation. Heaven is the goal of the earthly pilgrimage, just over the river which may be so low as scarcely to wet the feet. Christ is spoken of as both immanent and transcendent with such unstudied and easy references that the reader may "fancy but thinly the veil intervenes between that fair city and me." Nothing that is not on the path between heaven and earth has any positive significance. Those who leave it go to speedy ruin and are soon lost sight of. The dynamism which creates the single "straight and narrow" track is sustained with unflagging vigour, particularly in the first book. Great releases of energy, both good and evil, attend each stage of the unfolding journey. Bursts of struggle and violent conflict alternate with places and periods of refreshment and repose. Allowing for Bunyan's scale, there is more heroic action in *Pilgrim's Progress* than in *Paradise Lost*. There is also a more constant constricting pressure. The path is in places "fenced with a wall." As it climbs the hill of Difficulty, it lies between the two alternative paths of Danger and Destruction. It runs between chained lions: "Keep in the midst of the path and no hurt shall come unto thee." If the pilgrims so much as turn aside, "Our Lord the King will certainly hear thereof." And not only fear but a lively hope keeps Christian in the way; he presses toward the goal, the prize of God's high calling.

The path runs through magnetic centres and fields of force, now good, now evil. The archers in Beelzebub's strong castle are a threat to those who would enter the gate to become pilgrims. A door to Hell opens close to the Celestial City. Inevitably a dreadful exigent harshness characterizes all judgement of the wicked. "However, I have dealt plainly with him, and so am clear of his blood if he perisheth" is a common sentiment, and we are not entirely surprised to hear the Shining Ones say, as they conduct Christian and Hopeful to the gate of Heaven, "When he shall pass sentence upon all the workers of iniquity, let them be Angels or Men, you also shall have a voice in that Judgment, because they were his and your Enemies." The locus classicus, however, is provided by the girl Mercy: "No, no; let them hang, and their names rot, and their crimes live for ever against them."

It follows that temptation and moral choice are as vital to Bunyan as to Milton and the concept of Christian heroism central in both. But Bunyan's allegorical treatment of this heroism entails quite insoluble contradictions. There is confusion between physical and spiritual assault. Are we to understand that the martyrs destroyed by Pope and Pagan do not get to heaven? Are they not, like good Faithful done to death at Vanity Fair, carried there direct? Since this is their object, in what sense have they been persecuted? Heedless falls into a ditch and lies there dead. Is he damned? Furthermore, we are categorically told, "A Christian can never be overcome, unless he should yield of himself." Yet Gaius, in complete contradiction, speaks in glowing terms of Stephen, James, Paul, Peter, Ignatius, Romanus, Polycarp, who "suffered injuries and death for the love of a pilgrim's life." Less than ten pages later Mr. Feeble-mind is saying with Bunyan's approval, "Also, when he had got me into his Den, since I went not with him willingly, I believed I should come out alive again; for I have heard, that not any Pilgrim that is taken captive by violent hands, if he keeps heart-whole towards his Master, is, by the Laws of Providence, to die by the hand of the Enemy." There is confusion here arising out of a loose use of allegory, between assaults upon the Christian wayfarer which threaten his liberty or life and temptations which threaten his integrity or his immortal soul. The Interpreter bids the pilgrims be submissive as sheep being slaughtered, yet Christian is armed for his journey and armoured from head to foot. Bunyan's desire to unify Christian experience, to present it whole and moving in one continuum of struggle and suffering and success, has outpaced the logic of his allegorical applications of imagery.

The image of Christ himself appears in both figurative and literal senses on the same page. Or the shepherds in Emmanuel's land may tell the pilgrims, "The sheep are also his and he laid down his life for them."

There is little congruency in the presenting of images. We see Christian succoured by "a hand with some of the leaves of the tree of life," which is pure emblem, as in Quarles. We see the definitive image of the wicket gate, which is essential to salvation. Yet it is the entrance to a path in which the agents of destruction seem more present and pressing than in the City of Destruction itself.

It may be asked, in Bunyan's defence, why this defect only becomes apparent when one is going through the text with a comb, and why it is not perceived by the ordinary reader. The answer is the best possible tribute to Bunyan's genius. He triumphs over the defects of his mechanism because his own intensity of conviction burns through to set the reader's imagination on fire. Nowhere is this more apparent than in the encounter of Christian with Apollyon.

But now, in this Valley of Humiliation, poor Christian was hard put to it; for he had gone but a little way, before he espied a foul Fiend coming over the field to meet him.... Now the Monster was hideous to behold; he was clothed with scales, like a Fish (and they are his pride); he had wings like a Dragon, feet like a Bear, and out of his belly came Fire and Smoke; and his mouth was as the mouth of a Lion. When he was come up to Christian, he beheld him with a disdainful countenance, and thus began to question with him. Whence came you? and whither are you bound?

In spite of the *mélange* of incongruous elements which make up the description of the fiend, we are instantly convinced of his reality because of the speed and urgency of Bunyan's prose. There are occasions when this sense of urgency crystallizes a narrative element into a single unforgettable image.

What a fool, quoth he, am I, thus to lie in a stinking Dungeon, when I may as well walk at liberty. I have a Key in my bosom called Promise, that will, I am persuaded, open any Lock in Doubting Castle. Then said

Hopeful, That's good news; good Brother, pluck it out of thy bosom and try.

Bunyan so intensely presents the Christian life, so urgently wishes to communicate actuality to the reader, is such a psychological realist and didactic in so evangelical a fashion, that the convention of mediaeval allegory is given new shape and new pressure, losing its point by point applicability, shifting rapidly, passing from figurative representation to actuality and back again as easily as scripture does and making each episode mean the whole. There are incongruities but there is complete unity of theme, intention, plot, characters, ornaments, illustrations, biblical references, and allegory. Every character may be the reader.

Bunyan's bold acceptance of logical incongruity, his willingness to disregard decorum, is a direct outcome of his sole reliance upon the scriptures. His overmastering image of pilgrimage, his urgent belief that a current of power flows from the eternal world into this one and magnetizes the minds of Christians to point only towards their celestial home—these elements in Bunyan's narrative are the direct outcome of his experience of the Bible. His figurative language he justifies in his Apology by pointing to the precedent of scripture and he can interpolate in the current of his story: "I make bold to talk thus metaphorically, for the ripening of the wits of young readers; and because in the book of the Revelation, the saved are compared to a company of musicians that play upon their trumpets and harps, and sing their songs before the throne." His feeling that what he conceives as scriptural imagery never fails to justify itself leads him, in an attempt to follow St. Paul's description, awkwardly to add "all-prayer" to the list of Christian's tangible armoury.

It need scarcely be argued that Bunyan's Puritanism issues in religious individualism and in the strongest of emphasis upon the inner life of the spirit. Mercy, in the Valley of Humiliation, says to her guide: "Methinks here one may without much molestation be thinking what he is, whence he came, what he has done, and to what the King has called him; here one may think, and break at heart, and melt in one's spirit, until one's eyes become like the Fishpools of Heshbon."

From this individualism proceeds a sense of responsibility for one-self—and for others up to the point where they decisively reject the gospel. This responsibility makes for fearlessness. "There are two things that they have need to be possessed with, that go on pilgrimage: courage and an unspotted life." Sometimes Bunyan renders this decisive inner direction with the absolute certainty born of his own experience. "Set down my name, Sir," said the man in Interpreter's tableau, then cutting and hacking most fiercely hewed his way through all opposition, to enter the kingdom. "Then Christian smiled and said, I think verily I know the meaning of this."

As we should expect, Bunyan is both anti-sacerdotal and anti-sacramental. The sacrifice of Christ is not stressed when the cross and the sepulchre are encountered. It is made, rather, a matter of the pilgrim's continuous experience. At no point are we given the impression that an event in the story corresponds to an established sacrament or a priestly office. The inner spirit is all.

Against this background of general resemblance to Milton startling dissimilarities develop. Bunyan possesses an abundant sense of Christian fellowship. Christian cannot rise from his fall till Faithful comes up to help him. After Faithful's martyrdom, Hopeful enters into a brotherly covenant "to be a companion with Christian in his pilgrimage." This sense of love between brethren is the flower of a deep-rooted experience of the love of Christ. He is a lover of poor pilgrims, who love him for what he has done for them. The children "cried out unto Him that loveth pilgrims." "For, to tell you the truth," said Christian, "I love him, because I was by him eased of my burden." And the word that finally repulses Apollyon is that we are "more than conquerors through him that loved us."

It is not surprising to find, even amid the exigencies of the pilgrimage, a sense of joy, even of gaiety. "Can you think who is at the door?" cries Innocent. "There is Christiana and her children, and her companion, all waiting for entertainment here. Then they leaped for joy, and went and told their master." When the pilgrims gather in Gaius' house, "Then were they very merry, and sat at the table a long time, talking of many things" and cracking nuts—which are the secrets of Christian life.

There is in Bunyan a humility which takes many forms. It seems at times the humility of the poor. It is certainly associated with the deepest sense of sinfulness and the need of forgiveness and redemption. It produces a sense of Christian ministry both like and unlike that of Milton. Bunyan, like Milton, resists ecclesiastical authority and vigorously asserts the all-sufficiency of scripture. But Bunyan, out of his humility, goes on to welcome the ministry of the gifted. "Thy company, O sweet Evangelist, how desirable it is to us poor pilgrims." At the same time, Bunyan qua minister disavows through Great-heart any pretentions to special powers. "It is my duty, said he, to distrust mine own ability, that I may have reliance on him that is stronger than all." Ministry is only an especially effective form of fellowship.

Bunyan has an intimate sense of the actualities of the pilgrim's life. Though the continuous purposeful journey is always in view there are numerous and swift changes of pace, changes of tension and mood. Once in a great while the pilgrimage itself is seen as it were in reverse. "Why, my wife was afraid of losing this world, and my children were given to the foolish delights of youth: so what by one thing, and what by another, they left me to wander in this manner alone."

In the latter part of the second book passages abound which suggest a lessening of the tension and terror of the journey. We are told of the most pitiful aspirants to pilgrimage that if they have even the weakest faith they shall reach the city of their desire. Feeble-mind explains, "Because the Hill Difficulty was judged too hard for me, I was carried up that by one of his servants." Soon after, Great-heart reassures him:

You must needs go along with us; we will wait for you, we will lend you our help, we will deny ourselves of some things both opinionative and practical for your sake, we will not enter into doubtful disputations before you, we will be made all things to you rather than you shall be left behind.

To drive home his message, Bunyan doubles his example. When Mr. Fearing passes along the Valley of the Shadow the evil powers in it receive "a special check from our Lord" till he has passed through. With beautiful insight Mr. Fearing's death is described:

When he was going up to the gate, Mr. Great-heart began to take his leave of him, and to wish him a good reception above. So he said, I shall, I shall. Then parted we asunder, and I saw him no more.

This ministering compassion for the weak extends itself also, in the second book, to what might be called the family situation. Christiana's four boys, Matthew, Samuel, Joseph, and James, show themselves from the beginning willing little travellers on the road, and Great-heart is given to them as a guide. Yet as time goes on it becomes apparent, as the boys in turn marry and have children, that some abatement of the rigour of Christian's original and archetypal journey must be conceded. Long sojourns take place at the houses of rest and refreshment. At one of these, by a wrenching of the allegory, children are left in the care of Christ himself while their parents go on. The concept of the Christian family propagating in the world has already been admitted. "Let Christiana look out some damsels for her sons, to whom they may be betrothed, &c., that the name of their father and the house of his progenitors may never be forgotten in the world." The world itself is ameliorated. The great Beast is repelled and "it is verily believed by some that this beast will die of his wounds." Giant Despair's Doubting Castle is, after the giant's death, demolished. There are parts even of Vanity Fair where, after Faithful's witness and martyrdom, religion is "counted honourable."

To complete the tale of Bunyan's divergence from Milton we must recall his beautiful tribute to women.

I will say again, that when the Saviour was come, women rejoiced in him before either man or angel. I read not, that ever any man did give unto Christ so much as one groat; but the women followed him, and ministered to him of their substance. It was a woman that washed his feet with tears, and a woman that anointed his body to the burial. They were women that wept when he was going to the cross, and women that followed him from the cross, and that sat by his sepulchre when he was buried. They were women that were first with him at his resurrection-morn; and women that brought tidings first to his disciples that he was risen from the dead. Women, therefore, are highly favoured, and show by these things that they are sharers with us in the grace of life.

The passage is worth record and consideration, for although it is on the face of it a scriptural mosaic its whole tone is of a tenderness and sense of fellowship in Christ in marked contrast to Milton.

We have seen that some of the methods by which Milton achieves unity of effect are employed, in his own more simple but no less effective way, by Bunyan. The single straight line connecting antagonistic poles; the reliance upon "diametrically opposed" moral values; the urgent sense of irrevocable choice ever imminent; the timed releases of energy, constructive or destructive, which themselves constitute a kind of quanta procession; the all-embracing nature of the plot: these are as familiar to the reader of *Paradise Lost* as to the reader of *Pilgrim's Progress*. In their use of still another device Milton and Bunyan show themselves children of the same age. They employ argument, in a continuous web from beginning to end of their work. Narrative, description, dramatic passages, exposition—all are given the tone and purpose of argument. Argumentative dialogue is Bunyan's most instinctive method. Even his frequent recapitulations, less than vistas yet more than summaries, are intended to persuade, to convince, by reiteration. Yet the arguments are often far from logical and, avoiding both scholastic refinement and scientific rigour, rely upon the *obiter dicta* of sacred script and on appeals to common experience of the converted. "Come away, prove my words," said Christian to Obstinate. "And do you think," asks Pliable, "that the words of your book are certainly true?" Christian replies, "Yes, verily; for it was made by him that cannot lie." This is the driving force of Bunyan's discourse. Even less than Milton does he need to qualify or hesitate. "Let a man have one of these blades, with a hand to wield it and skill to use it, he may venture upon an angel with it. He need not fear its holding, if he can but tell how to lay on. Its edges will never blunt. It will cut flesh and bones, and soul and spirit, and all. (Ephesians 6: 12–17, Hebrews 4: 12)"

In both Milton and Bunyan argument is more (and less) than reason. It is a verbalized dynamic issuing with overpowering conviction from a belief in revealed truth and a consciousness of determining experience.

Bunyan, in blending romance, allegory, and Puritan intensity to form a new and unforgettable form, is as palpably moved by the spirit of his age as Milton, who makes of classical and Christian elements a new kind of epic. How often Bunyan operates as a point of comparison with Milton has, it is hoped, been indicated. One of the more striking differences between them lies in Milton's almost complete lack of the evangelistic spirit. He avoids the real problem of hell. He thinks of heaven as a place of recognition, fame, beatitude rather than of safety. Where Bunyan thinks of sinfulness, Milton thinks of wilfulness.

In any broad consideration of Milton it is a great help to have Bunyan as a point of comparison. Doctrinally the two men are very close, temperamentally very different. Bunyan's method of composition owes nothing to Italy or to antiquity. It is possible therefore to regard what they express in common as belonging to basic Puritan ideology. The parts played by this complex of ideas and by Milton's own individualistic temperament in shaping *Paradise Lost* as a poem both intensely Puritan and intensely Baroque become easier to assess.

Another useful point of comparison with Milton is furnished by Defoe, whose *Robinson Crusoe* is the story of Everyman, besides being a veiled record of the crises of its writer's own life.

It is easy to read the story of Robinson as the story of man's struggle with nature or as a triumph of individualism in adversity. Defoe's own emphasis, however, is religious and the religion he works within is closely akin to Bunyan's in its essential features, though differing in its emphases. His family were Nonconformists. He was educated at an academy presided over by a dissenting minister.

Robinson is born in York, in 1632. His family is of German extraction. One brother, a soldier, is killed fighting the Spaniards. The Crusoe family belongs to "the upper station of low life." It appears to be associated with no religious, cultural, or social institutions.

Robinson's father intends him for the law and urges him not to go to sea. His advice is prudential: "that temperance, moderation, quietness, health, society, all agreeable diversions, and all desirable pleasures, were the blessings attending the middle station of life."

But Robinson, with a causeless obsession for travel, runs away. Later he is to refer to this act of rebellion against his father as "my original sin." He is enslaved by the Moors, escapes, becomes a planter in Brazil, foolishly goes on an unnecessary trading voyage, is shipwrecked, and finds himself on the island, as sole survivor.

He has now ample time for reflection but it is not until he is shaken first by an earthquake, then by an ague, that he becomes conscience-stricken. In a dream saturated with the terrors of apocalyptic judgement, he is threatened with divine punishment for his failure to repent. What follows is a religious conversion, recounted with absolute conviction. His rebellion against his father lies heavily on his mind, together with the general course of his wicked life and and his present sins. An internal dialogue of question followed by expository answer sets itself up in his mind. Looking in a sea-chest for tobacco for his ague, he finds a Bible, opens it, and reads "Call on

me in the day of trouble, and I will deliver thee; and thou shalt glorify
me." As he recovers he begins seriously to go through the New
Testament and finds repentance and faith. This episode is all of a
piece with *Pilgrim's Progress*. It is subsequently that the inherent
differences between Crusoe and Christian appear.

In an account of his feelings while still solitary on the island, he
blames himself for not having in the first place been satisfied with
the station in which God and nature had placed him; for his opposition to his father's will, "which was, as I may call it, my original sin";
and for his later mistakes of the same kind. So far, so good. But he
continues:

Had that Providence, which so happily had seated me at the Brazils as a
planter, blessed me with confined desires, and could I have been contented
to have gone on gradually, I might have been this time—I mean in the
time of my being on this island—one of the most considerable planters
in the Brazils; nay, I am persuaded, that by the improvements I had made
in that little time I lived there, and the increase I should probably have
made if I had stayed, I might have been worth a hundred thousand
moidores: and what business had I to leave a settled fortune, well stocked
plantation, improving and increasing, to turn supercargo to Guinea, to
fetch negroes, when patience and time would have so increased our stock
at home, that we could have bought them at our own doors from those
whose business it was to fetch them? And though it had cost us something
more, yet the difference of that price was by no means worth saving at
so great a hazard.

This is a comedown with a crash from Christian's single-minded
pursuit of the path to the Celestial City. Yet we seem to be employing
the same terms and concepts. There is lament for waywardness, for
impatient straying from the divine will; there is a going over of the
blessings we have lost by our folly. But prudence and moderation
have succeeded to the old Puritan élan. Blessings are financial. Slavery
—though Crusoe has been a slave and known captivity—is accepted;
even the slave-trade from Guinea is not condemned. What has happened is that Defoe is employing the bottom half, so to speak, of the
ladder of Puritan thought, the prudential, practical, money-making
virtues with which the concept of Puritanism has ever since his
generation been all too unhappily tagged. This devotion to the lower
rungs of the ladder leading from earth to heaven persists in the second
part of Crusoe's history and was undoubtedly derived from Defoe's

own experience. The old strenuousness of spirit is gone. Christian, fingers in ears, crying, "Life, life! eternal life!" is the image of the past. Belief accommodates itself to prudent reasonableness.

This limiting change, however, does not entail a loss of Puritan doctrines and values. Though deprived of their tension, their vigorous aspiration, their sustained intensity, they persist. Crusoe, for example, enjoys, in a way Bunyan would have approved, an evangelistic concern for Friday's salvation and, after Friday's conversion, a warm sense of fellowship with him.

The conversation which employed the hours between Friday and me was such as made the three years which we lived there together perfectly and completely happy, if any such thing as complete happiness can be found in a sublunary state. The savage was now a good Christian, a much better than I; though I have reason to hope, and bless God for it, that we were equally penitent, and comforted, restored penitents. We had here the word of God to read, and no farther off from His Spirit to instruct than if we had been in England.

If we read Defoe's story page by page, noting the resemblances between his ideas and Bunyan's, the list becomes impressive. The same intense, pervasive individualism appears. Man lives between celestial and infernal poles and the gospel of repentance toward God and faith in Christ is his sole directive to salvation. Truth is revealed and, while reasonable, is above reason. The Bible, interpreted by the Holy Spirit to the individual soul, is the means of grace. We are ever under God's eye and beneficent direction whether we acknowledge it or not. Liberty of conscience is essential if we are to serve God. Both Christian and Crusoe fear priestcraft and regard Catholicism as a persecuting power.

Certain habits of sensibility occur both in Bunyan and in Defoe. There is supersensitiveness to alienation of the mind from God, whether this leads to flagrant sin or no. Bunyan's remorse over a state of mind that led visibly to nothing worse than bell-ringing, tip-cat, and some profanity is matched by Crusoe who tells us, "I was all that the most hardened, unthinking, wicked creature, among our common sailors, can be supposed to be, not having the least sense, either of the fear of God in danger, or of thankfulness to God in deliverance." Yet nothing, after his initial flight from home, seems really to support the statement. This scrupulous sense of the great Taskmaster's eye is undoubtedly related to a whole scale of virtues, such as punctuality and sobriety, and to habits of thought, such as arguing, reckoning, recording. Crusoe is nothing if not self-disciplined. "First, my duty to God, and reading the Scriptures, which I constantly set apart some time for, thrice every day; secondly, the going abroad with my gun for food, which generally took me three hours every morning when it did not rain," and so on. As for debate, Crusoe, having not a soul to discuss anything with, is the best possible test of the Puritan's ability to produce argument out of the substance of his own mind and out of its relation with God.

Thus I lived mighty comfortably, my mind being entirely composed by resigning to the will of God, and throwing myself wholly upon the disposal of His providence: this made my life better than sociable; for, when I began to regret the want of conversation, I would ask myself, whether thus conversing mutually with my own thoughts, and, as I hope I may say, with even my Maker, by ejaculations and petitions, was not better than the utmost enjoyment of human society in the world.

The natural form of Crusoe's thoughts is revealed early in his story on the island when he draws up a list, as he says, "like debtor and creditor, the comforts I enjoy against the miseries I suffered." Six points follow, under Evil, and six counterbalancing points, under Good.

But neither Defoe nor Crusoe is as straightforward as this brief glance at the lower echelons of Puritan ideology would suggest. Crusoe exhibits in a kind of blueprint outline one of the cruxes of Puritan feeling which also disturbs the consistency of *Paradise Lost* and *Pilgrim's Progress*. It is a problem also for the Counter-Reformation sensibility, as we shall see in due course.

Briefly, it is disparity between complete passive submission to the will of God, on one hand, and vigorous defensive or punitive action against evil on the other. Neither Milton nor Bunyan appears to recognize the nature of the difficulty, but Defoe through Crusoe does. Crusoe is debating with himself whether to attack any cannibals who may land and he concludes it would be a rash and unwise act.

Religion joined in with this prudential resolution, and I was convinced now many ways that I was perfectly out of my duty, when I was laying all my bloody schemes for the destruction of innocent creatures—I mean, innocent as to me: as to the crimes they were guilty of towards one another, I had nothing to do with them; they were national punishments to make a just retribution for national offences, and to bring public judgments upon those who offended in a public manner, by such ways as best please God.

After this, the fluctuations of Crusoe's mind and the disguises assumed by his impulses make a breathless story of emotional ups and downs. All his calm of mind and resignation to Providence is suspended and his desire to escape from the island becomes "an impetuosity of desire, that it was not to be resisted." He becomes fevered and falling asleep dreams of rescuing someone who shall be the companion of his escape. He awakes, recalls that to fulfil his dream he must kill the whole band of savages that may come. "My heart trembled at the thought of shedding so much blood, though it was for my deliverance." After many secret disputes and after much perplexity as the arguments "struggled in my head a long time" he is resolved to get a companion cost what it may. A band of savages arrives, and as every child knows Crusoe rescues Friday, killing two of his pursuers. With this induction into defensive violence he and Friday make a splendid and almost complete slaughter of the next party (who bring the Spaniard and Friday's father). From now on, Crusoe is a different man. "My island was now peopled, and I thought myself very rich in subjects; and it was a merry reflection which I frequently made, how like a King I looked." Crusoe's fusillades have destroyed the wicked, rescued the good, provided him with companions and subjects, opened the probability of leaving the island. The mood of total submission to God, of happiness alone in God's company, or of fellowship with Friday as they speak humbly of repentance and divine grace—all this seems to have gone down the drain. Subsequently he quells a mutiny, blasts a fleet of canoes containing Indians, and all across the width of Asia, on his way home, is ready at the defensive or offensive without the least hesitation.

It has been said of France that no country is more truly Catholic, because among the roll-call of notable Frenchmen are names which perfectly evoke all the varieties of Catholic excellence. It can equally be claimed for the British Isles that in the course of their history every variety of Puritan sensibility has appeared.

Spenser exhibits a Protestantism on the way to Puritan positions. Milton, Bunyan, Fox represent the high-water mark of Puritanism, which it has never since regained. Defoe records the rapid subsidence of Puritan endeavour to the less exalted of its designated levels.

High Puritanism itself possesses variants it does no harm to think of in theological terms, which was after all the way in which Puritans conceived their own ideas. Milton, we have seen, centred his thoughts upon God the Father and subordinated all else to this passionate unity of aim so that he became as it were an involuntary Arian. No one has ever been much distressed by Milton's Arianism, it so unmistakably proceeds from a desire, not to denigrate the Son, but to glorify the Father. Bunyan as even the most cursory reading of *Pilgrim's Progress* will show, was filled with thoughts of the Son, the Christ who died for men and lives to save them, with whom they may enjoy a life everlasting. And Fox, founder of a communion relying upon the inward light and avoiding all external show, was one in whom there shone the over-powering experience of the Holy Spirit. Fox's definitive protest during the church service in Nottingham in 1649 was prompted by an inward voice and its purport was that doctrine must be judged not by scripture alone but by divine light. Puritan thought, putting as little stress as possible on church government and on the delegation of divine authority to men, necessarily concerned itself in a practical way with the character of God, under whose instant direction the independent Puritan had to make his decisions. And accordingly as God was apprehended—whether in paternal majesty, or as redeemer and saviour, or as ministering to a new life of the spirit—so differences of temperament could be allowed to find expression and expansion within the fixed terms of Christian belief.

Milton gives embodiment to the ideals of the Puritan Independents in "their finest hour." From the historian's stance it may seem a pitifully brief and confused tenure of greatness. From the viewpoint of the conservative, either in politics or in religion, the two or three decades involved will seem not merely confused but disastrously so. And in the minds of many who regard Milton as a great poet there is the belief that Milton's value lies in his being a forerunner of liberalism and democracy. One reward of even a brief recognition of Milton as Baroque is to supply concepts over and above these, particularly of the triumph and glory of the Independents' vision.

In contrast to Bunyan, Milton possessed not only immense learning but also an intimate and practical knowledge of literary forms, of artistic conventions, of classical traditions and of tricks of the writer's trade. Given other incentives, he could therefore encompass the requirements of the Baroque style. Nothing in his structure of doctrinal belief hindered him. That structure had indeed been modified into something less than orthodoxy by the imperiousness of his unifying mind. And his mind now opened upon the vision of Puritan glory, in this world and the other world, which to the Puritan are in truth one world, of spiritual struggle and fulfilment, of illustrious achievement, concerning which his imagination presented him with "nothing but very happy and very possible according to best wishes; if God have so decreed, and this age have spirit and capacity enough to apprehend." And if in the course of events he had at last to express a fear, all too well grounded, that "the people be so affected as to prostitute religion and liberty to the vain and groundless apprehension that nothing but kingship can restore trade," if his view of human history became by the time the last books of *Paradise Lost* were being written even less hopeful than Bunyan's, still there shone with undiminished brightness to the last pages of his writing and the last days of his life the vision of divine glory, of the triumph, in a new heaven and a new earth, of everything he had believed in and striven for.

The world of Milton's poetry, therefore, is in the most unequivocal fashion Baroque. The scenes he depicts, the insinuating significance of which is emphasized by every device of scholarship and literary art, are radiant with the divine omnipotence, omniscience, and omnipresence.

As for the unity of Milton's style, we have only to look across the Channel and observe the unity imposed upon artists by Louis XIV's agents such as Colbert and LeBrun to find it credible that Milton's desire to do for his country what the greatest and choicest wits of Athens, Rome, or modern Italy had done for theirs should have brought his style too, in every detail, into conformity with absolutism, the absolutism of God's immutable will.

Among the most perceptive critics of Milton as a Puritan poet is Malcolm Ross, whose *Milton's Royalism* and *Poetry and Dogma* together present a picture of Milton employing traditional concepts to unexpected ends.

He will pilfer from the Fathers and the scholastics, as from Luther, Calvin, and Boehme, but always to his own peculiar purpose. He will twist the economy of redemption to fit his own private intuition of the nature of things. Thus his doctrine of free-will is more Catholic than Protestant, yet for Milton the consequence of man's freedom is as dark as if man in the mass had been predestined to damnation. Milton's free conceptualization (and improvisation) of dogma permits a parallel freedom in the use of rhetoric which startles us, not by the incongruity which we might expect to result from these montages of Catholic, pagan, and Protestant surface, but by the incredible propriety of the mongrel effect. For Milton neither negates nor affirms the images of particular and exclusive dogmatic traditions. He uproots them; he rearranges them. And they come somehow to cohere in living novel patterns.[2]

Ross's analysis of Milton admirably demonstrates that in Milton's poetry we see the absolutes of Christian doctrine changing shape under the compulsions of his personal and Protestant needs. He comments sharply on Milton's repeated references to God as though he were a character rather than the creator of all things, upon the poet's disregard of Christ's "Eucharistic strategy for redeeming the time," upon the lack in Milton of a sense of sin, of self-depreciation, and of the significance of sacraments.

Milton's strength lies in his grasp of the unity of all things and the primacy, in a God-sustained universe, of individual responsibility and inner rectitude. He may have emphasized the restrictive virtues, but he did conceive of man's will linked with God's will in moral dynamism. He may have lacked sympathy and even charity but he had the recipe for abolishing fear. If he had small sense of sinfulness, he had an intense feeling for regeneration.

He may be viewed historically as a unique soul, associated with Independents, within the larger ring of Puritanism, itself concentrically enclosed by Protestantism and by Christianity. From beginning to end his simple reliance upon God's will is abundantly evident. His eagerness in *Ad Patrem* to satisfy his father is in this context of interest to the psychologist. From his real and immediate apprehension of God's will arises the distinguishing quality of his greatest works. He is constrained to treat God as a directly acting Absolute accessible in some sense to reason. Priests, sacraments, and mysticism he passes by. In *Paradise Lost*, Satan must be given some kind of comparable status as a combatant to God, and to the reader's embarrassment God must explain his own actions. In *Paradise Regained* we should not be surprised at the Son of God's rejection of Athens, but rather at

2. M. M. Ross, *Poetry and Dogma*, 219.

Milton's ability to avoid an outright condemnation of humanism. In *Samson*, the explicit nature of God's dealings with the hero and the demonstration that he is indeed "favouring and assisting to the end" make impossible the normal effect of tragedy, either Greek or Elizabethan. Milton's view of God of its own accord makes his major works expand toward breaking the bounds of their recognized forms.

Milton's highly personal variety of Puritanism was uniquely suitable —among all the varieties of Protestantism in seventeenth-century England that readily identify themselves—to mount the Baroque chariot and ride in splendour. If naturalism, allegory, grandiose dignity, severe tensions, Counter-Reformation doctrine, and courtly life are found to be marks of Italian Baroque, Milton is not behind in producing their transposed equivalents. His belief in reason and in the goodness of matter, his play with symbolic actions on the part of ideal characters, his reliance upon a supernal will in which ideological tensions may be contained, the rolling splendour of his scenes in *Paradise Lost*, of the vision of God's greatness and of the very verse itself—all these combine to form and foster the grand style.

Ross's analysis of Milton has the special value of helping us to identify English Protestant Baroque. In this region the struggle to achieve unity is a sharp one, the necessary adjustments all the more amazing, the techniques of composition those of a virtuoso. The resistance at every level is great and the art-forms which eventuate are, as we might expect, less freely flowing and emotionally expansive if no less impressive than those of Bernini.

Before leaving the question of Milton's Puritanism and its relation to Baroque, we might look briefly at still another index of his sensibility, the summary one of his educational ideal.

All ideal schemes of education are immensely revealing. They permit and indeed encourage the writer to reveal his mind, for his ideal scholar cannot fail to be a projection of his ideal self. They oblige him to imply, if not to state, his views of man, the world, and human destiny. We may therefore look into Milton's little tractate on education, written at the request of Hartlib, with confidence that Milton will reveal the fundamentals of his own thinking.

The first thing that strikes the modern reader is the totally self-contained design of Milton's academy. It is not part of a system of education. It offers education absolute. The boys come in at about the age of twelve, having presumably learned their letters at home, and remain until the age of twenty-one when all but the few who intend to be physicians or lawyers are ready to go out into the world. It is "under the government of one, who shall be thought of desert sufficent, and ability either to do all or wisely to direct and oversee it done."

The object of Milton's scheme of education is eqally unitary. It is to lead the student to know God. And if it is asked how history and literature lead us to God, Milton's answer is ready: "Our understanding cannot in this body found itself but on sensible things, nor arrive so clearly to the knowledge of God and things invisible as by orderly conning over the visible and inferior creature [i.e., creation]." The habitual movement of Milton's mind begins to proclaim itself at this very outset of his discourse. Under his direction, familiar ideas realign themselves to achieve a new emphasis. The ideal of courtly education, supremely realized in Castiglione, reappears in Milton but the ruler to be served is God. The interest in languages displayed by Cheke and Lily continues undiminished into Milton's pages but only, and he labours the point, only because language is "the instrument conveying to us things useful to be known." Yet nothing, as we shall see in a moment, can be farther from Milton's mind than utilitarianism.

The boys, then, are to learn to know God and serve his purposes. In the practical realization of this ideal a powerful concept of nationalism is introduced. A reform of education, "for want whereof this nation perishes," is, quite seriously, an "opportunity to try what God hath determined." If the years of our adolescence are to be spent in learning and using foreign languages, we must adopt the pedagogical method "whereby we may best hope to give account to God of our youth spent herein." What in practice may be expected of the graduates of Milton's academy? The incidental remark that by getting some knowledge of physic any one of them may "save an army" suggests the answer. First, last, and always, public service. The study of history and politics is to serve this end, "that they may not in a dangerous fit of the commonwealth be such poor, shaken, uncertain reeds as many of our great counsellors have lately shown themselves, but steadfast pillars of the state." Some are to be literally statesmen: "whether they be to speak in parliament or council, honour and attention would be waiting on their lips." Others are to fill the pulpits.

But their education must be "equally good both for peace and war." They are to be military captains, with some knowledge too of fortification, navigation, and fighting at sea.

Milton's intense desire for comprehensive and organic wholeness is nowhere better illustrated. The one object of his scholars must be to serve God in a godly commonwealth and each of them must be capable of fulfilling all the functions that education fits men for. In Milton's day it was perhaps just still possible to conceive of a man fit to undertake all the offices of peace and war.

The comprehensiveness of Milton's curriculum is incredible. There are no survey courses. Every subject is mastered and the list of authors to be studied would seem ludicrous if we did not know that Milton himself had absorbed them. Even so, the familiar incongruities attending too resolute an attempt at all inclusiveness show their heads. "Sundays also and every evening may be now understandingly spent in the highest matters of theology and church history ancient and modern; and ere this time the Hebrew tongue at a set hour might have been gained, that the scriptures may be now read in their own original; whereto it would be no impossibility to add the Chaldee and the Syrian dialect." This and the vision of Milton's hopeful scholars listening to music of organ or symphony while "unsweating themselves" strain our credulity. Milton, in fact, seems to be putting forth a programme for the young idealist similar to that which brought disaster to young John Stuart Mill.

Clearly some extraordinary incentive is needed to carry the boys through this tremendous course, "which fits a man to perform justly, skilfully, and magnanimously all the offices, both private and public, of peace and war." And what this incitement of the will is Milton reveals almost casually, as something the reader will of his own accord know. The scholars are pictured as "stirred up with high hopes of living to be brave men and worthy patriots, dear to God and famous to all ages." This will "gain them to an incredible diligence and courage, infusing into their young breasts such an ingenuous and noble ardour, as would not fail to make many of them renowned and matchless men." Dear to God and famous to all ages: with what naturalness it comes from the pen that wrote *Lycidas*. The fusion of absolute faith in another world and desire for fame in this world is perfectly, and without hint of facility or evasion, achieved.

But if the will of Milton's scholars is to be formed under this heat and pressure into more than a match for the enemies of England, the true bearing of Milton's aim is at a still higher level. His conclusion is an overwhelming resolution of the contradictions implicit in his scheme. As the great curriculum has unfurled itself, the reader must become aware of its practical impossibility. And Milton, with one side of his mind, is aware of this too: "I believe that this is not a bow for every man to shoot in that counts himself a teacher, but will require sinews almost equal to those which Homer gave Ulysses." But all practical difficulties are swept away in the torrent of divine power to which here as everywhere Milton makes his final appeal. The stream of human endeavour need only turn itself into the cosmic channel; "not more difficult than I imagine, and that imagination presents me with nothing but very happy and very possible according to best wishes; if God have so decreed, and this age have spirit and capacity enough to apprehend."

There are worse interpretations of Milton than the old statement of Coleridge in his *Literary Remains*: "He was, as every truly great poet has ever been, a good man; but finding it impossible to realize his own aspirations, either in religion, or politics, or society, he gave up his heart to the living spirit and light within him, and avenged himself on the world by enriching it with this record of his own transcendent ideal."

It is hoped that the reader will not find this long excursus into English Puritanism too tedious a detour in our path toward Roman Baroque. It will at least have preserved us from the easy and false assumption that Milton, who knew and loved Italy both through books and at first hand, merely assumed some Italian elements of style when he came to write his great poems. "By what buildings in Rome was Milton influenced?" is only the most naive form of a question often asked. It is necessary to insist that, remaining all the while as English as Shakespeare or Wordsworth, Milton by mighty acts of transposition and reconstitution was able to do for his own country what the choicest wits of Italy had done for theirs. The high tide of English Puritanism taken at the flood carried Milton's art over insular sandbars to the fruitful coasts of European High Baroque.

ii. *PARADISE LOST* AND ROMAN BAROQUE

GIANLORENZO BERNINI (1598–1680) has been called the Michelangelo of the Seicento. To juxtapose *Paradise Lost* directly with his architecture is to compare great things with great and to gain by this immediacy what might be lost by more conventional approaches. Bernini, expressing the triumph of ecclesia and curia, achieves the major statement made by Catholicism in the Baroque manner. Milton, proclaiming the triumph of the will of God and of the individual soul devoting itself to God, creates for Puritanism a corresponding supreme statement. It is tempting to regard the two men as united only by the art-form they chose to employ and differing in both the essentials and the particulars of their respective beliefs. But on the contrary they were both fervent Christians, living eight hundred miles apart in a Europe more conscious of its common heritage than now, with only some twenty years separating their dates of birth. Many elements of their artistic practice run parallel. Both begin with Mannerist techniques. Both go on to large-scale organization of traditional or given materials to produce a new and startling effect of unity and power. Both show the typical movement of the creative mind found in a Baroque milieu, the combination of strict obedience and vast independence. That Bernini was a fervent post-Tridentine Catholic, a friend of Jesuits, and a protégé of popes need not inhibit us now from comparing him with the greatest of English Puritans. The power of God Milton is concerned with is absolute and arbitrary ("I am that I am"). Yet it is legitimate because God is the creator and his creation is an act of will. This arbitrary but reasonable possession of power is justified, largely by a rough and ready reasoning in the smooth garb of rhetoric. The justification proceeds without recourse either to mysticism or to sacraments or to ecclesiastical authority. Bernini, although deeply committed to all three of these, does work by reason and rhetoric to display the arbitrary, absolute, divinely bestowed, irrefragable power of the Church, which from the point of view of Catholicism is the same power, but delegated to the vicar of Christ. These general resemblances induce a great many incidental points of resemblance. (It is fascinating to find Milton and Bernini sharing with Mr. Dick a concern with King Charles's head.)

St. Peter's, as Bernini left it, like *Paradise Lost* issuing from Milton's mind, is a fresh organization of already existing and disparate materials, by additions and manipulations of the most skilful kind, into a totality of impressive grandeur and unity expressing ultimate authority. This is achieved in the face of great difficulties, such as the pre-relation by tradition of formal and ideological elements; it is in part effected by the consistent impress of a high style, personal and persuasive to the least degree.

We may at this point remind ourselves of the obvious fact that both Milton and Bernini worked with sets of structures they were obliged to accept. Religious art is always difficult and for artists with so exalted a sense of vocation as Bernini and Milton there was, in their handling of sacred subject, very little leeway, so to speak. They could only press on toward their supreme concepts as matters of "highest hope and hardest attempting."

A problem of the greatest interest, which Bernini successfully solved, presents itself as one approaches St. Peter's. It is the formation of the piazza. This had to hold as vast a crowd of the faithful as possible, to suggest by its form that they were not merely assembled but embraced by the arms of the church and to make it possible for them all to be conscious of receiving, from the pope standing high up in the façade of St. Peter's, the blessing bestowed *urbi et orbi*. Bernini's solution, in the form of enormous columns set in two quadruple colonnades and graduated in size for the correct optical effect, crowned by an entablature crowded with figures of saints and martyrs, is too well known to need description. In addition to the function of ritual unification just mentioned, the colonnades unify the approach to St. Peter's by refusing (because not arranged in arcades) the suggestion that they are themselves a palatial entrance, and, furthermore, by presenting an extremely massive and relatively low structure they make the façade of Maderna, which is by itself too wide for its height, appear more lofty. To stand well back in the piazza and look first at the separate elements surrounding it, then at the whole, is to realize the sheer magic of Bernini's performance. (It might be added as a matter of interest that Maderna was hardly to blame for the proportions of his façade. By the Pope's orders his original finished front was extended in width by the addition of a tower at each end; yet, because the death of Paul V caused these to be abandoned as substructures, the necessary flanking effect was never achieved. Bernini later attempted to add similar towers but by unhappy experiment it transpired that the foundations were inadequate for the weight.)

A final effect of unification which Bernini had in mind for his piazza but which circumstances did not allow him to complete was the addition of a third colonnade, constructed like the two existing ones but designed to run across the open end of the oval, some distance back from the point where the ends of the two main colonnades face one another. Had this scheme not been brought to naught by the death of Alexander VII in 1667, it would now be possible to experience what Bernini intended—a view, from the forecourt or ante-piazza thus created, of the whole piazza and façade at one *coup d'œil*. The spectator would be at the same moment himself within the complex and part of it, yet empowered to view it as a totality from his point of vantage. (In exact contradiction to Bernini's intention, a wide roadway has been cut which permits the approaching spectator to see the space between the colonnades presenting an awkward opening, whereas Bernini intended that the pilgrim approaching, having first seen the splendour of the dome as he crossed the river by the Ponte S. Angelo, should move through narrow streets, and then successively into the forecourt, the vast piazza and the great nave of St. Peter's.)

Milton employs the same device of taking us into the plot suddenly and in such a way as to make it our own story, yet allowing us to see the whole which is to be unfolded.

Of Man's First Disobedience, and the Fruit
Of that Forbidden Tree, whose mortal taste
Brought Death into the World, and all our woe,
With loss of Eden, till one greater Man
Restore us, and regain the blissful Seat,
Sing Heav'nly Muse. . . .

Bernini's concern is with concepts of unity and power in his handling of the whole complex of forms in and about St. Peter's. Wittkower's analysis of Bernini's achievement evokes both the intentions of the artist and the response which an ideal pilgrim to Rome might make, in a passage where criticism of its own impulse becomes lyrical. From this passage we must abstract the main argument as having a direct bearing on the similarity of Bernini and Milton.[1]

After half a century of work in and around St. Peter's, Bernini completed a complex of old and new architectural units which expressed the totality of effect he had from the beginning desired. Nowhere else shall we find the spirit of the Counter-Reformation and the formal requirements of Baroque so completely unified and fully expressed.

From the time that he crosses the Ponte S. Angelo, between two rows of angels bearing the insignia of Christ's crucifixion, the pilgrim is drawn steadily on toward a designed climax of spiritual and emotional experience. Crossing the bridge, he has seen the domes of the cathedral against the sky and, moving toward them, he is plunged into an area of small and narrow streets. From these he emerges into the piazza and then, mounting the steps, looks down the enormous nave of the cathedral itself to Bernini's Baldacchino. From a distance, its four gigantic bronze columns appear to frame the Cathedra. Upon nearer approach, they are seen to be covered with a profusion of sculptural elements emblematic of ecclesiastical triumph and papal splendour.

Reaching, at last, the Cathedra itself, the pilgrim is at the end and apotheosis of his journey. Flanked by four of the greatest of the Fathers, who supported the claims of Rome—Augustine, Ambrose, Athanasius, and Chrysostom—the chair high above the ground is absolutely central and dominant. Above it are the tiara and the keys

---

1. R. Wittkower, *Gianlorenzo Bernini*, 19ff.

and above these again the image of a dove descending in stained glass with a blaze of glory.

Bernini's mastery of his media is absolute. "Despite the multitude of impressions any of these works may evoke," says Wittkower, "he achieves the total subordination of architecture, sculpture and decoration to an overriding spiritual conception."

Bernini, like Milton, was both able and willing to bend old conventions to the service of new effects. The traditional view down the nave to the altar, which in a mediaeval church was an alignment of worship, a direction and guide toward the mystery of redemptive incarnation, becomes under Bernini's handling a device for demonstrating a glorification of power and submission.

In seeking to unify the complex of St. Peter's, Bernini had as many technical problems as Milton in unifying *Paradise Lost* and for the same reasons. Like Milton, he was accepting a traditional Christian structure of ideas embodied in forms, and treating it, perforce yet willingly, as an unchangeable absolute. This fundamental form had been shaped, century by century, into a system which reached Milton initially as the doctrine of the Anglican Church, and came to Bernini as a cathedral which Michelangelo and Maderna had designed. Milton drove a single axis through received Christian doctrine so as to reveal all its components in a relationship with God's will, which, if submitted to by the individual believer, becomes his will too. Bernini created one axis down which the pilgrim of reverend and submissive mind could move, from the moment when he stepped out of the crowded streets of ordinary life into the piazza (ideally, into the ante-piazza) until he stood before the Cathedra behind which the Dove was descending upon this symbol of ecclesiastical authority with which his own will might now be at one.

The irony of these two great successes need not be suppressed. Most readers of *Paradise Lost* are sooner or later rendered uneasy, either for aesthetic or for doctrinal reasons, because Milton is treating God as a character. The real decisions seem to be Milton's own. And few who visit St. Peter's with open eyes, passing through the great galaxy of attestations to papal power, can fail to feel uneasy. The obelisk in the piazza may proclaim "Christus vincit, Christus regnat, Christus imperat, Christus ab omni malo plebem suam defendat."

But the dominant impression is of papal rather than divine supremacy. Coming away from St. Peter's one has a strong desire, at once and as a corrective, to visit Chartres or Beauvais.

If the omnipotence inherent in "the ways of God" is Milton's theme and if the delegated power which makes true of the Church "securus judicat orbis terrarum" is Bernini's, then to each there is a necessary correlative of obedience. Power, like nature, abhors a vacuum and must have the means of exercising itself. In Bernini's world the martyr is a leading figure. St. Peter was himself martyred. The mark of the martyr is a passionate willingness to suffer even as Christ suffered, a longing to be found worthy so to suffer. Counter-Reformation inconography laid emphasis on the glory of martyrdom and on martyrs as exemplars of heroism.

Bernini's profuse and penetrating use of the conventions of martyrdom Milton parallels in a fashion all his own and with consistent differences of treatment. Whereas Bernini follows Ripa, Milton shows no interest in the decorative, diverse iconography of Catholicism. He simplifies, unifies, energizes.

We might pause to notice the inherent difficulty in dealing with martyrs in a context of the heroic. Since they refuse to retaliate, martyrs exhibit a kind of immobility unsuitable for drama; they fight in their own way for the right, but not for their own rights, and for them death is all victory. In the eighth chapter of his commentary on Aristotle's *Poetics*, Butcher has interesting things to say about this problem:

Blameless goodness has seldom the quality needed to make it dramatically interesting. It wants the motive power which leads to decisive acts of will, which impels others to action and produces a collision of forces.... In refusing to strike back it brings the action to a standstill. Even where it has no lack of strong initiative, its impersonal ardour in the cause of right has not the same dramatic fascination as the spectacle of human weakness or passion doing battle with the fate it has brought upon itself.

Differences between Catholic and Protestant concepts of martyrdom were sharp and led to open controversy on matters of principle. In chapter iii of his monumental work on the art of the Counter-Reformation, Mâle demonstrates how changes in iconography were induced as a deliberate answer to Protestant denigration of saints and martyrs. In Milton there is early visible an emphatic dislike for the deliberately shocking presentation of the agonies of those done cruelly to death. Over such matters he himself is content to pass quickly as he views the martyrs of history (XII, 493–5),

> not afraid,
> Though to the death, against such cruelties
> With inward consolations recompens't.

His emphasis is all on something else, summarized by Zephon in his defiance of Satan (IV, 854–6):

> Thy fear, said Zephon bold,
> Will save us trial what the least can do
> Single against thee wicked, and thence weak.

This attitude seems to be inherent in Milton's temperament and early training. At the age of eighteen, in the fourth Elegy, he sounds a note which will resound later in his mature works.

> Sis etenim quamvis fulgentibus obsitus armis,
>   Intententque tibi millia tela necem,
> At nullis vel inerme latus violabitur armis,
>   Deque tuo cuspis nulla cruore bibet.
> Namque eris ipse Dei radiante sub aegide tutus;
>   Ille tibi custos, et pugil ille tibi.

Milton has a passion for "heroic fortitude" to martyrdom, but neither he nor the heroes he presents us with have any intention of being martyred. They are all in the mood of the sonnet "when an assault was intended on the city." They expect their superior virtue to protect them from harm. The Lady, Abdiel, Ithuriel and Zephon, the Son of God in *Paradise Regained*, and Samson (given the initial situation, his captivity): it is always the same story; no one lays a finger on them. They seem neither anxious for martyrdom nor to anticipate its possibility. They all show great moral courage in the asseveration of the truth and their show of steadfastness repels Comus, Satan, Harapha, alike. Such was Milton's own experience when warned in Italy of plots against him. With the Jesuit concept of martyrdom, with the ideology which saw in Charles "a Glorious King or a Patient Martyr," Milton has nothing to do. Nor does he appear, like Puritans of an earlier generation, to have been imbued with the

spirit of Foxe's *Acts and Monuments,* which in 1571 had been
ordered to be placed in every church. The Miltonic view is summed
up in the well-known lines,

> Servant of God, well done, well hast thou fought
> The better fight, who single hast maintain'd
> Against revolted multitudes the Cause
> Of Truth, in word mightier than they in Arms;
> And for the testimony of Truth hast borne
> Universal reproach, far worse to bear
> Than violence. . . .

(It is doubtful whether in practice it is really harder to bear vilification
than, say, being torn to pieces.)

Bernini's practice has distinct affinities to Milton's. While a few
of his earlier sculptures represent the actual experience of the pains
of martyrdom—"St. Lawrence on the Grill" (about 1617), "St. Sebas-
tian" (about 1617–18)—the great bulk of his more mature work has
for its subjects figures whose vigour and energetic attitudes put them
at a remove from the tradition of the martyr being done to death. As
we have already seen, there is an inherent discrepancy between the
martyr utterly resigned to the will of heaven and meekly submitting
to death and the martyr as an heroic figure filled with spiritual
energy. Doctrinally the two concepts are easily reconciled and perhaps
they are psychologically compatible but it is very difficult to produce
an iconographical type in which the two elements are simultaneously
expressed. As one would expect in a High Baroque context, both
Milton and Bernini produce images of vigorous affirmation.

Sometimes, however, Bernini effects a union of elements quite
outside Milton's range. If we consider the Cornaro Chapel (where
Bernini achieved an effect of limitlessness in a shallow false transept
less than seven and a half metres in width) we find much that is well
within Milton's customary scope. We see a virgin saint devoted to
the heavenly Bridegroom; an angel sent to assure this soul of the
love of God; other characters on a lower plane of the action who are
more like ourselves and bridge the distance; a sense of momentary
vision into heaven and the divine purposes. All this is clearly in
Comus. But Bernini includes other experiences outside the scope of
Milton's sensibility—a mystical experience of union with the heavenly
Bridegroom in which the sexual symbolism is barely concealed and the

representation of orgasm scarcely avoided. Milton, as we have seen, worked in quite another way. He could express union between the human and the divine will—for example, in Samson—by formal devices as startling as anything Bernini could achieve. But his emphasis on this identity of wills precluded, as we have shown, the exploration of other sides of the relation between man and God.

Milton was not happy with representations of conventional martyrs, and given the *réclame* which Catholic martyrs, trained at Douai, at Rheims, and finally at the English College in Rome, had received, it is difficult to see how he could have employed the conventional concepts in a Protestant context. He chose his own methods of reasserting the familiar elements. Abdiel, his own creation as an iconographic figure, may be interpreted as a combination of the familiar martyr— willing to suffer all for the faith—with the traditional accompanying angel, confident, invulnerable, holding the palm, pointing to the heavenly reward. In many paintings these appear, demonstrating how earth and heaven may be united. In Abdiel, so like ourselves in his peril, his potency to resist, and his reward, the same unity is shown.

We might remind ourselves, too, that just as Milton produces, within the recognizable intentions of Baroque style, a type of martyrdom and heroic fortitude based on will, so his variant of mysticism retains both Baroque features and a personal predilection. The conventional mystic reaches God by the route of intuition aided by revelation. The Counter-Reformation had its ecstatics: Loyola, Philip of Neri, Teresa, John of the Cross. And its artists delighted in representing the ecstasies of traditional saints like Francis of Assisi and Catherine of Sienna, and of biblical characters such as Mary Magdalene and Paul. Milton, we have suggested, worked within a Puritan range of sensibility, in which the will predominated. It would be impossible, however, to regard Milton as an exponent of High Baroque if some version of mysticism, transposed or redefined, were not among his dominant ideas. And he does indeed possess a kind of personal equivalent for the mystical rapture of Mediterranean saints. It is the ecstasy adumbrated (and no more) in the Lady:

> Yet should I try, the uncontrolled worth
> Of this pure cause would kindle my rapt spirits
> To such a flame of sacred vehemence. . . .

This is the active side, which when expressed in gentleness and music awakens even in Comus a "sober certainty of waking bliss." It springs from will. But, even so, when its full note is sounded later on it is a by no means contemptible substitute for intuitive revelation:

> So much the rather thou Celestial Light
> Shine inward, and the mind through all her powers
> Irradiate. . . .

Where Milton's doctrinal or national concepts do not inhibit him from particular practices it is surprising how close he and Bernini may come in the handling of a problem. The moment of change was a favourite Baroque theme. Bernini, as we have noticed, represents Anchises and Proserpine at the instant of their being carried off, Daphne as the bark folds round her body and her fingers put forth leaves. The action looks both ways and we know from the extreme and subtle expressiveness of Bernini's modelling (the anxious old eyes of Anchises, the gripping fingers of Pluto upon Proserpine) both what the subjects have been and what they will be. Milton similarly, and unlike Dante or Spenser, gives us the moment of change—in Satan the moment when the realization of hell bursts upon him, not less than archangel fallen; in Eve when we have been thoroughly prepared to see the moment of eating the fruit as an index pointing to past and future. Furthermore, Milton's interest in this device extends widely into his delineation of places. Heaven we see as a great expulsion takes place. Hell, as a capital city is founded. Earth, as sin sweeps over its perfections. Chaos, as it is cut back and pierced by a causeway. As all these may be taken not only as scenes in the epic but also as psychological states, this reference is perhaps not out of place. It may be pleaded, in support of referring to Baroque structures as though they were organisms, that they appear organic to their devotees. A Baroque building looks alive, in comparison with the business block on the opposite corner, because its weight-bearing members are emphasized, compressed spaces on the façade appear to expand upward, recessed areas suggest vital movement, centralizing escutcheons, finials, and so on trace the path of vectors of power.

It has been advanced as a criterion of Baroque art that it freely employs allegory. Milton's use of allegory is not only severely restricted but in *Paradise Lost* is carefully contained, as we have seen, so as not to mingle with the progress of the grand argument. This apparent contradiction disappears, however, if we consider the use by both Milton and Bernini of a group of conventions wider than the simple employment of allegory but all concerned to present figures or characters with explicit and typical moral content.

Bernini sometimes produced a figure in which the allegorical element is without doubt predominant. His sculptural representation of Truth, it has been shown by Mâle, was taken directly from the pages of Ripa's *Iconologia.* The nude figure holds in her hand a sun with rays and rests her foot on a terrestrial globe. Yet, as one might expect from Bernini, the intention goes beyond the simple allegory intended by Ripa, who explains that Truth is represented nude because her very nature is simplicity, she hold the sun to show that she loves the light and is herself light, the globe is beneath her feet to show that she is worth more than the things of this world. Bernini's intention was to incorporate this figure of Truth into a monumental structure illustrating the unveiling of Truth by Time. Ripa's purely conventional strip of drapery is developed by Bernini into a large and dramatically flowing veil in process of being removed from above. Truth looks ecstatically up toward her deliverer, offering her rayed disk to him. We know also that the whole structure was intended by Bernini to express his personal feelings after he had suffered a professional disaster and been subjected to personal vilification. This intention remained with him although the whole complex was never completed; he recorded in his will that the piece should descend as an inalienable legacy in his family to testify to the value he placed upon Truth. In this employment of an allegorical concept Bernini has changed drapery, gesture, and facial expression to integrate the figure into a larger whole of profound religious significance. And this significance has a peculiar urgency and poignancy because of his personal feelings, deeply disguised as these may be by the convention selected to express them. Finally, the figure represents a crucial moment of change, from one stable state to another, like the moments of change Bernini had already represented in the figures of Daphne and Proserpine.

If we may next consider Bernini's representations of Louis XIV, we may see how he handled other formal types. The portrait-bust of Louis is "probably the grandest piece of portraiture of the Baroque age";[2] this is Wittkower's phrase and it opens a masterly analysis of Bernini's procedure in this instance. The artist accumulated sketches of the King, taken from life, in the tennis-court or at meetings of the cabinet. He made version after version of a small clay model, seeking to convey his concept of royal grandeur, heroism, and majesty by the general configuration, including that of the drapery. When he combined these two concepts, that of realism and that of ideal form, he introduced a third influence, the face of Alexander as represented on Greek coins. Yet the ideal elements were not allowed simply to absorb the realistic first-hand impression of the King. Toward the end of his task Louis sat for the artist many times to allow the detail of his features to be recorded. By hollowing parts of the forehead, chiselling the eyeballs, and forming the lips in a speaking position, Bernini suggested both colour and movement. This struggle to incorporate into a new whole the components supplied by a variety of sources is completely and characteristically Baroque. There was also to be an allegorical meaning expressed by the pedestal in the form of a globe with a cryptic inscription suggesting that even this was too small for the exercise of so much heroism, the display of so much glory. In his portrait-bust Bernini has worked, so to speak, in the opposite direction from his adaptation of Truth, where he submitted allegory to the demands of realism. In the King's portrait he begins by accepting, and never to the end denies, the requirement of realism, yet all the while is imposing traditional ideal forms and ideas and finally an allegorical conceit.

The lost bust of Charles I showed much the same approach on Bernini's part. He had only the Van Dyck triple portrait to work on but he modified the outlines to depict an heroic sovereign, dominant and Italianate.

The equestrian statue of Louis (which the King disliked and which was ultimately disguised so as to persuade the onlooker that it represented Marcus Curtius) also bears testimony to the consistency of Bernini's artistic intentions. He employed a stance for the horse which can be traced back to Leonardo. The figure of the King expressed supreme regal dominance. And, once more, the combination of realism, formal traditions, and concepts of magnificence is made to serve an allegorical function. At the summit of a rock Louis was to suggest

2. R. Wittkower, *Bernini's Bust of Louis XIV*.

Hercules at the peak of the attainment of power and splendour. Even in its present transmogrified condition it presents, to the visitor who walks the length of the Pièce des Suisses to the remote point where Louis banished it, an aspect of controlled energy and magnificence which renders the rest of the garden statuary insipid by comparison.

It may be postulated with reasonable confidence that Bernini habitually moved across the limits which had defined the conventions he employed and that with immense effort and technical skill he created a new type of expressive statuary in which realism, allegory, and, above all, concepts of majestic power and heroic devotion were totally combined.

Several features of Bernini's sculpture conduce to the similarity of effect they produce, their air of being all members of one family. There is no attempt to produce a separate plane of allegory; on the contrary the allegorical figures can, so to speak, mix freely with the others. So much so that we may not be sure a face we are looking at is allegorical or not. The features of Bernini's "Anima Beata" and "Anima Damnata" are so extremely life-like as to suggest portraits, yet so devoted to the embodiment of a theological conception that they might be called by abstract names such as Expectation or Despair.

Bernini's realism is twofold. States of mind and emotions are realistically conveyed by dramatic attitudes realistically rendered. In the statue of Constantine, which serves to remind the visitor entering the Vatican of the glory brought to the Church by his conversion, the Emperor, whose steed is rearing in terror, gazes in reverend amazement at the vision in the sky. An enormous wind-blown drapery behind him accentuates the effect. Bernini took pains to give the statue features which traditionally were Constantine's. The psychological moment is caught between Constantine pagan and Constantine Christian. That the horse, rearing in alarm, palpably cannot see the vision emphasizes the inward effect upon the emperor.

Bernini's realism is related to the extreme expressiveness of High Baroque and to a combination of complexity and clarity which is not always understood. He endeavours to express as many facets of his subject as possible and therefore loads his forms with significance. At the same time he intends that the significances, however complex, shall invite logical understanding. Whatever he intends must be, in the end, rationally clear.

We have already seen that Milton's use of allegory is highly selective and that he refrains from intruding allegorical figures into the main highway of the narrative. Like Bernini, he avoids the establishment of a separate allegorical plane. The careful reader of *Paradise Lost* will notice that Sin and Death are Satan's daughter and Satan's son by incest. Now the reader is expected to believe in the literal reality of Satan without any doubt, for even if it were conceded that the story of Eden might take on some qualities of myth, there remains the Satan of *Paradise Regained* who, as tempter of the Son of God, must by the seventeenth-century reader be literally accepted. It follows that the allegorical figures are given a semblance of actuality and this is strengthened by their meeting Satan at the gates of hell in the most dramatically realistic fashion. We cannot regard as pure allegory a Death who is using his traditional dart to threaten Satan in whose mission we have become ourselves emotionally involved and who is literally the tempter of our first parents. This degree of realism acquired by Sin and Death is carefully limited. They are permitted before our eyes to fashion the incongruous causeway in Chaos but as soon as their activities, in the tenth book, bring them into the region of our own heavens, the thread of the narrative turns abruptly, leading to a realistic, almost mathematical account of celestial mechanics. Sin and Death quietly disappear.

As Milton's allegories are mingled with realism, so his real actors are given an element of allegory. He would be a naive reader of Genesis who supposed that the sin of Adam and Eve was simply the eating of a forbidden fruit. Milton is scrupulously careful, as for every reason, doctrinal and aesthetic, he must be, to treat the event as literally true. Nevertheless the allegorical possibilities stand thickly in the wings ready to come on at the slightest invitation and when in the end we reach the paradox of the fortunate fall and the realization of a Paradise within, happier far, the figurative nature of this second Paradise induces us to think less literally of the first. If this is true of the garden and the human pair, it is even more easily believable of the archangels, of whom Raphael is dealt with in the greatest detail. Milton's handling of Raphael is a triumph of unobtrusive fusion; he is realistically rendered, eating with Adam and Eve, confessing that heaven is much like earth, yet in his momentary appearance with six wings as an angel of prophetic vision, in his participation in the war in heaven still closer to allegorical action, and in his quite extra-canonical name and manner he is a fit figure for some charming allegory of divinely approved knowledge. In a similar way the single-heartedness of Abdiel or the courage of Ithuriel and Zephon have both realistic and exemplary elements, the latter of which give them a link with allegorical method.

It is reasonable to interpret all these devices which merge one tradition into another as efforts to achieve unity. Instead of creating a plane of allegory within his epic or making his complete work an allegory on a plane separate from the reader, he gives to all his characters without exception explicit moral significance, so explicit that it relates to a formal scheme of doctrine and is intended to lead towards virtue. But the reader, instead of standing back to regard an allegory, is closely involved. When, for example, Raphael—with whom the reader has probably had no previous literary contact—descends into Eden, he stands there like Maia's son (and Mercury was a figure every school-boy did know); he is on familiar terms with Adam our progenitor, yet a few minutes before he had been receiving his orders directly from God the Father. The enormous competence of Milton's style conceals the audacity of this transition. It is assisted by the poet's employment of unmistakably allegorical figures (such as Chance or Chaos) only sparingly and at a distance from Eden.

We might at this point summarize, all too baldly, some of the ideas developed in the last few pages.

The essential fact about a martyr is that he belongs to both worlds and is engaged in uniting them. He is a witness on earth of heaven's message; he testifies to earth's cruelties under the direct eye of God and the immediate presence of angels. He is about to leave a body on earth and enter heaven as a spirit but these will at the last judgement be united. His witness and his voluntary sufferings are in every sense dynamic. At the moment of his change, his putting on of immortality, there is a great release of spiritual energy. Milton's substitute for martyrdom is prompt, fearless witness to God's truth.

The mystic also unites both worlds but in a private rather than public manner. His path is that of intuition, seen from beneath, or revelation, seen from above. His moment of vision or of ecstasy is equally a uniting of heaven and earth. Milton's substitute for mystical vision is dedication and the belief that his offer of himself and all his powers is acceptable to God, that the Spirit of God will dictate the very substance of his great work.

Allegory unites this world and the world of eternal truths by presenting figures derived from the life about us, with familiar things as their accessories, and persuading us that they are the embodiments of eternal values and the objects in their hands emblems of truth. Both Milton and Bernini achieve effects of allegory but generally either inextricably involved with other elements or else transposed into exemplary contexts. They are most reluctant to let allegory develop a plane of its own.

Another architect of the period worthy to be considered beside Bernini is Francesco Borromini (1599–1667). One of his churches, S. Carlo alle Quattro Fontane, has been characterized as among "the incunabula of Roman High Baroque." It exhibits a dynamic and successful effort to unify three kinds of architectural tradition.

Bernini, as we have seen, desired to embody *concetti* in his sculpture or architecture and in this way provides a bridge to the verbal arts. Among his surviving sketches are several which demonstrate that the circular piazza before St. Peter's was intended to represent the world at large. A figure within a plan of the piazza has its four extended limbs labelled "Europa, America, Affrica, Asia." Another sketch shows the curving colonnades as the embracing arms of what is probably the figure of Christ. Still another suggests the church and the circular piazza as a cross surmounting an orb.[3] But we must face the fact that these verbal and diagrammatic proofs of Bernini's preoccupation with unity and totality are fortunate accidents. It is not to be expected of architects that they will furnish statements of their intentions except as these are already stated in architectural language. In briefly considering Borromini's Church of S. Carlo alle Quattro Fontane, we may hope to find the architectural statement sufficiently clear in its own right.

It follows that between Bernini and Milton there are often explicit parallels in the realm of ideas but that between Borromini and Milton the parallels are chiefly formal. This may seem to present a difficulty but as Wölfflin has observed, "Anyone who concerns himself exclusively with the subject-matter of works of art will be completely

3. R. Norton, *Bernini and Other Studies in the History of Art*, 287.

satisfied with it; yet the moment we want to apply artistic standards of judgment in the criticism of works of art we are forced to try to comprehend formal elements which are unmeaning and inexpressible in themselves."[4] When the artist has gone through the looking-glass into the world of representation, from there he may like Alice go through a door into regions which obey their own law and seek their own line of development, though still in some intricate way related to the actualities of his starting place. The critic would do well to follow him and not remain on the mantlepiece from which only the simple reflection of ideas can be seen. Milton and Borromini resemble one another less in doctrine than in the effects they produce with given conventions, their sensitiveness to the texture of materials, their exquisite care in detail and design, their mixture of craftsmanship and the afflatus which projects the lofty dome or rhyme. The ninth edition of the *Encyclopædia Britannica* says of Borromini, "In his style he affected originality and richness, which corrupted the noble simplicity of the older schools, though his compositions are occasionally imposing," which means, in modern terms, that Borromini took the conventions of Renaissance architecture and recombined them to produce Baroque structures.

The architecture of sacred edifices is a difficult subject. They are characteristically not utilitarian and questions of function are not the only ones. Even the simplest arrangements—a circle of chairs in a bare wooden room round a table with a loaf and a cup of wine—may have significances which vibrate through eternity. Certain extremely ancient associations are likely to be present in the design of almost any Christian church. The enclosure itself is magical or sacred. It may be in the literal sense of the word oriented about an axis or it may cohere about a central area beneath a dome, or simultaneously both. It is a house of God and, by easy transposition or by survival of the concept of a priest-king, there may be in the transept or elsewhere an episcopal throne. Certain features possess immemorial significance. We shall find, preferably at the eastern end, an especially sacred liturgical area. The dome will suggest a cosmic sky opening into heaven. Columns, as the statue columns of Gothic portals suggest, recall saints and prophets and other pillars of the Church. In Abbot Suger's account of the building of St. Denis we discover this equiva-

4. H. Wölfflin, *Classic Art*, 287.

lence: "The midst of the edifice, however, was suddenly raised aloft by columns representing the number of the Twelve Apostles and, secondarily, by as many columns in the side-aisles signifying the number of the [minor] Prophets, according to the Apostle who buildeth spiritually."[5]

A Christian church by Borromini's time had become a complex convention capable of being modified to emphasize various aspects of the evangelical, mystical, liturgical, confessional, and other functions of the ecclesia. What Borromini does in S. Carlo is to affirm in a kind of absolute rhetoric one version of the Christian theme.

Borromini and Milton conceive of space in the same way. The space of *Paradise Lost* is not composed of the aggregation of determined areas or volumes but by indicating these within an already conceived total continuum and hastening to prevent by various means the isolation or too close bounding of any one of them. This feeling for space as a unified whole comprehending all locations that may be postulated is shared by Borromini. Pevsner remarks of S. Carlo, "space now seems hollowed out by the hand of a sculptor."[6] The feeling for space as total is associated with the sense of a total unified purpose in the universe. *Paradise Lost* is the story of the fall, led into by the story of creation and innocence, led out of by the promise of redemption and final re-creation. There are obedient angelic hosts above, rebellious devils below. God is omnipotent and omnipresent, pervading the totality. Borromini departs radically from Renaissance practice, his working method being to manipulate a preconceived logical whole. "In the one case the overall plan and its divisions are evolved by adding module to module, and in the other by dividing a coherent geometric configuration into geometric sub-units."[7]

The total configuration which Borromini proposes to himself is the result of plan after plan and the amalgamation of several traditions. The columns of the interior are in a general sense classical; the curved walls are clearly of a late classical type; the ground plan provides a Greek cross; over this is contrived a Renaissance dome the outline of which is refined into a Mannerist oval. The traditional cruciform plan represents old Christian tradition and leads toward

5. Suger, Abbot of St. Denis, *The Abbey Church of St. Denis* (trans. Panofsky).
6. N. Pevsner, *An Outline of European Architecture*, 182.
7. R. Wittkower, *Art and Architecture in Italy, 1600 to 1750*, 133.

the divine mystery present upon or symbolized by the altar. The dome, centralizing and unifying all, lets in a flood of clear light, encouraging the gathering of the congregation under the pulpit for instruction. At the same time the vigorous assertion of the columns and the elusiveness of the curving walls behind them give power and a sense of unconfined space. It is an effect of mastery, not mystery, yet in the words of Borromini's employer: "Everything is arranged in such a manner that one part supplements the other and that the spectator is stimulated to let his eye wander ceaselessly."[8]

Borromini's effort in S. Carlo alle Quattro Fontane may be taken as an active piece of reconstitution, after the Mannerist revolt against Renaissance convention. The new unity involves more elements, a wider recognition of conflicting claims, a more strenuous and skilful effort to achieve wholeness. He cannot return to Palladio's kind of simplicity, a simplicity that saw the round plan as the ideal, "because it is the only one amongst all the figures that is simple, uniform, equal, strong, and spacious. Therefore let us make our temples round."[9] Wittkower has insisted on the relation between the shapes of Christian churches and the concepts of Christ held by those who planned them: "The builders of the Middle Ages laid out their churches in modern crucis—their Latin Cross plan was the symbolic expression of Christ crucified. The Renaissance, as we have seen, did not lose sight of this principle. What had changed was the conception of the godhead: Christ as the essence of perfection and harmony superseded Him who had suffered on the cross for humanity; the Pantocrator replaced the Man of Sorrows."[10]

In Lomazzo we find the anthropometric concept of church building associated with the cruciform plan. He develops the first of these at considerable length. We learn that "the measures of ships, temples and other things were first drawn from the imitation of man's body." The shape of a cross "cometh nearest to the shape of man's body" and the proportions of the ideal church are such that the human figure visualized would equal in height the top of the vault or if stretched horizontal would reach from the middle of the vault to the west end.[11]

8. Quoted in Wittkower, *Art and Architecture in Italy*, 135.
9. Quoted in R. Wittkower, *Architectural Principles in the Age of Humanism*, 21.
10. *Ibid.*, 27.
11. G. Lomazzo, *A Tracte Containing the Artes of Curious Paintinge, Carvinge, Buildinge* (trans. Haydocke).

Both Borromini and Milton burst through such anthropomorphic conceptions into larger and more complex concepts of structure. It is not that they ignore the Platonic circle. The perfectly balanced round is the world of Adam's Eden under the dome of heaven, the revolving spheres, and the Platonic ladder up which Adam's sons may move "by degrees of merit rais'd." It is the world of Adam's last afternoon of innocence in a perfectly centralized parterre from which Raphael ascends straight up to the presence of God. But for neither Borromini nor Milton is this simplicity the whole structure, nor can it remain unmodified by other and more ambiguous considerations. The principle of Renaissance architecture was the harmonious arrangement of parts into a whole, parts which were themselves composed of modules having some relation to the human body. Borromini approaches the problem differently, by providing an over-all total geometrical form for his ground plan, within which he can manoeuvre his various possibilities. Milton in *Paradise Lost* fits the story of Eden, scaled to the physical and psychological stature of Adam and Eve, into a preconceived totality beyond the scope of the human module and in any case existing always as a whole in the mind of God—a fit arena for "things unattempted yet in prose or rhyme."

In addition to employing classical walls and columns, a Greek-cruciform scheme above these, and finally an oval dome, Borromini employs two other devices, one internal, one in his façade, to repeat the theme of unity achieved by difficult but successful association of conflicting conventions. Milton's employment of classical epic and classical similes with a Christian theme and a Puritan ideology is on all fours with Borromini's achievement. And Milton, like Borromini, adds other parallel schemes of resolved oppositions to strengthen, diversify, and enrich his poetic statement.

Borromini makes spectacular use of what has been called "overlapping triads of bays." These permit or indeed compel the spaces involved, between the columns, to combine simultaneously in two different ways. To this deliberate conflict, of a Mannerist type, he has added unifying elements, first a strong continuous entablature running through the midst of the ambiguous area; second the dynamism of the columns themselves which by their vigorous, weight-bearing parallel presences counteract any appearance of disunity. Milton relies on the strong continuously unfolding biblical plot, familiar as sacred story to all his readers. He relies too on spaced releases of dynamic energy, as we have already shown. Were these devices missing, the strain on Milton's structure might well be disastrous. As it is, we really are induced to see the eating of the apple and loss of innocence as parallel, simultaneously, to a vast rebellion of angels in remote time and space, and in quite another sense to the recovery by Adam of a Paradise within him. We are persuaded to give credence to Satan as a rebel blasted by divine wrath, as a sultan in hell, as entering a snake to tempt Eve. We have already noticed one special and beautiful instance of this kind of operation in the union of all the disparate roles of Messiah—Son, Avenger, Judge, Creator, Mediator, Sacrifice, Deity incarnate—under the simple aegis of his total, glad obedience to the Father.

Borromini's handling of the façade of Carlo Fontana has been the subject of acute analyses and has been shown to consist of "diversity, even polarity, within a unifying theme."[12] Simple methods of uniting the two storeys are avoided and deliberate reversals of concave and convex serve to make the façade a structure of extreme but aesthetically satisfying tension. Yet every component is handled in a manner reflecting Borromini's personal and inimitable dexterity. Only his inspired manipulation makes it possible to surround the statue of St. Charles Borromeo by herms with cherubs' heads and anatomically preposterous wings. Only his peculiar instinct for the combination of incongruities within a totality could make possible the balancing of this statue in the lower storey by a very large oval medallion in the storey above. We might remind ourselves how much of the cohesion of *Paradise Lost* derives from Milton's compelling, highly individual use of the high style, how, for example, anticlimax is avoided at the end of Book IV by the sudden introduction of the constellation Libra and a verse from the Book of Daniel; or how the Trinity in heaven is daringly balanced by Satan, Sin, and Death; or how the departure from Eden is given exactly the melancholy dignity required by the use of vague but allusive words like "world," "Providence," "wandering."

Returning to the words of the Procurator General of the Order which employed Borromini, "Everything is arranged in such a way that one part supplements the other and that the spectator is stimu-

12. Wittkower, *Art and Architecture in Italy*, 135.

lated to let his eye wander about ceaselessly." We recall, too, that *Paradise Lost* is a structure of such scope, such richness of design, such subtlety, such power to combine traditions, such ever renewed freshness of effect that we can move about freely within it and regard it from constantly changing viewpoints. Sometimes it will seem like its avowed theme, a justification of God's ways; at others it may seem the paradox between the fall as forbidden and as fortunate; equally well, it is an account of the nexus between God's will and man's will; it may be accepted as the theme of obedience, with rebellion as its dark shadow; or as the story of rebellion, with which Milton is perhaps unconsciously and with one part of his nature in sympathy.

The impression left by S. Carlo alle Quattro Fontane upon the observer who surrenders to its persuasions is ineffaceable. Seen head on it looks disjointed, the storeys of its façade not hanging together, just as *Paradise Lost* read literally seems an assemblage of incommensurable elements. But Borromini could not have intended, given the narrowness of Via Quirinale, to have his façade viewed in any way but obliquely. Seen thus, in an oblique afternoon light, his curves come into motion as the spectator moves; they supply an interplay which brings the whole alive. The interplay is between two storeys. These are separated by an entablature, so strong and salient as to constitute the principal unifying feature. Its sinuous movement, sharply and diagonally cut off at each end, follows the undulation of the storey of three bays below it, the central one convex, the others concave. Above the entablature are three concave bays. The unexpected concavity of the central one is compensated by its possessing the pill-box projection mentioned above, over which the very large oval medallion sustained by angels cuts heavily into the upper cornice. Scarcely any wall, as such, can be seen. The whole field of one's vision is taken up by structural and decorative elements contending to produce an effect of strenuous and triumphant unity. The medallion is now completely defaced; dirt and some delapidation join with electric wires and the rush of Roman traffic to distract from the pure architectural experience. But the triumph of this façade is so indubitable, the fascination of its effect so powerful, that Borromini, who ended his own life in a fit of depression, must assuredly from the heaven of Platonic forms look down and reap his reward.

The interior is even better than the façade promises. Its area is, unbelievably, no bigger than the cross-section of a single pier of St. Peter's but the effect is nothing short of monumental. Several devices contribute to this end. The ground plan is formed by two equilateral triangles on each side of a common base circumscribed by two circles whose circumferences form the substance of an oval. About this oval stand sixteen impressive Corinthian columns, arranged in pairs, which are in turn grouped in pairs. Painted cream and standing on green marble bases delicately faceted and curved to follow the oval plan and the openings of the chapels, these columns take possession of the total space, moulding it as though with the fingers of the hand. The effect of a bounding wall is lost by the existence of six chapels, in addition to the entrance and the high altar. The columns take control and support a heavy cornice which changes direction every few feet. Above this unifying band of cornice the pendentives briefly suggest a cruciform and then the dome, with its long axis terminating in some-what flattened and strongly curving ends, draws the eye up. Deep and sharply cut coffering in the shapes of octagons, crosses, and lozenges diminishes in size upward and lengthens the perspective. After a time the eye accepts this combination of diverse traditional elements made to answer one another with such skill and it would happily explore this space for ever, stimulated by the ceaseless play of combinations and soothed by the dominance of the columns, the continuity of the cornice, and the grandeur of the dome, so lofty for its size.

Borromini set out deliberately to produce an absolute unity of effect, a new totality in which traditional components combine to give a novel impression. If proof is needed, it is furnished by the Church of S. Giovanni in Laterano where he was commissioned to convert the nave of an ancient basilica into a contemporary seventeenth-century style. He intended to build a vault over the nave but was prevented by circumstances; the old flat wooden ceiling remains. Here we may see Baroque imposed on a mediaeval building and the two styles standing distinct with perfect clarity.

In S. Giovanni, Borromini created very wide pillars by combining pairs of the old columns. He filled the space between and added enormous pilasters, only a cornice and frieze intervening between their capitals and the ceiling. Twelve tabernacle-niches between these pilasters are of varied marbles, very large and salient. Over each tabernacle a rectangular panel of sculpture surmounted by a large oval oil painting adds further emphasis. The twelve apostles in dramatically expressive attitudes stand out in white contrast to the coloured marbles of their tabernacles. Two of the apostles are out of line by being placed on the bevelled corners of the nave by the portal. This tends to close the nave in and reduce its longitudinal effect. The unity of the nave is further emphasized by the double functioning of the arches, which simultaneously appear as low compared with the pilasters and high compared with the statues. A further effect conducive to unity is the redecoration of the arches and aisles in Borromini's inimitable personal style. How a mind filled with such exquisite cherub faces can have given way to suicide is inexplicable.

Further illustrations of Borromini's power to unify and to centralize are offered by the two exquisite churches, S. Agnese (in Piazza Navona) and S. Ivo della Sapienza.

12. *PARADISE REGAINED*

PARADISE REGAINED, quite apart from Ellwood's testimony, is palpably a sequel to *Paradise Lost*. The cast of characters is almost unchanged: God the Father, Satan, angels fallen and unfallen, and a perfect Man, the second Person of the Trinity, now in the role of "the second Adam." It is also, in Milton's own view, an example of the epic, of which he considered "the book of Job a brief model." The action is epic, if we allow for a transposition, familiar to the reader of *Paradise Lost*, from the courage of the warrior to that of the witness and martyr. Needless to say, the division into books, the verse form, the high style, the similes, and much else go to confirm the epic pattern. The theme of temptation is at the outset made a link between *Paradise Lost* and *Paradise Regained*; we are invited in the first half-dozen lines to regard the two works as parallel.

Milton chose Luke's account of the temptation in the wilderness rather than Matthew's. It has been shown[1] that the temptations as given in Luke—to turn stone into bread, to take the kingdoms of the world as a liege of Satan, to leap from the top of the temple—have a certain cumulative effect and that the first and the last are respectively incitements to distrust Providence and to presume upon Providence. This linear development of the theme is, however, subjected to the superimposition of still another pattern which we must now consider, noting at the outset that the issue of the combat between the Son and Satan is never, in any possible sense, in doubt.

Certain fixed features of the scriptural text appear, upon a first

1. A. S. P. Woodhouse, "Theme and Pattern in *Paradise Regained*," *University of Toronto Quarterly*, XXV, 167–82.

examination, to govern Milton's handling of the verses in Luke. The
first and third temptations resist poetic expansion, while the central
temptation invites it. To turn stone into bread might stir the imagination of an organic chemist but to any other reader past or present it is
likely to suggest, by its arbitrariness, only the demonstration of absolute and divine power. This, of course, it is intended to do but the
effect is simple and summary. The last temptation offers a similarly
limited scope but for a different reason. To any straightforward reading it is ambiguous in an awkward manner. If the Son of Man can
keep his balance on the top of a spire at all, he is superior to ordinary
dynamics and can descend at will; there is therefore in this case no
temptation to cast himself down. If, on the contrary, he cannot keep
his balance he has no choice but to fall; it is not an act of volition
and no temptation is involved. It has been thought that this temptation was an incitement to perform a feat of magic and so win the
allegiance of the crowd but neither the evangelists nor Milton make
any such suggestion.

If the first and last temptations offer little to the extrapolating
power of poetic imagination, the middle one on the contrary is capable
of infinite extension. To a practitioner of the Baroque style this second
temptation is a gift from heaven. It offers the spectacle of vast authority extended with great splendour through enormous panoramas, the
whole unified and driving force being the object of a single overwhelming moral decision.

What Milton has chosen, then, is a theme which encourages the
subordination of its initial and final components to an expansive
development of its central one. And whether rationally or instinctively
made, this choice permits the deployment of techniques associated
with Late Baroque.

Paradise Regained commences with an invocation and statement
of theme similar to those in *Paradise Lost* but with such significant
forecasts of difference in style of treatment as raise a lively curiosity
in the ideal reader. The note of very quiet assurance, of a firm
obedience and resulting edification, is in striking contrast to the
varying plangency of Milton's opening cry in *Paradise Lost*. Next the
theme is denominated heroic, as epic demands, but not as in *Paradise
Lost* an indeterminate mingling of conventional, if idealized, warfare
with "patience and heroic martyrdom." It is the latter only and "in

secret done," in the desert. What transpires from this spiritual victory is to be a demonstration that the hero is "by proof th'undoubted Son of God."

As a prologue to the narrative we are now shown with synoptic brevity (fifteen lines) John's baptism of the repentant in Jordan, to which the Son of Man comes and at which he is revealed to all, by the descent of the Spirit in the shape of a dove and by the confirming voice of the Father, as the Son of God. It is surely not by accident that the object of the whole action—to bring forth proof that Jesus is the Son of God—is achieved at the very outset in the most public manner by the joint witness of the Spirit and the Father. If ever there was in a work of art a designed distribution of stress, this is it.

Now comes the description of an infernal council, a link with similar councils in *Paradise Lost*, but whereas they are filled with the tension and excitement of purpose becoming plan, this finds Satan, "with looks aghast and sad," recapitulating the evidences of the Son's Messiahship. He sets off on "a calmer voyage" to essay the temptation; it is almost the calmness of despair and his legion is left in "deep dismay."

As in *Paradise Lost*, the infernal council is followed by a heavenly one, brief and radiant. The purpose of God's permitting the temptation of the Son is explained, it is "to show him worthy of his birth divine," to "lay down the rudiments / Of his great warfare." It reaffirms, in other words, the divine demonstration of a unity of purpose between Father and Son and its potential saving power for man.

The main thread of the action is now picked up. It is simply, and stupendously so, what goes on in the mind of the Son. His soliloquy (of about a hundred lines) reveals him fully cognizant of his divine parentage, his destiny on David's throne, his redemptive death for all mankind, and the imminence of his period of public ministry. Why he is led into the wilderness he does not immediately know but knows it will be revealed. With skill and care, Milton is offsetting tendencies either to drive the narrative forward or to achieve suspense and tension, by showing how completely the Son is initially aware of his divinity and redemptive purpose.

Now Satan appears and his pastoral guise is in sharp contrast with the serpent who tempted Eve. With startling suddenness he puts the first temptation. It is instantly rejected (fifteen lines). That either

Satan or the Son is unaware of the other's identity is disposed of by the Son's final words: "Knowing who I am, as I know who thou art."

The extreme abruptness of the first temptation cannot be without significance and the formal explanation will bear examining. While undertaking to tell an epic story, in three episodes, and while obeying the convention of an heroic struggle and a denouement containing a recognition scene, Milton is at the same time boldly shifting the emphasis and manipulating the given components to produce another effect. What this is now commences to appear.

The brief account of the first failure of Satan is succeeded by a fairly lengthy debate (140 lines). Here none of the sense of clash persists but Satan's status as a tempter is examined. He represents himself as an unfortunate and disowned but still effective servant of God, admiring what is "excellent in good, or fair, / Or virtuous." The Son's reply is to stigmatize Satan as a liar, "a poor miserable captive thrall," "a Fawning Parasite." Satan whines that his ill deeds come from "not will but misery," admits the Lordship of the Son, and begs for continued access to his presence. The Son's brief reply refers all action of bidding or forbidding to the Father but asserts full knowledge of Satan's purpose: "I know thy scope." Satan's position has been weakened. The Son appears invulnerably strong and his spiritual energies are completely undeployed. His knowledge of Satan's intentions and limits is what it always was and always will be: complete.

The first book produced two councils, one infernal and one heavenly. Book II now introduces two more. The first is among the disciples and has a tone of pastoral complaint as the "Plain Fishermen, (no greater men them call)" gather in a cottage among reeds and willows. Appended to this is a soliloquy by the Virgin in which the conservation of spiritual energy is a main theme: her Son has led a life "Private, unactive, calm, contemplative" and now "some great intent / Conceals him."

The minor key of this passage is followed by another infernal council in "the middle Region of thick Air" but between the two there is struck a major chord of resounding strength, as a reminder of the continuing theme of the work, for meanwhile the Son

> Into himself descended, and at once
> All his great work to come before him set;
> How to begin, how to accomplish best
> His end of being on Earth, and mission high.

The effect of the second pair of councils is to reduce the cosmic scale of *Paradise Regained*. In a sequel to *Paradise Lost* a heavenly council is, let us say, essential but it is made brief, early, and unremarkable. The true theatre of action is the mind and spirit of the Son to which the wiles of Satan, the hopes of Mary, and the fears of the disciples are closely linked in space and time.

The second infernal council, in which a weakened Satan, all his old natural predominance lost, begs for aid and advice, turns into the projection by Belial of a temptation never in fact attempted, the parade of women. It is deployed nevertheless for over seventy lines as Belial and Satan discuss its expedience. The passage is of great interest, being decorative and serving to define the character of the Son only by exclusion: "Therefore with manlier objects we must try / His constancy." It is quite outside the terms of the gospel narrative and Milton is careful to keep it so.

It is in accord with epic tradition that the Son's combat with Satan should be in three stages on three successive days, but no stress is placed on these divisions. After passage of the first night, Satan renews his attack, as a courtly figure in a pastoral setting, inviting the Son's attendance at a *fête champêtre* of imperial luxury. The nymphs appear, but they are in the distance and are of Diana's train; the figures of Ganymede and Hylas, so seductive in Milton's seventh Elegy, are reduced to a pictorial notation. The scene absorbs the situation into itself by its formal beauty like something out of Poussin or Lorraine. Satan's renewed invitation to the Son to eat and the almost gentle refusal he receives are muted into harmony with the sylvan-courtly setting. Its scenic qualities are emphasized by its vanishing like the stage banquet of *The Tempest*.

Book II is completed and the decorative episode rounded out by Satan's offer to the Son of money, of wealth to secure power. These succesive offers of women, food, and money are all of a piece and all on the same level; no dynamism exists and no one, not even Satan, expects his "weak arguing and fallacious drift" to succeed.

By this time the true centre of the poem has been reached and the dominant scene, "the Kingdom, the power and the glory," is about to be displayed. In a set of speeches filled with energy, Satan and the Son discuss the concept. The word "Glory" (or "Glorious") appears some thirty times, usually paired with itself, like a colonnade of coupled columns (with a briefer coupling of Zeal and Duty).

And now the great panorama of power, central to the whole design of the poem, is revealed. The topography of the biblical and the classical traditions, over which the poet's imagination has from his childhood exercised itself, is once more projected upon the panoramic screen. On this side the valley of the Tigris-Euphrates and on the other Rome central in the Mediterranean world. But it is worth noting that in comparison with the view of the world afforded by Michael to Adam this view is circumscribed, befitting Satan's lesser power and the reduction of the external scene. Adam's sight was strained to the utmost; Satan's panorama may be viewed "with easy eye."

A curious discrepancy of emphasis now develops. The scene itself brims with the ingredients of powerful action:

> He saw them in their forms of battle rang'd,
> How quick they wheel'd, and flying behind them shot
> Sharp sleet of arrowy showers against the face
> Of thir pursuers, and overcame by flight;
> The field all iron cast a gleaming brown,
> Nor wanted clouds of foot, nor on each horn,
> Cuirassiers all in steel for standing fight.

Action, however, is totally absorbed into the spectacular demonstration. Satan's annexed arguments are by any count extremely feeble, about as convincing as those put by Disraeli into the pages of *Tancred*. He is repulsed with ease and the mood in which he proceeds to the second half of his allurement, the spectacle of Rome, should be closely observed. He is "Perplex'd and troubl'd," going on only out of spite, though to his greater shame; he resembles a swarm of flies or the froth and bubbles of assaulting waves. No survival of the sympathy aroused for him by Milton in *Paradise Lost* now remains as his "vain importunity" proceeds without a trace of his pristine energy in hell.

The scene itself retains all its splendid vitality as we turn to view Rome:

> Turrets and Terraces, and glittering Spires...
> Praetors, Proconsuls to thir Provinces
> Hasting or on return, in robes of State;
> Lictors and rods, the ensigns of thir power.

But Satan's attack declines into the greatest feebleness and he is no more than "impudent" in defeat when he makes the proposal that the Son fall down and worship him in return for kingly power. The Son's answer, as befits this impudence, is given with "disdain." Satan, "with fear abasht," has only one more scene to offer, Athens the eye of Greece.

This spectacle, of surpassing beauty and supremely attractive to the twentieth-century reader, is rejected by the Son in terms whose finality should not surprise anyone familiar with *Paradise Lost*. In such a passage as that in Book I beginning "thus they relate Erring," in the careful relegation of classical materials to subordinate positions such as similes, in a scrupulous reliance upon the Bible for the frame of narrative for which credence is demanded, there is ample reason to anticipate the rejection here, by the Son, of pagan wisdom as a path to the Kingdom of God. And for all its extraordinary beauty and attractiveness, the scene is not effective as a true temptation. It comes after the decisive rejection of Satan's conditional offer of power. The learning and wisdom of Greece are not in any case within Satan's gift but open to all, as his words admit, "These here revolve, or, as thou liks't, at home." The presentation of Athens, for all its charm and all its indirect revelation of the mind of the Son, is not seriously to be regarded as a temptation any more than were the procession of nymphs and the sylvan banquet. The two presentations, one on each side of the main thematic picture of power and glory, are indeed a complementary pair, one appealing to simple feelings, the other to the intellect, while the central splendour of realized power appeals directly to the will.

The Son is returned now by the baffled tempter to the wilderness. He passes the night amid a storm provoked by the Prince of the power of the air and at dawn a pastoral peace returns. Satan too returns but "with no new device, they all were spent" for the Son is "Proof against all temptation as a rock." Enraged, he sets the Son on the pinnacle of the temple. It is a desperate act, perhaps an attempt at murder, for Satan is "in careless mood" and "swoln with rage." But it is only in a nominal sense a temptation. What is superbly done is to underline in one short, sharp stroke what has all along been demonstrated, that this is the Son of God over whom Satan has no power. "He said and stood, / But Satan smitten with amazement fell."

Now the angelic choir conveys the victorious Son to a pastoral valley and heavenly anthems attend the breaking of his fast. Lost Paradise has been regained, Satan's impotence demonstrated. The full potential redemptive power of the Son is apparent and he will from this point "begin to save mankind." That this power is not, within the bounds of the poem, released is made clear in the final lines: "he unobserved / Home to his Mother's house private return'd."

Paradise Regained extends the complexity of Milton's concept of the Second Person of the Trinity. In *Paradise Lost* he has been presented with overpowering effect as the coadjutor of the Father, regal in his vice-regency, mild, mighty, merciful, rational. At the climax of the war in heaven he appears righteously angry with the Father's enemies, overwhelming in his descent upon them. As Creator he is powerful, purposeful, beneficent. And always, as obedient Son of the almighty Father, he is worthy of all praise and glory.

In *Paradise Regained* the assertion of inconceivable and beneficent power is compressed, so to speak, into a concept of will. This simplification has important results. The mysterious birth of Christ is muted; nowhere is the great mystery of incarnation allowed to assert its mysterious nature. The betrayal and humiliation of Jesus are given no prominence and it is to be remembered that the Lady in Comus and Abdiel in the north of heaven suffered no physical violence. The suffering of the Son in the wilderness is blurred; a strong ambiguity pervades the discussion; one concludes that he is sustained, perhaps without suffering or debilitation, by will. The relation of Church and Saviour as bride and bridegroom is suppressed, as not related to power and will. (Milton is, of course, not insensitive to this truth as the marvellous moment of "unexpressive nuptial song" in *Lycidas* testifies.)

The Son of God is no less the exponent of unity, of power, and of will in *Paradise Regained* than in *Paradise Lost*. But new relations and combinations of elements are apparent. The epic model has been changed. The element of Puritanism now being elaborated is not a dynamic exercise of personal choice but a demonstration of inflexible inner rectitude as a preparation for future action. Whatever models may contribute, whatever may be acquired from Renaissance prototypes such as Spenser's Guyon or Fletcher's Christ, all is adjusted to the sensibility of Late Baroque.

The unity is one of centralized demonstration. Any narrative progression the story possesses is designedly slowed down. The weak polarity of Satan, as he tries to avoid worse trouble, prevents any

alternating surges of power, such as the war in heaven permitted.
There is a recognition scene, but placed beside Euripides' scene where
Orestes is recognized by Iphigeneia it reveals Milton's refusal to make
the act climactic or in any real sense the resolution of suspense. And
this is not wilfulness or caprice on Milton's part. There would be
something vulgar, irreverent, and contrary to the spirit of the gospels,
some excessive rationalization of the mystery of the incarnate Word,
if Jesus discovered suddenly that he was indeed the Messiah. We may
be assured that Milton does not intend to tell the story of a man who
found out one day that he was the Second Person of the Trinity. The
element of progressive revelation in *Paradise Regained* is for the best
of reasons most scrupulously confined.

The unity with which Milton is concerned in *Paradise Regained*
is not the unity of many elements fused in the heat of imaginative
power. It is a unity of form growing naturally out of the demonstration
of a divine unity of purpose among the Persons of the Trinity. To
this will the will of the poet and of the reader cannot but be
subdued. The super-ego becomes a demonstrated source of deliverance for the ego and the id suffers complete defeat. Indissoluble
from the concept of unity is that of divine power to defeat Satan and
save mankind. This potential of beneficent efficacy is ready, as the
poem closes, to take effect in the salvation of the world. Its point of
focus is the mind of the Son, a still centre between the renunciation
of wrongly motivated action and the true action of saving mankind,
which is about to begin.

No longer is Milton's muse striving toward a justification of the
ways of God to men. It achieves here a demonstration of the avail-
ability to man of God's Son, to the likeness of whose invulnerability
and inner power all may attain if God have so decreed and the age
have spirit and capacity enough to apprehend. Milton's ideal Son of
God shines forth. That he is not entirely the Christ crucified of Paul's
epistles need occasion no surprise.

The particular devices by which Milton produces his effects are
calculated, like the technical felicities of Baroque architects, to give
exquisite pleasure to the recipient of the effect. If we compare the
first seventeen lines of each poem, the care with which Milton has
avoided in *Paradise Regained* the forward thrust of the verse in
Paradise Lost becomes apparent. In each instance these lines deal

with the invocation and the statement of theme. *Paradise Regained* has separate paragraphs instead of a single carefully amalgamated one. The resounding proper names are missing; the scope of the scene is reduced. Gone is the characteristic Baroque coupling of complementary opposites (Oreb or Sinai; both of these against Sion Hill and Siloa's Brook; the Muse or the Holy Spirit; and so forth). There is a renunciation of the great vistas ("till one greater Man..."; "...Rose out of Chaos"; "pursues / Things unattempted"). The two climactic lines in the opening of *Paradise Regained* are carefully toned down. "And Eden raised in the waste wilderness" is flattened by the vowel of "raised"; Milton declines to raise tectonic sensations: the Kingdom of God is within you. The final line, "Worthy t'have not remained so long unsung" is muted by its double negative.

That *Paradise Regained* is eminently visual should be apparent. We have noted the pervasive employment of synoptic, image-provoking reviews; of visual demonstrations; of optical effects; and how the lower edge of the projection screen is kept level by a border of pastoral devices.

The narrative is turned into scenes, and, somewhat similarly, the action becomes a demonstration that the kingdom of God may be realized within, timeless and transcendent.

The concept of Late Baroque should not disturb the unbiased reader. It is now freely used in histories of European culture. There is a wide measure of agreement among art historians that after, say, 1660 certain elements of Baroque hitherto subordinated became prominent or that their dynamic complementary elements retired. Fokker has demonstrated that the same artists may employ High and Late Baroque schemes close together in time. All students of English literature are familiar with rapid changes in Shakespeare's style. It can be argued that his style passed by a natural and quick development from Renaissance to Mannerist or Baroque modes.

In considering the devices used by Late Baroque architects we must avoid the supposition that a façade can be directly compared to a plot-structure or that there is some direct, simple analogue in literature for, say, the use made of light in a Baroque chapel. As Panofsky's comparison of Gothic buildings to Scholastic thought has demonstrated, everything depends upon the existence of a controlling intention in the creative consciousness of the period and its realization in different but comparable ways by practitioners of the various arts.

It has been shown that unity of form corresponding to an ideological unity was a hallmark of Baroque, that this formal unity was achieved in the face of difficulties deliberately incurred by a desire for complete and total experience, and that the realization was effected within the bounds of Christian and classical conventions manipulated by past-masters of their craft.

One variant of this process, assuming greater importance with the passage of time, was the search for unity by means other than dynamic fusion of elements. It may be illustrated by Pietro da Cortona's Church of SS. Luca e Martina. The façade was begun between 1635 and 1640. It had perhaps reached the first entablature before 1644. There is conflicting evidence as to when the building was completed.[2] It seems to have been later than 1674. Cortona died in 1669. Existing plans show that the two wings of the façade were not completed in accordance with Cortona's first plan and the mode of their completion may be regarded as an example of modification in the direction of Late Baroque practice by an unknown architect.

The ground-plan of the church is that of a Greek cross. If we disregard the four apses for the moment, the proportion of the longer axis of the church to the shorter axis is about 7:6. As we should expect, Cortona has not allowed the axial tendency to prevail but has skilfully converted it into a centralized effect by devices devoid of tension. The walls refuse their usual office of defining space, by assuming several distinct planes none of them presenting any substantial area to the eye. Columns in the apses retreat into the walls while eight columns defining the area beneath the dome stand out clearly. A free use of pilasters of the same order as the columns assists in unifying the total effect but without contrasts or clashes. The whole church is white except for the marble surrounds of the altars. The cornice is not employed, as in Borromini's S. Carlo, to create a vigorous continuity, but, by creating an ambiguity between the real and apparent depth of various bays, it serves to draw attention toward the emphatic central area under the dome. The dome itself is decorated with motifs of a floral softness in contrast to the hard geometry in the dome of S. Carlo. The floor is of modest brick, in which bands

2. R. Wittkower, *Art and Architecture in Italy, 1600 to 1750*, 155, and T. H. Fokker, *Roman Baroque Art*, I, 166 ff.

of marble suggest concentric circles within a square beneath the dome. There is chastity and restraint in the Ionic columns, the clear glass windows, the absence of colour.

The façade employs analogous devices to similar ends. It is divided into three parts, of which the central one is by far the most extensive, almost equal to twice the other two combined. The two wings, in fact, consist of little more than a pair of pilasters apiece in each storey. The central section, a flattened convex curve, is divided into three shallow bays, of which the central one is strongly emphasized by containing the single door and, above, the single window, and by being surmounted by the usual shield, above which are the tiara and keys. In the other two bays decorative elements appear in both storeys; large and realistic decorative panels represent flowers and palms. These, particularly in the upper storey, vie with structural elements for attention.

To sit down in SS. Maria e Luca after experiencing the impact of Borromini or Bernini is to bid farewell to all compulsion of the eye or mind, to accept a unity of structure achieved by a selection from the familiar elements of Baroque, but quietly done, by self-restraint rather than domination, by using palms and flowers instead of violent statuary, by persuading the eye to stay with the centralized unity of the scheme.

This persuasion of the eye is even more palpable in the Venetian S. Maria della Salute, begun in 1631 by Baldassare Longhena and consecrated in 1687, after his death. He is said to be the only Venetian architect of the period who can stand comparison with the great men in Rome. His method in this church has been fitly called scenographic. We see everything with the greatest of clarity, often at some distance. "Instead of inviting the eye—as the Roman Baroque architects did— to glide along the walls and savour a spatial continuum, Longhena constantly determines the vistas across the spaces."[3] Longhena's innovations were immensely influential and his S. Maria, besides being salient on the Grand Canal, is a structure of high architectural intentions abundantly fulfilled.

The three separable elements of S. Maria are the main body of the church, an octagon with six chapels; a sanctuary having two apses; a choir, dominated by organ and loft. These are in a sense three build-

---

3. Wittkower, *Art and Architecture in Italy*, 194.

ings side by side. Their separateness is quite pronounced from an external view, the large dome, the smaller dome, and the towers of the choir clearly belonging to separately conceived fabrics. Yet both from within and from without a remarkable unity is achieved by devices of perspective. From the central point of the octagon, head-on views into the six chapels are possible and the framing columns have bevelled bases which lead squarely into each. From the same point a long axial view through the sanctuary, over the high altar, and into the choir pulls all together into one relationship. Externally the visual effects are superb and include more than the church itself. Situated near the entrance to the Grand Canal it is most often viewed across the water from the St. Mark's side. The octagonal form shows up boldly and asks for the recognition of its separate façades (those best seen from this point of view being elaborately finished). High and salient buttresses shaped like scrolls and supporting free-standing statues once more emphasize the octagonal plan. The enormous dome is echoed by the smaller dome of the sanctuary, behind it, and complemented by a tower of the choir behind that. The very site proclaims that unlike certain of the Roman churches which seize the viewer as he moves in a narrow street, this variety of Baroque may be explored and comprehended even from a distance.

That Longhena's contemporaries understood and appreciated his intention to organize vision is apparent from the use made of his eightfold viewpoints in the construction of the Reggia, at Caserta. The building and park are dominated by the desire—far more fully realized here than at Versailles—to achieve comprehensive clarity by providing explicit vistas. Very long tree-lined avenues of approach lead to an immense axis of vision, which, rising the full length of a steep cascade at the extremity of the gardens, comes to rest in a small garden temple at its source, from which point in reverse the gardens, castle, and whole countryside are exposed. Inside the palace, eight views diverge symmetrically from the landing at the top of the grand staircase, four of them into the courts. The courts themselves permit diagonal as well as rectangular views into each other. Their relationships are from every side revealed.

It is perhaps not inappropriate here to mention the Invalides, not in its present form of a shrine for Napoleon's tomb, but as Mansart planned it, in the year that Milton died. From the central point under the dome, lines of vision extend, not only along the main axis of the nave but also through the centre of each of the six chapels and upward through an inner dome into the outer one. Not only so, but to stand in the centre of any one of the four corner chapels is to command vistas into the other three, vistas which establish clearly the relation of each to all. The façade of the Invalides achieves unimpeachable unity by retiring from the central portico, the columns being stepped back in stages so that no conflict or tension arises.

In this kind of architecture, as in the structure of *Paradise Regained*, Baroque feeling is predominant and Baroque aims are clearly achieved. A unity is contrived with care, to express absolute power. S. Maria della Salute is a votary offering to the Virgin, whose divine powers stayed the plague in Venice. The Reggia at Caserta and the Invalides express each in its own way the pride of princes. *Paradise Regained* is concerned to reveal that the power of God to save man has been reposed in the Son of Man, who is invulnerable to Satan's attacks. The kingdom of God is the backdrop against which every scene is played and resonant overtones concerning the rule of the saints in England are audible to anyone who listens.

Milton in this late (perhaps last) poem renounces much that he had employed in *Paradise Lost*. The power he presents is all held in reserve so that even a sensitive reader may feel that Milton's "Christ is actionless, the poem expressive of a frozen and paralysed will to good."[4] There is deliberate renunciation of dramatic effect as the apparently sensible proposals of Satan for Israel's deliverance are rejected. Looked at simply from the humanistic and dramatic point of view, "Christ becomes an increasingly unsympathetic figure, a pusillanimous quietist in the temptation of Parthia, an inhuman snob in the temptation of Rome, a peevish obscurantist in the temptation of Athens."[5] There is also loss of narrative effect, as we have already shown. All that has happened is that we have been permitted to see, as Satan has been forced to see, that the fulfilment of God's great purposes for Israel and for mankind is about to begin and that in the Son of Man is the total resource that the great work demands. The scenes that have passed before our eyes, the banquet in the wilderness,

4. Wilson Knight, *The Burning Oracle*, 82.
5. Northrop Frye, "The Typology of *Paradise Regained*," *Modern Philology*, LIII (4), 234.

the Parthian kingdom, the empire of Rome, the city of Athens, none of these has had power to draw us into it, and none has disengaged any force that will change the course of events. In meeting the eye of the Son, or the inward eye of the reader, who is the central point of the sublunar world, they have performed their function. Forces are deployed, identified, reviewed, and assessed, but they are not engaged. It is a grand marshalling and parade preliminary to hostilities.

13. *SAMSON AGONISTES*

IN CONSIDERING *Samson Agonistes* in the context of Baroque, we
might begin by reminding ourselves of the thematic resemblances
between this work of Milton's and the other two of his great trilogy.
It is apparent that *Samson* is concerned with the unity of God's purposes, with the absoluteness of his power, and with the problem of
relating human to divine will. The dealings of God with a single
representative person adumbrate his dealings with his people as a
whole. God's presence is powerfully felt at the mundane level; at the
same time the human actors are elevated far above the common level;
nor is this effect achieved by giving to gods human attributes, for
Milton's God retains the absoluteness and awfulness of the central
Christian tradition.

In form, too, the resemblance to *Paradise Regained* is too palpable
to need elaboration. A classical model of great dignity and antiquity is
reshaped, though with care to maintain the observance of the required
conventions, so as to create a new effect. The very obviousness of the
resemblances may hinder their recognition. Thus the three great
works of Milton are all biblical in plot, characters, and setting. They
are all heroic, in that only great and universally significant deeds are
in view. The will of the one God and its demonstrable rightness are
never out of view, as the intention of each member of this trilogy
unfolds.

Milton's method of making his mixed sources yield an absolute unity
of effect has been admirably demonstrated by Krouse in *Milton's
Samson and the Christian Tradition*.

What Milton found in the Book of Judges was a story resting on oral folk-lore, redacted through written folk-lore containing historical matter and now become sacred scripture to Jews and Christians alike. And in another part of the sacred Christian text the old folk-hero judge of Israel becomes a Christian saint, one of those "who through faith subdued kingdoms, wrought righteousness, obtained promises, stopped the mouths of lions, quenched the violence of fire, escaped the edge of the sword, out of weakness were made strong, waxed valiant in fight, turned to flight the armies of aliens."

In the early centuries of the Christian era Samson was treated as a saint who had fallen by the wiles of a woman and been redeemed, or alternatively as a figure of Christ. Certain difficulties arose: Samson's final act was of mass homicide combined with suicide, and his whole story was what publishers now call a lusty one and *ipso facto* incongruous with his status as saint. Augustine freely used allegory as a way out and Samson's visit to the harlot followed by his bearing away the gates of the city became a prefiguring of Christ in the bonds of death preparatory to the Harrowing of Hell. Samson thus became a link between the Old Testament and the New. He was also a useful bridge over which pagan typology could be carried into Christian thinking. His affinity with Hercules was too good to be passed by and indeed modern attempts have been made to trace them to a common solar myth.

In the period of scholasticism this complex figure of Samson was given all the authority of tradition. (The *Summa* established the fact that "Samson killed himself as we are told in Judges 16; however, Samson was numbered among the saints, as is clear from Hebrews 11. Therefore it is granted to some to kill themselves.") There were poetic treatments of Samson in the later Middle Ages in the manner of a mediaeval tragedy. A great man falls from high estate because of woman's perfidy. Literal and allegorical interpretations went side by side throughout the period.

During the Renaissance a strong note of rationalism was introduced into exegesis of the Samson theme. How did Samson carry away the gates? How could he catch threee hundred foxes? How could he demolish a temple by dislodging two pillars? Answers were provided, in some instances with diagrams beside the text. But allegorical interpretations persisted. Samson's strength as residing in his hair might mean literally that the strength of any Nazarite lies in faithfulness to vows; allegorically that Samson was a figure of Christ, Head of the Church; tropologically that sound thoughts spring from a sound mind; and anagogically that special endowments from God are ours only so long as we keep from sin.

We should expect Milton to unify the concept of Samson, to do so not by a process of selecting one aspect or strain and discarding the others but by a vast effort of retention and intricate subordination. We should expect, moreover, that, however classic and clear the forms might be through which his concept was realized, the whole would be suffused by a sense of violent power and the tension of the elements involved would be extreme. If the analogues with Baroque architecture, which suggest that the arts of this period have all put their roots into an underlying sensibility, have any validity, this is at least one of the effects we might anticipate.

The available tradition made it easy for Milton, as a starting point, to see in the tribal hero of the Book of Judges a tragic hero. Tragic dramas had already been written, both in Latin and in vernacular languages, with Samson as subject. Most of us would postulate that Milton's method consisted in his arbitrarily selecting, rejecting, and subordinating the incidents in the Judges account. Krouse, however, argues convincingly that his "emphasis on the later and more sober aspects of Samson's career is entirely in keeping with the whole body of the Samson tradition"; "ever since the early part of the patristic period— primarily because of the changes of emphasis needed in his story to make it possible to absorb him in Christianity—attention had been concentrated increasingly on Samson's later career and on the more tragic aspects of his life."[1]

When he comes actually to shape the plot, Milton shows himself an artist of his own century. Anagogical and tropological interpretations are quietly dropped. The allegorical interpretations occur as overtones to a fudamentally rational treatment of the Samson story. The prefiguring of Christ by Samson is left to the reader as an easy implication. It is not developed as allegory.

On a rational basis, therefore, Milton re-erects the familiar tale, subordinating with absolute singleness of purpose all other elements to the dominant concepts of Samson as hero of high and serious purpose. His exploits against the Philistines, which seem so adolescent and

1. F. M. Krouse, *Milton's Samson and the Christian Tradition*, 88.

boisterous, become warfare in the cause of Jehovah. The foxes and firebrands episode is omitted; others are elevated by Milton's controlling diction to the proper level.

The devices, and above all the tact, by which he secured depth of interpretation without risking obscurity of meaning or confusing layers of interpretation are worth considering. *Samson Agonistes* is not political allegory. But Milton was immensely concerned and engaged in politics; he found the Samson tradition shaped so as to make the political significance of the story easily seen; he presented it to his readers thus; the air is full of overtones of political implication. Yet the treatment is so unified that no separation of planes, as in Spenser, is allowed to appear.

The emphasis on Samson himself, which never falls away during the whole course of the play, gives him a colossal stature. The chorus, discovering him eyeless in Gaza, can think of nothing but his heroic deeds:

> Can this be hee,
> That Heroic, that Renown'd,
> Irresistible Samson? whom unarm'd
> No strength of man, or fiercest wild beast could withstand;
> Who tore the Lion, as the Lion tears the Kid,
> Ran on embattled Armies clad in Iron,
> And weaponless himself,
> Made Arms ridiculous.

A Baroque work typically packs its meaning to a high degree of density and a variety of meanings may be implied at the same time in a fused wholeness of implication. *Samson Agonistes* achieves such an effect by having two intricate and interrelated sets of implications, neither of which is allowed to achieve any independence as an interpretation: first the political implication mentioned and second the startling number of correspondences between Samson's life and Milton's—dedicated youth, God-fearing parents, struggle against an intestine enemy, success followed by failure, unfortunate marriage, blindness, defeat and contumely, "abating not a jot of heart or hope," and so on. And not only is the political implication a simple use of tradition; so also is the biographical application: the tradition of Samson's life is preserved intact and the resemblances to Milton's own life are never forced upon the story or upon the reader. It is true that the rude and violent Samson, the hairy harlot-visiting folk-hero, would not correspond to the Lady of Christ's. But the sublimation of this Samson into a figure of consecrated virtue had already taken place, as we have seen, to serve the concept of the saint and martyr.

In the title of his play, which has been shown to have manifold meanings, Milton suggested that Samson was a model of virtue, a hero and a champion and a martyr-saint. He is cast in the same pattern as the first Adam and the last Adam (Christ) in being subjected to three temptations in a traditional pattern and order: the flesh, a temptation of necessity; the world, a temptation of fraud and persuasion; the devil, a temptation of violence or fear. Samson's conversation with Manoah constitutes the first of these; the old man promises relief from the weariness of the flesh, a means of complying with necessity; Dalila, filled with fraud, promises to bring Samson back into the world; Harapha, tempting him to a display of violence and a despair in God's mercy, completes the picture. Now here it seems that Milton has unnecessarily departed from his source, in inventing a character. But no reader will feel Harapha an intruder or incongruous, so exactly does he remind us of the archetypal Philistine giant, Goliath of Gath. The slight transposition from Samuel to Judges is scarcely noticed. And Harapha is needed in the play to round out still another insistent association, that between Samson and Hercules. Antaeus and Hercules, Satan and Christ, Harapha and Samson: the themes merge in the mind of the instructed reader into a complex fraught with moral significance.

We should look for a moment at the formal side of *Samson Agonistes*, its place in the roster of Greek tragedy. But before doing so let us remind ourselves, by a simple example, of the inherent difficulty of putting a Christian theme in a pagan classical form. In the conclusion of *Samson* we have a double resolution, one Greek (or at least classical) and one Hebraic, so deftly compounded as to produce a single effect of remarkable depth:

> Nothing is here for tears, nothing to wail
> Or knock the breast, no weakness, no contempt,
> Dispraise, or blame, nothing but well and fair,
> And what may quiet us in a death so noble.

This is followed by classical burial: laurel and palm, trophies and a monument; the valiant youths, the lamenting maidens. Then we pass to the inwardness and mystery of an Hebraic Jehovah.

> Oft he seems to hide his face,
> But unexpectedly returns
> And to his faithful Champion hath in place
> Bore witness gloriously; whence Gaza mourns
> And all that band them to resist
> His uncontrollable intent;
> His servants he with new acquist
> Of true experience from this great event
> With peace and consolation hath dismist.

The unifying element for these two very differently motivated laments seems to be Milton's phrasing and rhythm, which have already taken a leading part in the long process, now completed, by which Samson the Christian saint has become Samson the tragic hero. Certainly we feel no incongruity. Milton has resolved more than a drama and more than a moral question; he has brought into an equilibrium the demands of two fundamentally irreconcilable traditions. And his equilibrium is a tension.

Milton invites us to think of *Samson Agonistes* as Greek tragedy, specifically asking that we compare his disposition of the fable with Aeschylus, Sophocles, and Euripides. His reverence for the masters of antiquity is absolute. They are, he says, "the three Tragic Poets unequalled yet by any, and the best rule to all who endeavour to write Tragedy." His debt to the great triumvirate has been exhaustively explored by W. R. Parker,[2] who says in the course of his conclusion:

In saying that the influence of Sophocles predominates in the *Samson*, I do not mean to call Milton's drama "Sophoclean". Our whole study, if it has taught us anything, has made such a loose and misleading summary no longer possible. *Samson Agonistes* is "Greek" in the sense that a tragedy written in the days of Aristotle might have been. It is a revival, a re-creation, of an art which has found its climax, and it represents borrowings from each of the great masters. . . . *Samson Agonistes* was not written merely as an experiment in Greek poetic form. It was written because the Greek was the right form for something that Milton wanted to say. And because the English poet had intellectual or artistic affinities with each of his three models, he wrote—not as an imitator of one of them, or two—but as a great successor of all three, borrowing freely, synthesizing boldly. . . .

2. W. R. Parker, *Milton's Debt to Greek Tragedy in Samson Agonistes.*

This tribute contains several points which bear on our present argument. Milton's homage to traditional form, his familiarity with its conventions, are clearly recognized; so is his ability to select and combine elements from various masters of the tradition and his transcendence of anything that could be called discipleship by his ability to weld his borrowings into something new, something unmistakably his own and of his own age.

The Baroque feature predominant in *Samson*, if our analysis is on the right track, is the achievement, under enormous and voluntarily accepted difficulties, of total unity of the most expressive and grandiose kind, by the subordination of all the material to a contrived and triumphant singleness of impression. Some of the subordinated elements exhibit relations among themselves so paradoxical as to make the logical mind wonder how they could be made to co-exist within the same framework, let alone subserve a total unity of effect.

The apparent simplicity of Milton's result is in fact a further proof of the dexterity of his technique. He achieves extreme concentration upon a single character and a single theme: Samson completely overshadows the remaining characters; he is always at the centre of our attention, even when absent from the stage. The episodes of the biblical story, moreover, are manipulated so as to provide unity of action; they are alluded to at various appropriate moments of the play and their materials distributed so that they cannot distract from the central theme—what is happening in Samson's heart and mind during the last hours of his life.

The new rationalism supplies another unifying agent. This Milton uses with a delicate touch, out of deference to his supernatural materials but there are clear signs of that new appreciation of reason which (whether in the Society of Jesus or in the Royal Society) was pervading seventeenth-century thought. The miraculous elements in Samson's story are not stressed; his feats of strength are made reasonable; his acts, however strange, are rationally accounted for. At the centre of the drama is Samson's will, and it is the part of reason to bring his will into alignment with the will of God.

Milton has realized with complete success that Baroque quality which critics refer to as tension of opposites, as ambiguity or paradox. Much of it comes easily out of the fundamental paradox of biblical material and classical form. Samson to the seventeenth-century reader is irresistibly reminiscent of Hercules, the strong man who coped with all enemies, even death, yet at the same time Samson is a type of Christ who by his own death destroyed our enemies. Samson is also a martyr, whose function it is to witness and to suffer, and simultaneously a divine avenger who invokes and brings down wrath upon his enemies. It has already been shown that he was regarded as a saint, from which category Milton was careful not to remove him. Yet he committed suicide, an abhorred crime. Within the structure of the classical drama Samson must function as the hero, with a "flaw" that leads to his tragic end. The lament for *Samson Agonistes* is, as we have pointed out, both classical and Christian. And the philosophic conclusion is similarly ambivalent. The suggestion is never dispelled that the hero has been unjustly treated by Providence: he has endured —"Samson hath quit himself like Samson." At the same time we are told reassuringly "With God not parted from him as was feared / But favouring and assisting to the end."

It is apparent that Milton is handling the theme of energy, will, and the control or release of power in a form which is a recognizable variant of his method in *Paradise Lost*. Samson's energy is at the end wholly kinetic in a most absolute fashion. It is enormous, it is totally expended at one moment. It causes the complete demolition of the temple and the annihilation of the ruling castes of the Philistines. In this respect *Samson* is the perfect complement of *Paradise Regained*. In the one is demonstrated the careful resuscitation, conservation, direction, and then sensational total release of energy. In the other the extreme example of continence is shown: "in quietness and confidence shall be your strength." It is tempting to ask whether the Son is not a projection of Milton the poet-prophet and Samson a projection of Milton the controversialist. It is perhaps wiser to keep within the works themselves and point out that Samson's likeness to the Son in both his victorious execution of God's judgement and his achievement of victory over the Tempter by patient fortitude is implied by the chorus:

> Hee all thir Ammunition
> And feats of War defeats
> With plain Heroic magnitude of mind
> And celestial vigour arm'd
> Thir Armories and Magazines contemns,

Renders them useless, while
With winged expedition
Swift as the lightning glance he executes
His errand on the wicked, who surpris'd
Lose their defense, distracted and amaz'd.
    But patience is more oft the exercise
Of Saints, the trial of thir fortitude,
Making them each his own Deliverer,
And Victor over all
That tyranny or fortune can inflict.
Either of these is in thy lot.

The irony of the "either" is that Samson was enabled to follow the archetype of the Son of Man (though not in time) and to fufil both destinies.

Milton's capacity to achieve unity is supported by an inexhaustible series of devices. The natural unity of the Greek tragic form is dovetailed into the achieved unity of Samson's character. The complete dominance of the play by the relation between Samson's will and God's will is sustained where the wills become one "with God not parted from him as was feared." The simple strength of the Hebrew Samson becomes identified with God's uncontrollable intent.

The conventions of Greek tragedy bend a little, as we have seen, to conduce to this totality of effect. The Aristotelian "middle" seems inadequately developed. The character of Samson absorbs all the minor characters. The time represented is only a very few hours. The play is intended, Milton tells us, to be read, so we have no producer like Lawes in *Comus* to consider.

Samson Agonistes brings to mind as its most natural analogue in architecture, Bernini's S. Andrea al Quirinale, in considering which we must keep in mind the dual opening which Bernini habitually offers to the student of literature. He presents an idea, a *concetto*, and he expresses this in a formal architectural idiom which has its own grammar and syntax. It is not to be expected that Bernini will tell the story of the apostle Andrew but rather that he will seize the moment of martyrdom to which this faithful fisherman's life has brought him, the moment of metamorphosis between earth and heaven, a moment which reveals both past and future, and this the disposition of his architectural units will bring home to us by devices beyond the power of words.

S. Andrea is a small but strikingly monumental church, the ground-plan of which is in the form of an oval. Bernini has boldly made the main axis of the church, from entrance to altar, the short axis of the oval. As one enters, a sweeping curve of very large, predominantly white pilasters seizes the gaze and conducts it round the circumference of the oval to where, behind a massive screen of four columns of dark red marble, the high altar stands. This unity of effect is compelled. The eye wishes to explore the longer, lateral axis but cannot, for each end of this axis terminates, not in the opening of a chapel, but in salient pilasters. The chapels, moreover, are relatively dark and their degrees of illumination are varied so as to divert the eye to the high altar. This movement is assisted by a massive, sweeping entablature, which the pilasters support.

The large, heavily framed altarpiece represents St. Andrew's martyr-dom by crucifixion. With heightened realism it presents an intense and anguished struggle. The apostle's eyes are raised to where an angel points him on. The great marble frame is set into a burst of gold rays with a group of angelic figures in full relief. Two golden angels sup-port the corners, and a third, above, holds out to the struggling saint the martyr's crown. The gold figures of putti are in attendance and one of these, ascending into the oval golden aperture to the dome above the altar, holds out a palm. Others lean over the edge to welcome the saint. On the upper rim of the aperture appear some winged heads of cherubim. Light from concealed windows of white frosted glass streams down from the drum of the dome. This sacred and mysterious action by which the martyr's soul is drawn up toward heaven is separated from the main body of the church, where, as spectators, we must remain. But lifting our gaze we see, set in an opening in the pediment over the aedicule, the white marble figure of the saint ascending to heaven upon a cloud. In this region, above the entablature, all is white and gold. Winged heads form a complete circle just below the lantern of the main dome and some ascend into it toward a likeness of the holy Dove. On a sunny day, brilliant light pours in through the gold glass of the lantern and the whole dome, into which the spirit of the saint has been released, glows with splendour. The white figure of the martyr, now triumphant and ascending, captures the mind. Putti and reclining figures disposed high in the dome suggest by emblematic reeds and nets the past life of the fisher of men but they are marmorial and relaxed as though in the mind of a spirit.

The façade reasserts the intention of the interior. Two curved walls in the form of quadrants (abbreviated since Bernini's day) invite entrance. The portico also curves out in invitation and proffers, above its heraldic decoration, the martyr's crown. The austerity of the façade as a whole and its effect of movement add to the expectations of a revealed mystery within.

Differences within likenesses, between Milton and Bernini, multiply in the mind. The theme of the saint triumphant engrosses them both. Both see the moment of dissolution and reconstitution as an outburst of enormous energy. Milton, an Englishman, a Puritan, and a poet, emphasizes the moral struggle of Samson. Bernini, an Italian (with a Neapolitan mother), a Roman Catholic, and an architect, conveys the passionate suffering of St. Andrew and his apotheosis.

In neither of these great representations of spiritual energy fully released is there the slightest hint of the facile. Unity has been secured and triumph conveyed by means that take full account of complexity and diversity. Samson the folk-hero, the judge of Israel, the Hebrew Hercules, the saint, the martyr, the suicide, the hero of Greek tragedy, the exemplar of better fortitude, and the type of Christ has emerged as a single unified character. As regards Bernini, we may quote here the words of a Dutch critic:

Of all the churches of the period, S. Andrea probably realizes most completely the aims of the Full Baroque. The contrasts between the two axes of the elliptical interior, between the enclosing vault and the lively white figures situated where it becomes oppressive, between the gloomy chapels and their mysterious glowing vaults, between the cage of the presbytery and the free flood of life within, all combine to produce the impression of limitless space. The enchantment of the light effects brings the contrasts between the clear structure and the sudden escape from its limits to perfection.[3]

Much more could be said in support of the parallels in intention, execution, and effect between Bernini's S. Andrea and Milton's *Samson*. But the reader who has consented to follow the argument to this point will be willing to explore other resemblances for himself. The ramifications of the subject are of inexhaustible interest, although the object of the foregoing pages has been not to develop intricacy of analysis but to put as simply as possible the reasons for regarding Milton as a great exponent of the Baroque style.

3. T. H. Fokker, *Roman Baroque Art*, 1, 158.

Bibliography

Quotations of Milton are taken from M. Y. Hughes's edition of the *Complete Poems and Major Prose* (New York, 1957) and of Spenser from the *Poetical Works* ed. by J. C. Smith and E. de Selincourt (Oxford, 1959).

Adams, R. M., *Ikon: John Milton and the Modern Critics*, Cornell University Press, 1955.

Adamson, J. H., "The War in Heaven: Milton's Version of the Merkabah," *Journal of English and Germanic Philology*, LVII (4), 690–703.

Allen, D. C., *The Harmonious Vision*, Johns Hopkins University Press, 1954.

BARKER, A., "The Pattern of Milton's Nativity Ode," *University of Toronto Quarterly*, X, 167–81.

Blunt, Sir Anthony, *Artistic Theory in Italy: 1450–1600*, Oxford, 1940.

Briggs, M. S., *Baroque Architecture*, London, 1913.

Bryskett, L., *A Discourse of Civill Life*, London, 1606.

Buffum, I., *Agrippa d'Aubigné's Les Tragiques: A Study of the Baroque Style in Poetry*, Yale University Press, 1951.

——— *Studies in the Baroque from Montaigne to Rotrou*, Yale University Press, 1957.

Bukofzer, M. F., "The Baroque in Music History," *Journal of Aesthetics and Art Criticism*, XIV (2), 152–6.

Burckhardt, J., *The Civilization of the Renaissance in Italy*, London, 1960.

Butcher, S. H., Introduction to *Aristotle's Theory of Poetry and Fine Art*, London, 1902.

Campbell, Colen, *Vitruvius Britannicus, or the British Architect*, 3 vols., London, 1717–1725.

Castiglione, Count Baldassare, *The Book of the Courtier* (trans. Sir Thomas Hoby), London, n.d.

Charles Borromeo, Saint, *Instructionum Fabricae Ecclesiasticae*, ed. E. van Drival, Paris, 1855.

Coleridge, S. T., *The Literary Remains*, London, 1836.

Croll, M. W., "The Baroque Style in Prose," *Studies in English Philology*, University of Minnesota Press, 1929.

Cumberland, R., Introduction to *Comus*; *The British Drama*, vol. II, London, 1817.

Daiches, D., *Milton*, London, 1957.

Daniells, R., "Baroque Form in English Literature," *University of Toronto Quarterly*, XIV (4), 393–408.

―― "English Baroque and Deliberate Obscurity," *Journal of Aesthetics and Art Criticism*, V (2), 115–21.

Dumaresq, W., "The Epic and Tragedy of *Paradise Lost*," unpublished Master's thesis, University of British Columbia, 1956.

Enkvist, N. E., "Functions of Magic in Milton's *Comus*," *Neuphilologische Mitteilungen*, Nov. 1953, 310–18.

Fokker, T. H., *Roman Baroque Art*, 2 vols., Oxford, 1938.

Friedländer, W., *Mannerism and Anti-Mannerism in Italian Painting*, New York, 1957.

―― *The Rise of the Anti-Classical Style in Italian Painting*, New York, 1941.

Friedrich, C. J., *The Age of the Baroque: 1610–1660*, New York, 1952.

―― "Style as the Principle of Historical Interpretation," *Journal of Aesthetics and Art Criticism*, XIV (2), 143–51.

Frye, N., *Anatomy of Criticism*, Princeton University Press, 1957.

―― "The Typology of *Paradise Regained*," *Modern Philology*, LIII (4), 227–38.

Hatzfeld, H., "The Baroque from the Point of View of the Literary Historian," *Journal of Aesthetics and Art Criticism*, XIV (2), 156–64.

Hauser, A., *The Social History of Art*, London, 1951.

Heckscher, W. S., "Bernini's Elephant and Obelisk," *Art Bulletin*, XXIX, 155–82.

Hurd, R., *Letters on Chivalry and Romance*, ed. E. J. Morley, London, 1911 (first published 1742).

Jung, C. G., *Psychology and Religion: West and East*, tr. R. F. C. Hull, London, 1958.

Kelley, M., *This Great Argument*, Princeton University Press, 1941.

Knight, G. W., *The Burning Oracle*, Oxford University Press, 1939.

Krouse, F. M., *Milton's Samson and the Christian Tradition*, Princeton University Press, 1949.

Lees-Milne, J., *Baroque in Italy*, London, 1959.

Lewis, C. S., *A Preface to Paradise Lost*, Oxford, 1944.

Lomazzo, G. P., *A Tracte Containing the Artes of Curious Paintinge, Carvinge, Buildinge*, trans. R. Haydocke, Oxford, 1598.

Madsen, W. G., "The Idea of Nature in Milton's Poetry," *Three Studies in the Renaissance: Sidney, Jonson, Milton*, Yale University Press, 1958.

Mâle, E., *L'Art religieux après le Concile de Trente*, Paris, 1932.

Martin, J. R., "The Baroque from the Viewpoint of the Art Historian," *Journal of Aesthetics and Art Criticism*, XIV (2), 164–71.

Maxwell, J. C., "The Pseudo-problem of *Comus*," *Cambridge Journal*, I, 376–80.

Mayerson, C. W., "The Orpheus Image in *Lycidas*," *Publications of the Modern Language Association*, LXIV, 189–207.

Meissner, P., *Die geistesgeschichtlichen Grundlagen des englischen Literaturbarocks*, München, 1934.

Murray, P. and L., *A Dictionary of Art and Artists*, Penguin, 1959.

Mutschmann, H., *Der andere Milton*, Bonn, 1920.

Norton, R., *Bernini and Other Studies in the History of Art*, London and New York, 1914.

Panofsky, E., *Abbot Suger on the Abbey Church of St. Denis*, Princeton University Press, 1946.

—— *Gothic Architecture and Scholasticism*, Latrobe, 1951.

Parker, W. R., *Milton's Debt to Greek Tragedy in* Samson Agonistes, Johns Hopkins University Press, 1937.

Pevsner, N., "The Architecture of Mannerism," *The Mint*, ed. G. Grigson, London, 1946.

—— *An Outline of European Architecture*, 5th ed., Penguin, 1957.

Praz, M., *Secentismo e marinismo in Inghilterra*, Firenze, 1925.

Prince, F. T., *The Italian Element in Milton's Verse*, Oxford University Press, 1954.

Pützer, F., *Prediger des englischen Barock*, Bonn, 1929.

Rathborne, I. E., *The Meaning of Spenser's Fairyland*, Columbia University Press, 1937.

Reynolds, H., "Mythomystes," *Critical Essays of the Seventeenth Century*, ed. J. E. Spingarn, Oxford, 1908–9.

Riegl, A., *Die Entstehung der Barockkunst in Rom*, Wien, 1908.

Ripa, C., *Iconologia*, 1593 (first edition, without illustrations).

Ross, M. M., *Milton's Royalism*, Cornell University Press, 1943.

—— *Poetry and Dogma*, Rutgers University Press, 1954.

Saurat, D., *Milton: Man and Thinker*, New York, 1935.

—— "The Occult in English Literature," *Listener*, XXXVIII, 262–3.

Selincourt, E. de, Introduction to *Poetical Works of Edmund Spenser*, Oxford University Press, 1959.

Sitwell, S., *The Gothick North*, London, 1950.

—— *Southern Baroque Art*, London, 1924.

Spens, J., *Spenser's* Faerie Queene, London, 1934.

Stechow, W., "The Baroque: A Critical Summary," *Journal of Aesthetics and Art Criticism*, XIV (2), 171–4.

—— "Definitions of the Baroque in the Visual Arts," *Journal of Aesthetics and Art Criticism*, V (2), 109–15.

Strich, F., "Der lyrische Stil des 17. Jahrhunderts," *Abhandlungen z. deutschen Literaturgeschichte*, München, 1916.

Suger, Abbot of St. Denis, *Abbot Suger on the Abbey Church of St. Denis and Its Art Treasures*, trans. E. Panofsky, Princeton University Press, 1946.

Sypher, W., *Four Stages of Renaissance Style*, New York, 1955.

Tillyard, E. M. W., *Milton*, London, 1930.
——— *Studies in Milton*, London, 1951.
Tolnay, Charles de, *The Medici Chapel* (Part 3 of *Michelangelo*), Princeton University Press, 1948.
Tuckwell, W., *Lycidas: A Monograph*, London, 1911.
Turnell, M., *The Classical Moment*, London, 1946.
Turner, W. A., "Miltons Two-handed Engine," *Journal of English and Germanic Philology*, XLIX, 562–5.
Vasari, G., *The Lives of the Painters, Sculptors and Architects*, 4 vols., London, n.d.
Waterhouse, E. K., *Baroque Painting in Rome*, London, 1937. Macmillan.
Wellek, R., "The Concept of Baroque in Literary Scholarship," *Journal of Aesthetics and Art Criticism*, V (2), 77–109.
Welsford, E., *The Court Masque*, Cambridge University Press, 1927.
Werblowsky, R. J. Z., *Lucifer and Prometheus: A Study of Milton's Satan*, London, 1952.
White, M. E. (ed.), *Studies in Honour of Gilbert Norwood*, University of Toronto Press, 1952.
Wittkower, R., *Architectural Principles in the Age of Humanism*, London, 1952.
——— *Art and Architecture in Italy 1600 to 1750*, London, Penguin, 1958.
——— *Bernini's Bust of Louis XIV*, Oxford University Press, 1951.
——— *Gianlorenzo Bernini: The Sculptor of the Roman Baroque*, London, 1955.
——— "Michelangelo's Biblioteca Laurenziana," *Art Bulletin*, XVI (2), 123–218.
Wölfflin, H., *Classic Art: An Introduction to the Italian Renaissance*, London, 1959.
——— *Principles of History*, trans. M. D. Hottinger, New York, n.d.
Woodhouse, A. S. P., "The Argument of Milton's *Comus*," *University of Toronto Quarterly*, XI (1), 46–71.
——— "*Comus* once more," *University of Toronto Quarterly*, XIX (3), 218–23.
——— "Milton, Puritanism, and Liberty," *University of Toronto Quarterly*, IV (4), 483–513.
——— "Pattern in *Paradise Lost*," *University of Toronto Quarterly*, XXII (2), 109–27.
——— "Puritanism and Liberty," review article, *University of Toronto Quarterly*, IV (3), 395–404.
——— "Theme and Pattern in *Paradise Regained*," *University of Toronto Quarterly*, XXV (2), 167–82.
Worringer, W., *Form Problems of the Gothic*, New York, 1920.
Zupnik, I. L., "The 'Aesthetics' of the Early Mannerists," *Art Bulletin*, XXXV (Dec. 1953), 302–6.

Index